DISCARD

D1264770

COURAGE AT SEA

Tales of Heroic Voyages

Naomi James

Salem House

Salem House Publishers
Topsfield, Massachusetts

First published in the United States by Salem House Publishers, 1988,
462 Boston Street, Topsfield, MA 01983.

Printed and bound in Great Britain

Library of Congress Cataloging-in-Publication Data
James, Naomi.
   Courage at sea.
1. Voyages and travels.   2. Seafaring life.
I. Title.
G540.J36   1988   910.4'5   87–16682
ISBN 0–88162–320–2

Contents

Acknowledgements

I would like to thank the publishers and authors of the following books which I used as source material:

The Strange Voyage of Donald Crowhurst, Nicholas Tomalin and Ron Hall (Hodder & Stoughton, 1970)
Ice Bird, David Lewis (Collins, 1975)
I Had to Dare, Tom McClean (Jarrolds, 1971)
Last Voyage, Ann Davison (Heinemann, 1953)
The Great Antarctic Rescue: Shackleton's Boat Journey, F A Worsley (Sphere, 1977)
A World of My Own, Robin Knox-Johnston (Cassell, 1969)
The Long Way, Bernard Moitessier (Translation © Adlard Coles, Doubleday, 1971)

Survive the Savage Sea, Dougal Robertson (Elek Books, 1973)
117 Days Adrift, Maurice and Maralyn Bailey (Nautical Publishing Company, 1974)
The Mutiny on Board HMS Bounty, William Bligh (The New American Library of World Literature)
Captain Bligh and Mr Christian, Richard Hough (Hutchinson, 1972)
A Voyage Round the World, Lord Anson (Everymans Library, Dent & Sons, 1911)
Fastnet Force 10, John Rousmaniere (Nautical Books, 1980)
Fastnet Disaster and After, Bob Fisher (Pelham Books, 1980, an imprint of A & C Black Ltd.)
Desperate Voyage, John Caldwell (Gollancz, 1950)

Photographic acknowledgements

The author and publishers are grateful to the following for permission to reproduce photographs:

BBC Hulton Picture Library, pages 13, 18 and 23; Mary Evans Picture Library, pages 8/9, 15, 19, 20/21, 28/29 and 33; Express Newspapers, pages 166/167, 171, 175 and 181; Grafton Books, a division of the Collins Publishing Group, pages 139, 143, 145, 150/151 and 153; National Maritime Museum, page 27; Photo Source, pages 154/155, 161 and 162; Pickthall Photo Library, photos by Bob Fisher, pages 159, 192/193, 199, 203 and 207; Popperfoto, pages 73 *below*, 78/79, 85, 91; Press Association, pages 163 and 165; Royal Geographical Society, pages 58/59, 61, 63, 64, 65, 67 and 70/71; *Times Newspapers*, pages 73 *above*, 81, 83, 86/87, 94, 95 and 99; University of Dundee, page 158; Weymouth and Portland Museums, page 111; *Woman's Own*, page 105.

Photographs on pages 127, 130, 132, 136 and 137 are from '117 Days Adrift' by Maurice and Maralyn Bailey, Nautical Publishing Co, 1974, now part of A & C Black (Publishers) Ltd. Photographs on pages 34, 39, 40/41, 42 and 43 are reproduced by kind permission of Curtis Brown Ltd, on behalf of David Lewis ©, 1975.

Illustrations on pages 100/101, 112/113, 125 and 182/183 are by Salim.

Colour section
The Governers of Dulwich College, page 3 *below*; David Lewis ©, 1975, page 8; National Maritime Museum, pages 1 *below*, 2 and 3 *above*; Pickthall Photo Library, photo by Bob Fisher, page 7; *Sunday Times*, pages 4, 5, and 6; Syndication International, page 1 *below*.

Introduction

I have never been able to explain to myself or anyone else exactly why I sailed alone round the world in 1978, but I hope the following stories provide some insight into the challenge of the sea. They include tales of immense heroism and courage, of triumphs over wave and water, scurvy and starvation, sharks and solitude.

But not all the stories are about triumphant heroism. Some, like the tales of the Baileys and the Robertson family, tell of a survival more awful than death itself, and some, like the tragic story of Donald Crowhurst tell of pain and failure and a sanity capsized, of seafarers who were daunted by their predicament or crushed by circumstance. I have included these darker stories, not to show how feeble or incompetent the more unlucky seafarers were, but to illustrate the many pitfalls awaiting us when we confront the might of the sea. And, much more important, to show how courage and resourcefulness can be discovered even in the very face of disaster.

Finally, I would prefer to disassociate 'A Round Britain Victory' from the title of this book. This race, however, gives an example of the trials and headaches the less than fanatical participants of the sport have to face.

Magellan's fleet off Tierra del Fuego

Magellan: Hazards of the Unknown

Most people know who Magellan was. That he was a
Spaniard, that he was the first man to sail around the
world some time in the sixteenth century, and that he
discovered the straits to which he gave his name. That was
the extent of my knowledge, and I very soon found one
grave error in even that meagre assembly of facts. He was
not Spanish, but Portuguese, though he sailed under the
Spanish flag.

It is not easy to uncover much about the personality of a man who lived so long ago. In the general turmoil that seemed an accepted part of life in those days – ships being seized, cities sacked, people being captured or dispensed with out of jealousy or intrigue – Magellan's own journals, as well as those of his captains, were lost. A handful of pilots' logs written at the time still exist, but they record only facts like distances run, navigational data, details of wind movements, and so on. In any case, the journals of the captains who commanded the other ships in the fleet would probably not have described Magellan as he really was, as most of them did not like him. Actually, only one captain survived the expedition and only then because he had returned to Spain several years earlier and was thrown into a dungeon. I am able to state that fact due to the existence of an account of the voyage by one of the few survivors, a man who was neither sailor, navigator, nor philanthro-pist. He was, rather, a 'fly on the wall', the equivalent of a modern reporter. His name was Antonio Pigafetta, an Italian scholar and a Knight of Rhodes. He had volunteered for the journey both to keep his masters informed of the discoveries of the new expedition, and for his own personal advancement. Pigafetta possessed an indefatigable curiosity, great courage and, even more important, a remarkable facility for survival.

Magellan was mounting his expedition under the patronage of the Spanish King, Charles V. He had first approached his own Portuguese King but Don Manuel had allowed himself to be swayed by his advisors who thought Magellan uncouth and a boaster. His fantastic plans were derided. Undeterred, Magellan went to Spain and found a more receptive audience.

It was the time of the great partitioning of the world by white men, who assumed the divine right to claim the ownership of foreign lands.

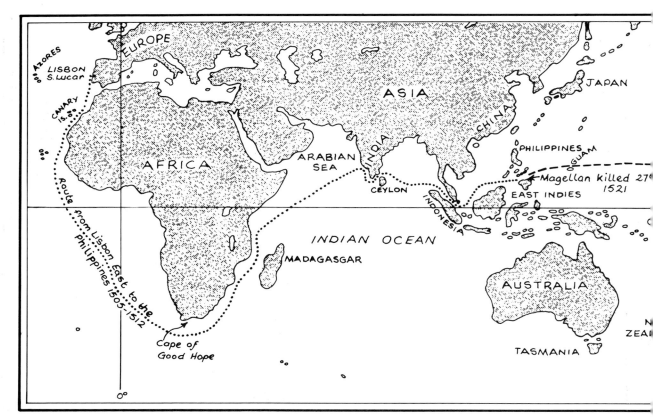

Because of the demarcation line drawn up by Pope Alexander the Sixth, showing which areas belonged to Portugal and which to Spain, it was a race to see who could extend their ownership beyond the Portuguese outposts of the Azores, Cape Verde Islands and the Canaries that guarded the route to the treasure-filled Spice Islands. As Spanish ships could not trespass in the above territory without the risk of capture, Magellan proposed to sail the other way, to the west, and attempt to reach the Spice Islands from behind, so to speak. He had heard of a globe of the world made by the astrologer Behaim before the voyage of Christopher Columbus 30 years earlier. There was no continent drawn on it between Europe and the East, only islands. Magellan believed that, going west, he could find a way through these into the unknown ocean beyond.

Along with a bewildered audience of ministers, Pigafetta was present at the Court of Seville when one of Magellan's associates demonstrated the astrolabe (one of the earliest instruments of celestial navigation) while Magellan attempted to explain the perplexing question of longitude and its great importance to his own theories. (It must be remembered that most people then thought the world was flat. As many ships set off and were never seen again, it was believed that they had simply sailed off the edge.) No doubt a considerable number of the men present thought he was mad, but all were willing to be swayed by the small chance that he might be right. Magellan banked on their greed and dwelt long on the profits of a successful expedition; their importance and wealth would be increased by inestimable proportions. They had everything to gain and Magellan was prepared to stake his own life on achieving his goal. It was an argument they could not resist. His plans were approved.

Magellan set sail from the Port of Seville on

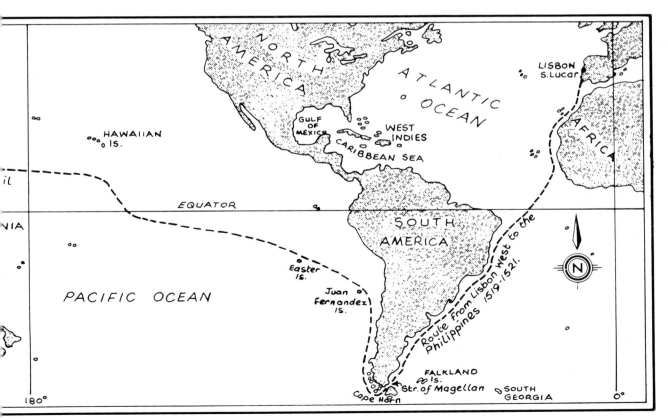

August 10, 1519, with five ships. The flagship, *Trinidada,* which was 78 feet on the waterline, had a 22-foot beam and a draft of 8 feet. The *San Antonio* was a little larger, and the *Concepcion, Vittoria,* and *Santiago,* considerably smaller. Never before had an expedition been so well prepared. Although the landsmen watching from the shore had labelled Magellan a trumped-up knight who had been lucky to find favour with the young king of Spain, those who witnessed him overseeing the preparations of the ships recognized a real sailor. He left nothing undone, and there was not a part of a ship that he did not know intimately nor any vulnerable quarter left unchecked or lacking reinforcement.

The crew of 240 or so included 35 Portuguese (a serious cause for dispute, it transpired), Moors from Gibraltar, Greeks, Spaniards, Frenchmen, Germans, Italians and Malays – and one Englishman. They were rabble, mostly, after the fashion of seaman of the day – hard drinking, uncouth, superstitious and only there, for the most part, because they were lured by a few weeks' wages in advance. Their number included spies and subversive elements, but a good proportion were loyal to Magellan. In Pigafetta he had an ardent admirer, who described Magellan as 'a wise and virtuous man, mindful of his honour' and he maintained a fierce loyalty for Magellan right to the end.

Magellan did not tell his captains precisely what he had in mind for the voyage, knowing they would not like it if he did, but commanded each captain to stick rigidly to a complex set of signals – by way of lanterns – to be used day and night while at sea so that the ships would not lose sight of each other. He led, they followed. If he wanted to shorten sail, halt, or alter direction, they must obey his instructions and follow suit.

The fleet, carrying full sail and firing their artillery, presented a stirring spectacle to the families, friends and thousands of spectators who lined the mole at Seville to watch them depart. At the mouth of the river they halted for a few days, to provision with fresh food, and confess their sins for the last time – at Magellan's insistence – before making sail for the Canary Islands.

These islands were quickly reached and more provisioning, including pitch for the decks and rigging, was undertaken. While this was going on a fast caravel (one of the first ocean frigates) arrived from Seville with a message from his father-in-law, only for the eyes of Magellan. It contained a warning that among his fleet were various infidels, including several of his captains, who had sworn to kill him when their chance arose. Speculation as to the contents of the mysterious letter was rife as Magellan calmly gave the order to weigh anchor and set course towards the south-west.

The Doldrums, the area of calm or contrary winds near the equator, held them up for more than the usual duration while that famous region fired electric storms and calms at them with the same tiresome regularity of today. Seamen were highly superstitious in those times and when certain phenomena occurred, like St Elmo's Fire (a green fiery glow caused by an electrical discharge and usually seen at the masthead) it was accounted for as a sign from the Gods – in this case a benevolent one as most believed that the fire was a protective presence. Mariners had an inordinate fear of storms and high seas: they did not view the weather as a natural phenomenon but as a supernatural force (their maps of the oceans depicted storms issuing from the cheeks of Boreus and others to whom they were attributed). For a reason he kept to himself Magellan clung to the African coast, exposing them to heavy offshore gales. These inexplicable tactics so incensed one of his captains – Julius de Cartegena – that he hailed Magellan and demanded to know why he did not sail to the west. Magellan roared at him to follow his lead and ask no questions. Cartegena retaliated with several conspicuous acts of discourtesy. Magellan bided his time for a few days in his cabin then went into action. On the pretext of an infraction of discipline by one of the common sailors he ordered all the captains to report to the flagship. They assembled in his cabin. Without warning he clapped Cartegena into irons, along with the King's treasurer, another traitor, and gave command of Cartegena's ship, the *San Antonio,* to a junior pilot.

Free of conspiracy from his worst enemy Magellan at once set course for the west (Cartegena was returned to duty as a plain officer but remained under nominal arrest). Soon they picked up the south-east trade winds which bore them steadily across the Atlantic Ocean to the coast of Brazil. On December 13 they entered the port of Rio de Janeiro and bartered with the natives for fresh fruit, vegetables and fish. Some days later they resumed the journey south to the latitude of the La Plata River where the weather became considerably colder and the natives markedly less friendly. Magellan was hugging the coastline of the now totally unknown terrain, searching every bay and inlet for the way through to the ocean beyond. For several days he sailed up the La Plata delta but, discovering that they were in a river, made his way out again and continued southwards.

The weather grew worse as they progressed at a snail's pace along the coast. Pigafetta reported seeing weird legless animals like wolves on the shore (sea lions and walruses) and flightless birds like goslings (penguins), and these they captured in large numbers to augment their rations.

After three months on the South American coast they had reached latitude 49 degrees south. It was March, and autumn was approaching. Everyone had grown afraid of Magellan's strategy of sailing so close inshore, believing that hidden rocks or reefs would put an end to their ships. The danger was greatly heightened by the savage 'pamperos' – squalls of quixotic suddenness and ferocity which struck the ships without warning and laid them over on their beam ends. One struck from the south east, catching the ships close to land. The sails were ripped from the yard by the ferocious gusts, forcing the ships to heave to under bare poles, totally at the mercy of the wind and seas driving them relentlessly towards the coast. By daybreak the ragged rock-strewn shore loomed closer with every wild roll of the straining vessels. Most of the men believed they were about to meet their maker and began to pray aloud. Not so Magellan. He gave the signal to hoist storm sails and stand in for the shore. Cautiously he moved his ship closer to a low

Ferdinand Magellan led an expedition to discover another way to the Spice Islands which resulted in the first circumnavigation

indentation in the cliffs, before which a reef threw up great clouds of spume. Above the noise of battering seas, flapping canvas, and screaming seabirds the leadsmen in the chains called out the depths and the lookouts above shouted warnings to the helmsman.

A way opened up between the reef. Magellan steered into it, signalling the other ships to follow suit. One by one the ships broke through the reef, barely visible because of the spume, to find the sea miraculously calm inside. They proceeded inland through a narrow bay and entered a kind of harbour where they dropped anchor. It was not, as hoped, the entrance to the Pacific Ocean but it afforded them shelter from the worsening weather. Magellan called the harbour Puerto San Julian.

It was March 31. Winter would soon be upon them and although they were temporarily out of danger their environs were bleak in the extreme. They could not see another living soul and nothing edible could be found growing on the shores. A strict regime of food rationing was ordered by Magellan. There was talk of harsh discipline and hard labour and soon the rumour began to circulate that he intended spending the winter there, at which the anger among those captains and men united in their hatred of Magellan burst forth. The displaced Cartegena, further incensed by the discovery that Magellan had made a Portuguese member of his own family the new master of the *San Antonio*, called upon the men to mutiny. He led a force of armed men against the *San Antonio* and captured it. Mendoza, the treasurer, and Quesada, captain of the *Concepcion*, had control of two other ships, having gained the crew's support for the mutiny. This left Magellan's flagship and one other.

Magellan, however, had been alerted to the trouble, and had had time to ponder and devise a plan. He dispatched a boat with his Master of Arms, Espinoza, and a few other men to Mendoza's ship on the pretext of arranging terms of surrender. They were allowed to board. While they were parleying on deck another boat drew up alongside unnoticed. Suddenly, Espinoza stabbed Mendoza in the throat with a dagger and killed him. His crew stood agape at the sight of their captain lying dead on the deck – and were even more amazed a second later when loyal seamen clambered over the rails, swords drawn. They surrendered without resistance.

With three ships on his side, Magellan now had the upper hand. Cartegena and Quesada planned to slip away in the dead of night on the ebb tide, which would have carried them past the three loyal ships anchored across the entrance of the harbour. But, when the moment came, a squall swept down just as the *San Antonio* was weighing anchor and she crashed into the side of the flagship, which immediately fired a broadside of cannon balls into her, followed closely by grappling hooks and Magellan's loyal marines armed to the teeth. A short struggle ensued but

when more reinforcements, in the shape of the *Santiago,* came crashing into the other side of the ship the *San Antonio* surrendered. The *Concepcion,* about to make her dash for freedom, was ordered to anchor and when she saw the fate of the *San Antonio* she, too, capitulated. The mutineers were rounded up and put into irons.

Magellan now chose to show his strength in no uncertain terms. The revolt had not been an impulse of the moment. He had known of the subversive elements in the fleet before leaving Seville, had been aware of it even on his own ship. Although the ringleaders of the mutiny were powerful and influential men at home, it was Magellan who possessed the power invested in him as Captain General of the fleet. In order to reinforce that power he dealt with the mutineers in the harshest possible way. He ordered that the body of Luis de Mendoza be drawn and quartered and his parts impaled on stakes ashore. Gasper Quesada, being next to Mendoza in culpability, had his head removed and was also quartered and placed next to Mendoza above the sands. This gruesome exhibition, showing stark against the dull grey skies, was enough to convince the rest of the men that their Captain General meant business. Magellan could not kill Cartegena outright as the Emperor Charles himself had made him captain. Instead before their eventual departure he was taken ashore along with his assistant, a priest, and abandoned to his fate. They were never heard of again.

The rest of the men were pardoned and returned to their duties. For Magellan accepted that fear of the unknown and the harsh deprivation the men were expected to face had inspired them to join the mutiny.

The fleet settled down for the winter. For two months they saw no one ashore but when Patagonian natives suddenly appeared, leaping and dancing, Magellan sent one of his men to greet them, and make friends by joining in their dancing. Magellan, whose instructions were to bring back specimens of the inhabitants of strange places, had to capture several natives – no easy matter as they towered above the

FERDINAN. MAGALA.

average European seaman. A plot was hatched, successfully, and though at first they went berserk when they realized they were captives, the natives were eventually subdued. In time they were converted to Christianity.

In May, shortly after the mutiny, Magellan sent the *Santiago* to reconnoitre the coast down as far as Puerto Santa Cruz. A storm blew up, catching her close inshore and she ran aground and was wrecked. All except one of the crew escaped and made their way overland to the fleet. Magellan sent back a large party and during the next few weeks it was able to salvage most of the wreck's cargo.

The enforced time in harbour was not entirely wasted. The vessels were careened so that the weed could be scraped off and pitch applied to the planking. Finally, the holds were restowed and the remaining stores checked, and it was found that half their provisions had already

This illustration of Magellan aboard his ship shows that superstition was rife among seafarers in the sixteenth century

been used up or spoilt. More might have been obtained from hunting and fishing but such trips had to be curtailed as the natives had become more and more unfriendly.

At last, in August, the ice began to break up in the harbour. Mass was said ashore, with the entire company prepared for a possible attack by the inhabitants, and a cross was erected on the highest point of land in the vicinity. The following day, August 24, 1520, Magellan gave the order to weigh anchor and proceed south. They soon reached a bay that had been discovered by the *Santiago,* where they remained for several weeks, buffeted by storms but reprovisioning, when the weather allowed, with water, wood, and whatever fresh food they could find.

Thus fortified they moved on south. Ice formed on the yards and rigging, the men grew haggard and afraid, reduced by their inadequate clothing and wretched food to a state of abject misery. Few now believed in the strait or saw any justification for continuing the push south into the fearsome unknown. Dissension again rose up around him, but Magellan grimly held on, calling on the loyalty of his key men to contain the subversion. He tacked continually towards and away from the coast, forcing the other ships to follow suit, not daring to go out of sight of land in case the elusive entrance might be missed. When contrary weather forced them out to sea he fought back northwards to a land-mark they recognized before continuing the painstaking search to the south. They had increased their latitude to 52 degrees when the shore trended sharply inwards. When the visibility improved they found themselves looking into a broad bay with a far shore on the south side and vast mountains to the west. Magellan believed this to be the entry into the channel through which they would reach the Pacific Ocean. A profoundly religious man, he went down on his knees in thanks to God for guiding them safely this far. He named the cape on the northern side, the Cape of Eleven Thousand Virgins.

Into this bay Magellan sailed, followed closely by his three escorts. They anchored a short way offshore and the captains boarded the *Trinidada* to take stock, but startled by the roar of a rising east wind, Magellan hastily dispatched them back to their vessels and got under way. Tacking cautiously from one invisible coast to the other, sounding depths, they moved ahead at a mere knot or two. By noon the next day the wind had eased and the fleet halted again. So far, the bay appeared to be land-locked, but Magellan refused to believe there was no way to the west. He sent two ships to search the extremities while he remained with two ships guarding the entrance. In the night the wind roared again out of the east, forcing the ships standing guard to weigh anchor and hold station away from the land. In the dawn light the returning ships could be seen sailing out of the gloom. Suddenly the vessels, which had been sailing in a straight line towards them, seemed to be seized by an invisible hand and were dragged sideways, abruptly disappearing from Magellan's view. In great agitation he tacked back and forth in the entrance, fearing the worst.

Unable to make way against the tidal pull, the ships were swept out beyond the sheltering cliffs and into the full fury of the storm. Nearer and nearer they were driven to the perilous coastline at the extremity of the bay, until the thunderous roar of surf overcame the wailing of the storm. The terrified shouts and prayers of the seamen welled up as the ships rocked violently, beam on to the shore. Even the captains had given themselves up for lost when a wild cry from the lookout of the foremost ship pierced the din: a gap could be seen dead ahead! Into a narrow channel they were swept by the racing tidal stream, borne along its length at furious speed and spewed out the other end into a wide bight of calm water.

Scarcely crediting their deliverance they dropped anchor. After a brief respite to gather their scattered wits and put their ships back in order they continued on until they found another narrow channel trending inland. In great excitement, flying banners and firing cannons, they raced back on the swift tide, now turned seawards, to tell Magellan of their discovery.

After giving thanks to God and the Virgin Mary, the Captain General called all his captains and officers to the flagship. Many now believed that, having found the strait, they should return to Spain, obtain new ships and provisions, and return again to carry on the quest. Magellan listened to their arguments but pronounced his determination to carry on. Pigafetta reports him as saying, 'If we have to eat the leather on the yards, I will go on and discover what I have promised the King.' Cowed by his conviction and recognizing the folly of standing against him, even the most unwilling gave way. On his orders, they followed the flagship inland to negotiate what was to become known as the Strait of Magellan.

At the first narrows, into which the *San*

Antonio and *Concepcion* had been unceremoniously hurled, they delayed to note the movements of the tidal race, finding it to vary in height by an incredible 40 feet and running at a speed of over nine knots at times. Then, successfully negotiating this first channel, they proceeded for some days due west to a point where the way split: a wide channel opened to the east, while the other continued south-west. To the *San Antonio* and *Concepcion,* whose crews harboured many elements unfriendly to the expedition, Magellan gave orders to explore the eastern channel as far as possible. If unsuccessful, they were to return to the divide and follow the south-western route until the ships met up again. They departed along what is now marked on the charts as Useless Bay.

As Magellan suspected, there *was* a plot brewing on the *San Antonio*. The pilot, another cousin or nephew of Magellan's, had reason to hate his Captain General. He, Esteban Gomez, had applied to the Emperor for funds to mount a similar expedition but the Emperor had chosen to back Magellan. As soon as Magellan's ships were out of sight, Gomez approached the captain, Mesquita, and convinced him of the wisdom of returning at once to Spain. Under cover of darkness and heavy snow showers they slipped away from their escort and sailed for Spain. Gomez' treachery was two-fold: on arrival in Spain he told of the Captain General's demise following his dreadful tyranny and executions. Mesquita was blamed also, and cast into a dungeon, where he remained for several years until the *Vittoria* returned.

Magellan, meanwhile, was proceeding cautiously along the south-west strait, past a magnificent snow-capped mountain with huge glaciers sweeping down its seven thousand feet – this was Mount Sarmiento. He slowly felt his way forward by day and halted during the hours of darkness which fortunately were short as it was the southern summer and only dark for a few hours. Even staying in the same place was difficult as the mountain sides plunged straight into the sea and no purchase could be found for their anchors: they were forced instead to run cables ashore. There was much in their sur-

roundings to frighten the most stout-hearted of mariners. The light shimmering off the towering mountains played strange tricks on imaginations distorted by superstitious dread. The still water reflecting the gigantic rock walls amplified the eerie silences which were broken only by the creaks and groans of the glaciers and the mournful cries of strange animals on the shore. In an instant the silence would be destroyed by the howling, snow-laden squalls which worried their ships like demons bent on their destruction. The squalls, accompanied by freezing snow, swept down from every direction off the surrounding mountains, tearing at the sails and yards and laying the ships over on their sides. Counter currents and tidal flows of tremendous force bore the ships forward at a furious pace, and then back again. All along the southern shores at night hundreds of lights flickered like stars, signalling the presence of natives – although none was seen. (These lights were native campfires. They had not learnt to kindle flame so the fires burned continually.) So extraordinary did the seamen find this, that the region acquired the name Tierra del Fuego, Land of Fire.

Sometimes the narrow and tortuous channel forced the labouring ships to tack constantly away from the shores, while the leadsmen and lookouts watched for underwater rocks and the navigators struggled to master the treacherous currents. Time and again they entered a side channel and, having worked their way painstakingly to a dead end of ragged shore line, were then forced back. At other times the strait increased to the width of a lake and they battled instead with a sea as rough as an ocean. After nearly a month of incredible work they had covered some 300 miles. Magellan felt they must now be near the ocean and called a halt, anchoring by the mouth of a river to await the arrival of the other two ships. After four days he grew tired of waiting. The suspense was too great. He ordered their biggest boat to be launched, filled her with as much food and water as she could bear and in her he placed some of his most trusted men. They set forth to negotiate the final stretch. Just three days later they returned, to

Now only a fleet of three ships, they beat back once more along the strait, this time exploring the southern coastline, which they found to possess good anchorages with fresh water, excellent cedar wood, and good fishing. On November 29, they reached the cape discovered by the men in the small boat, which Magellan called Cape Desire. Ahead of them lay the wide blue ocean.

It now remained only for Magellan to return to Spain and tell of his great conquest. Had he (or at least one of his ships) failed to bring back news of the discovery history would have been considerably reshaped – influenced by the accounts of Gomez. As it was many important political moves were made, lands were claimed, treasures were seized, none of which would have been possible without Magellan's Strait discoveries. In the immediate years following his voyage many other ships tried to trace his steps but failed. Some could not find the entrance to the strait; more perished in negotiating it; some mutinied – all of which only served to add weight to his extraordinary reputation as a navigator and leader of men.

Magellan's promise to eat the leather off the yards was prophetic. Instead of his estimated 600 miles they had to travel an incredible 11,000. At first Magellan marvelled at the abundance of sea life and extraordinary calm of the sea, so welcome to his men. He called the ocean the Pacific. But the weeks passed. The three ships grew weeds and barnacles and a dreaded presence began to make itself felt: scurvy. In the oppressive heat starvation beset the crew and they died. The ships' biscuits were turned to powder by weevils, and tasted of rat's urine. The rats themselves became the most highly prized and wholesome food they had. The hides intended for binding the masts and stays to reduce chaff were soaked for several days in the sea, laid on burning coals, then eaten. After 40 days an island was sighted but it had no food or water, nothing but birds and trees. The sight of it so disturbed the minds of the sufferers that many more died immediately.

At last they came upon islands where Magellan was able to obtain fruit to revive the

The Vittoria, *the only surviving ship of Magellan's fleet to return to Spain*

report the discovery of a new cape and, beyond it, a great ocean. At the news Magellan wept tears of joy and gratitude.

As the other two ships had still not appeared Magellan returned to look for them. He found only one, the *Concepcion,* but no one could tell him what had happened to her consort. After days of fruitless searching as far back as the first narrows, flags were left ashore at various points with messages and, finally, a cross was erected on a small island by a river that divided the majestic mountains. They could do no more for their companions, who, they believed, must have perished.

Magellan conferred with his remaining captains. The missing *San Antonio,* being the biggest vessel in the fleet, had carried the largest proportion of provisions. Without sufficient food or water, they would now be taking a greater risk venturing into unknown territory. But Magellan had calculated the distance to the Spice Islands as a mere 600 miles. If they sailed north first to decrease their latitude, he argued, the weather would be kinder and they would reach the Spice Islands in a few short weeks. The promise of warmth and easy sailing was alluring to the weary sailors: they agreed to go on.

company, now reduced to just 100 out of the original 240. He pressed on and found more islands, later called the Philippines, where he met traders from China and other parts of the Far East. He had by this time travelled more than halfway round the world.

Magellan, a zealot in religion as in all things, could not pass up the opportunity of converting the heathen savages to Christianity. In this respect he allowed his eagerness to override his good sense. Attempting to aid a converted chieftain in a battle against a heathen brother, he found himself and a handful of supporters (including the faithful Pigafetta) surrounded by hundreds of angry warriors – having failed to subdue them by burning their houses. The Spaniards fought as bravely as they could and tried to retreat to the waiting boats. But the natives were after Magellan's blood and aimed their spears particularly at him. Although he resisted (at the same time urging the rest of the company to make their escape) the sheer weight of numbers brought him down. Once on the ground he was hacked to death with lances and cutlasses.

The hero of the great expedition was dead and his survivors were still a long way from home. The natives massacred many more of the fleet's company before they could retreat to the safety of the ships and escape from the Philippines. As there were not enough men left to work all three ships the worn-out *Concepcion* was burned and the two remaining vessels sailed on to the Spice Islands where they loaded up with spices. At this point the *Trinidada* sailed east again to attempt another crossing of the Pacific to Mexico (which she failed to do), while the *Vittoria,* visiting many islands and countries along the way, returned by way of the Indian Ocean and the Cape of Good Hope, to arrive back in Spain on September 6, 1522.

There were 18 haggard and sick men on board – all that remained of the proud fleet. Off the port of Seville they discharged their artillery and sailed in to a tumultuous welcome from the incredulous Spanish who, of course, because of Gomez' testimony, believed them all to be dead. The *Vittoria* was laden with spices which more

than paid for the expedition costs but this was the least important cargo brought back by her survivors.

Their experiences influenced science, the economy and politics, but most important by far were the pilot charts and the information each (especially Pigafetta) could give. Most astonishing of all was an accomplishment that they had not set out to do in the first place: namely adding to the globe a third of the world's surface by the discovery of the Pacific Ocean. In crossing it and returning to Spain, they became the first to circumnavigate the world.

Magellan did not live to enjoy the full glory of his epic voyage. He was slain in the Philippines attempting to convert the natives to Christianity

Anson's Incredible Circumnavigation

In 1740, when war with Spain had been declared, Commodore George Anson led a squadron of Royal Navy ships to harass the Spaniards in their distant settlements in the Philippines and elsewhere along the route. It consisted of eight vessels and a total of 1,955 crew. Nearly four years later he returned with just one ship and a mere 145 men. About 500 or so had been killed in battle or through other causes; the rest had died of scurvy.

The Centurion, *Anson's flagship, engaging the gold-laden Spanish galleon off the Philippines*

Few lengthy voyages of the eighteenth century – and before – were free from an extraordinarily high fatality rate, the commonest cause of which was scurvy. Sea scurvy was first recorded as a serious outbreak in 1498 by Vasco da Gama but there were eyewitness accounts of the disease at the time of the Crusades in 1215. Whether as a result of sieges, being marooned, or spending long periods at sea, the failure to provide fresh food caused outbreaks of illness and deaths for as long as the deprivation lasted. It took many years before the exact nature of the problem was identified and even longer before anything positive was done to remedy it.

Although no known prevention existed for scurvy some navigators, Drake for instance, managed to avoid losing men in epidemic proportions, due, seemingly, to a higher standard of provisioning, better fortune in reprovisioning before long passages, and more living space allocated to each man. Anson's squadron, with the greedy and ambitious Navy behind it, was grossly overcrowded. Officers (and their servants), fighting marines, seamen, and a multitude of camp followers considered indispensable to the success of the enterprise, were packed into the small ships like sardines in a tin.

Much of the fighting force were men in their sixties drafted straight from Chelsea Hospital and given to Anson because they were too ill to fight on land. Of the 500 expected, only 259 reported for duty and those who were fit enough deserted when they discovered what was in store for them. Many of the others were in an advanced state of decrepitude. As Anson was allocated only half the number he had requested, the rest he press-ganged – a cruel and barbaric system of recruitment common at the time. A group of marines – under the captain's orders – would swoop on a merchant ship returning from several years abroad and round up all its able bodied trained seamen on to the new and unknown vessel. The effect of being sent back to sea when so close to home, unpaid and in appalling conditions, was traumatic. Small wonder that mutinies and desertions frequently occurred aboard Navy ships even though the penalty was death at the yard arm.

Why, then, this disregard for men's welfare and for the effectiveness of a fighting force? A separate Naval attack against the Spanish was being launched by the Admiralty in the Caribbean at the time of Anson's fitting out. It was viewed by the Admiralty as far more important than Anson's enterprise, which therefore received scant attention. Such an attitude conveys an avarice and ignorance of man management which is hard to imagine today.

Anson himself was reputed to be an indomitable and humane commander which suggests that the conditions his men suffered were not the result of his harsh treatment but simply those which were considered normal at the time.

Ships' provisions generally consisted of biscuits, salt beef and pork, pease, preserved butter and cheese, oatmeal, and large quantities of liquor – usually wine, brandy or beer. This official diet endorsed by the Admiralty was thought to contain sufficient calories and protein, especially as an adequate supplement of fresh foods, it was assumed, would be collected from foreign shores – though in practice this was seldom the case. A small amount of ascorbic acid (vitamin C) was present in the statutory diet but much more was consumed by the officers who could afford to bring such exotic items as marmalade and onions. This helps to explain why few of the men in charge went down with the illness – this, plus the greater spaciousness of their living quarters, which allowed for greater personal hygiene and a healthier frame of mind.

The provisions shipped aboard for Anson's circumnavigation had more than the usual shortcomings. He had informed the Admiralty that, in his experience, pease and oatmeal became inedible on prolonged passages and had requested 'Stockfish, grotts, grout and rice' instead. (He does not tell us exactly what these items were but it is academic since, in the event, he didn't get them.) Though permission was granted, dishonesty prevailed among the

Commodore George Anson's expedition suffered appalling loss of life from scurvy during its four-year circumnavigation in the eighteenth century

pursars and supply contractors. Unbeknown to him he was loaded up with a frightful assortment of victuals: old London work horses, whose texture and taste resembled old wood; 'pork' consisting mostly of bristly hide – which sweated and turned to slime in the tropics; and casked bread that went mouldy and crumbled away to dust.

Almost as much of a headache to Anson was the fitting out of his ships. The dockyard workers had pocketed the money paid to them for proper masts, rigging, etc. and supplied instead vastly inferior materials which posed a very serious danger to the ships once they faced the rigours of storms and high seas. Anson was unable to influence the Admiralty in putting these serious disorders to rights.

The squadron suffered endless delays. Even when the ships were ready to sail they were prevented from leaving by obtuse orders. Anson was instructed to shepherd a fleet of 140 mer-

chantmen and warships out of the English Channel. The company was so vast that only the most favourable of weather conditions would allow them to make progress – for this they had to wait many weeks. At last, after countless abortive attempts to organize the fleet and to impress the authorities with his untenable situation, Anson was allowed to leave separately. But the season was already far advanced and timing became yet another vital factor in the disastrous outcome of the venture. It meant arriving at the Horn in time for the equinoctial storms.

Instead of the usual 10-day passage to Madeira bad weather, rotten spars, and fouling on the ships' hulls stretched it to 40. They remained on the island for a week but the voyage had already made such serious inroads into the health of the elderly crews that within three weeks of clearing Madeira many of them died of a tropical fever. In their stinking holds, pitching

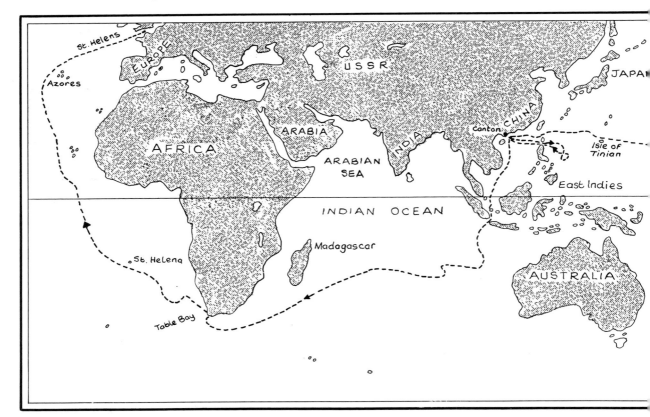

and rolling in the rough seas, each man's 14-inch space was putrid with vermin and human excrement. Devoid of suitable sanitation and even fresh air, it's no wonder that they lacked the mental resources to combat the scurvy waiting in the wings.

By the time the ships had reached the island of St Catherines, off the coast of Brazil, 171 deaths had occurred – none as yet attributable to scurvy. Anson delayed sailing for a month while the survivors of the fever recovered and the more able-bodied cleaned out the ships and reprovisioned with meagre supplies. There was plenty of fresh beef but virtually nothing else. Supplies were again sought at Port St Julian in Patagonia (now Argentina) but to no avail.

At St Catherines Anson received reports of a Spanish Naval fleet which had set off from Spain to intercept his ships. It was reported to be lying in wait somewhere along Anson's route to the Horn. They were not to know that the Spanish

commander, Don Joseph Pizarro, although aware that Anson's ships were ill-equipped, had decided not to give credit to the reports of its poor state. He believed it was a ruse and chose to delay his attack until after they entered the Southern Ocean, knowing that Anson would then have no back-up support from the considerable British fleets always cruising in European waters. Had he heeded the report he would have succeeded in dispatching all of Anson's ships with ease.

Anson's general anxiety was heightened by further reports that Pizarro had set off ahead of him through the Le Maire Strait, probably intending to attack him off the Patagonian coast. Knowing that his only chance against Pizarro was to slip by him undetected, Anson commanded every captain in the fleet to keep in proper company with its consort – no easy task as the wind often blew at storm force against them. However, in early March they entered the

Le Maire Strait and cleared it without incident, congratulating themselves as they viewed the open sea ahead that they had avoided the worst weather and, notwithstanding the continued Spanish threat, that their worst problems were behind them. (They did not learn until several years later that the Spanish fleet was devastated by storms as Pizarro lay in wait for Anson off the Horn; they too had inadequate provisions and suffered great losses from scurvy, mutiny and murder, till all but one ship and less than 100 hands remained.)

The same storm that had assailed the Spaniards was waiting for Anson. On March 7 the British fleet cleared the straits, only to be set upon by a furious tempest which drove them to the east, past Staten Island and on into the higher latitudes. They were swept along like flotsam for five days until the storm finally abated. But worse weather by far was yet to come. They had hardly time to put the ships back in order when a storm of hurricane intensity ravaged the fleet. Even the oldest and most experienced mariners on board were terrified. Never before had they experienced such violence from the wind and sea. All attempts to make headway were useless; just surviving the crazed rolling and pitching of the top-heavy vessels was beyond many of the crew and some were dashed to their deaths against the sides of the hull.

Any small lull in the wind induced Anson to hoist sail in an attempt to make northing but each time savage squalls carried away spars and ripped canvas from the yards. Seams sprang in the planking from the strain of supporting the rows of heavy cannon and let in deluges of water, and the most able men laboured on the pumps to keep pace with the inflow. Anson struggled to keep the fleet together, occasionally having to turn his flagship around in order to keep in touch with the slower vessels. On one such occasion he watched helplessly as one of their ablest seamen was flung overboard as the ship came about in the mountainous seas. He swam strongly towards the ship but they were powerless to offer him assistance. Their last view was of him fighting against the waves as the seas drove them apart.

The weather occasionally let up but never for long. At the end of each storm Anson learnt of fresh disasters, till there was not a ship left with a decent mast or set of sails. After 40 days they had clawed their way northwards to the latitude of the Straits of Magellan. By now out of the Southern Ocean they expected kinder weather, but when land appeared, instead of the latitude they imagined themselves to be in, they found they had misjudged their course and direction and were back at Tierra del Fuego. Many men were already ill and dying, and the depression they suffered at this discovery ensured a sharp rise in the death toll. More discouraging still was the news that two of their ships had gone missing in the most recent foul weather — whether lost or foundered, there was no way of knowing.

Misery and forebodings accompanied them back to the Horn. This time Anson was determined not to attempt a rounding until they were well clear of the land and lee shores. This turned out to be a good strategy for the seas were less violent and the wind less gusty. This time, they rounded without mishap and began to make good progress along the Chilean coast. But nothing could protect the crew from the wintry conditions. More died and the rest grew physically weaker. Towards the end of April Anson's flagship, the *Centurion*, was separated from the rest of the fleet and from then on they continued alone. In April, 43 men died of scurvy but once they had rounded the Horn and began to press northwards Anson hoped that the outbreak would abate. Of course it did not. By May twice that number had succumbed.

In his book, 'A Voyage Around the World', Anson describes the perplexing symptoms of the disease and how no two men seemed to be affected in exactly the same way. Some of the more common afflictions included large discoloured spots all over the body, swollen legs, and putrid gums. Other symptoms such as lassitude which totally debilitated the crew, caused Anson great consternation. He goes on to relate: ' . . . it is not easy to complete the long roll call of the various concomitants of this disease; for it often produced putrid fevers, pleurisies, the

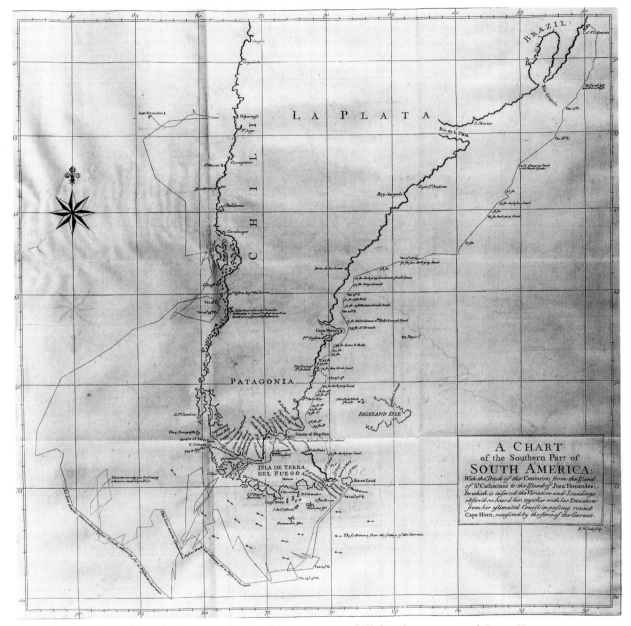

Anson's own chart of South America showing his tortuous and ill-fated route around Cape Horn

jaundice, and violent rheumatic pains, and sometimes it occasioned an obstinate costiveness (constipation), which was generally attended with a difficulty of breathing, and this was esteemed the most deadly of all the scorbutick symptoms; at other times the whole body, but more especially the legs, were subject to ulcers of the worst kind, attended with rotted bones, and such a luxuriancy of fungous flesh as yielded to no remedy.'

But the most peculiar symptom of all was the effect scurvy had on scar tissue. Scars or broken bones of a long forgotten accident, though previously perfectly healed, would turn into ugly wounds or fractures that appeared as though they had just been sustained. Another strange thing was the way a man would seem perfectly healthy, eating, drinking, and laughing loudly, but upon being moved at all, even in his hammock, he immediately expired.

Everyone was now affected by illness to some degree. Each new day claimed the lives of a half-dozen men while Anson strove with an ever-diminishing number of able hands to get clear of the Southern Ocean and into the Pacific. Each fresh gale left its mark of destruction on sails and rigging, although every day brought the hope that the winds would abate and there would be some compensation for the miseries sustained so far. It was not to be.

Once clear of the high latitudes the weather did indeed moderate for a time but Anson was forced to kick his heels for two weeks waiting for the other ships of the squadron to come up with them. When they failed to do so he sailed for the island of Juan Fernandes where they could refit the vessel and allow the sick to recover. Alas, the island did not appear where the chart led them to expect it. Frightened of missing it altogether, a course was set too close to the Chilean coast to obtain a position fix and a course on which to sail back. This fix was obtained within two days but with it came the bitter knowledge that had they kept to their previous course they would undoubtedly have found the island within a few hours. Now contrary winds and calms contrived to keep them at sea another nine days, during which time a further 80 men died.

Even when Juan Fernandes was spotted, the sick men could not be landed for another three days due to the weather and the shortage of fit helpers to prepare their accommodation ashore. The miraculous cure anticipated upon simply setting foot on shore also failed to materialise. A dozen more died on being exposed to the fresh air and although there was no shortage of fresh meat, vegetables and water, it was nearly three weeks before the deaths ceased.

On June 11, two weeks after their arrival, the

Tryal, a small sloop of the squadron, joined the *Centurion* at her anchorage. Most of her company had died or were too ill to move so she was manned only by two officers and three men. She was blown out to sea again before her anchor could be properly secured and more men were lost.

Ten days or so later another sail was spotted

carrying remarkable little canvas but before she could be identified she disappeared into the haze. Several days passed before she reappeared close to the bay entrance and was recognized as the *Gloucester*. Her distress was so obvious that Anson sent out one of his boats filled with provisions, and the following day, when it became clear that she could not make anchorage,

A view of the Commodore's tent on the island of Juan Fernandez where the fleet sought refuge from the ravages of the southern ocean

another boatload of provisions and fit men were dispatched to her. She tacked back and forth outside the bay for two weeks, unable to fetch the entrance, after which she once more disappeared. The plight of the men on board was pitiful in the extreme. For nearly a month they were tossed to and fro just out of sight of the bay but could not get in for lack of fit crewmen. At last, unexpectedly, the wind eased and within a couple of hours she was anchored in the bay. This situation graphically illustrates how unmanageable and inefficient the square-rigged ships of those days were when sailing against the wind, compared with today's yachts.

The next member of the squadron to arrive was the *Anna*, a merchant ship. She sailed breezily into the bay with her total crew of 16 apparently in excellent health, a circumstance later explained by the fact that by chance she had found a wonderful anchorage in which to recuperate, just as her crew thought they were doomed to shipwreck. They had stayed two months before sailing on to join the others. It puzzled Anson exceedingly (as it does me) to find that the *Anna*'s crew, although moderately affected, escaped without fatalities from both fever and scurvy.

The remaining ships of the squadron were the *Severn*, the *Pearl* and the *Wager*. The first two, after parting company with Anson's *Centurion*, put back to South America (this was learnt a year or so later). The *Wager* was wrecked off the Argentinian coast after her captain became disabled in a fall and the crew were so weak from disease and frustration that no one else could summon the wit or energy to keep her off the rocks. The majority of the crew then mutinied and decided to make their own way back to England by way of the Magellan Straits. However, it was not until five months after the shipwreck that 80 of the men set out in the longboat, leaving behind the captain and 18 who chose to remain with him. The mutineers left on October 13 and arrived on January 29 off the coast of Brazil, having left about 20 of their crew ashore at various places. A still larger number died at sea from hunger and thirst. Only 30 remained.

On December 14 the captain of the *Wager* and his remaining men put to sea in two small vessels and were struck by one disaster after another. Storms forced them to jettison pro-

visions. The wrecking of one of their boats at anchor resulted in the death of one man, and four more had to be left behind because there were too many to accommodate in one boat. Starvation and thirst, and finally defeat by the weather, forced them to return to the island from which they had started. Several canoes of Indians came by shortly after and agreed to take them to another island in exchange for their remaining boat, but on a brief stop for provisions, six of the crew who had stayed on board with one Indian, sailed off and did not come back, leaving the captain and four others behind. Luckily another canoe reappeared and fulfilled the Indians' promise of taking them to the island of Chiloe. They remained there for a year before finding a passage back to England.

Anson remained about three months on Juan Fernandez, refitting and provisioning his ships while the crews recovered. The merchant ship *Anna* was found to be unseaworthy so her cargo and crew were portioned out among the other ships and she was scuttled. Anson was quite determined to carry out the orders he had so far dismally failed to fulfill, i.e. to capture some prizes for his masters. As they sailed up the Chilean and Peruvian coasts he carried out some successful raids on coastal settlements and Spanish ships, although their pickings were not nearly rich enough for his liking. During these forays the *Tryal* lost all her masts and was leaking so badly that it was decided to scuttle her too and transfer her men to a Spanish ship now in their possession.

Anson had got wind of a Spanish galleon that plied a regular route from Acapulco to Manila in the Philippines. This galleon made the journey once a year: she was very large and heavily armed, and she carried a very rich cargo. He made his plans and laid a trap for her outside Acapulco Harbour but, unbeknown to him, one of his ships had been spotted and the sailing of the galleon was postponed till the following year. Extremely disgruntled after a long and fruitless wait Anson decided to cut his losses there and sail across the Pacific to China. Repairing first to a port in Mexico for fresh water he set off in the flagship *Centurion* with just the *Gloucester* for company.

They should have picked up the north-east winds at once, but these famous winds, so fulsomely praised by those who have crossed the Pacific, failed to materialize. They stood further south but did not find the expected wind and they began to have serious problems with their spars. The *Centurion*'s foremast began to split and no sooner was that strengthened with splints than the *Gloucester*'s mainmast began to crack. This mast was discovered to be so rotten that it had to be cut back to just a stump. Meanwhile, the ships lay becalmed and the dreaded scurvy began to reassert itself. After seven weeks at sea the disease was rife. As there did not seem any better reason to suppose that the trade winds would appear now than at any time in the past seven weeks, Anson and his officers feared that they would all perish, either of scurvy or their inability to sail the ship, should the wind ever arrive.

It is interesting to note here that Anson's chaplain (and the compiler of his memoirs) became convinced by the end of this voyage that the only cure for scurvy was for the men to be on shore or in the vicinity of land. It was generally assumed that scurvy had something to do with being deprived of fresh food – but they *had* plenty of fresh food on board in the shape of live pigs and fowls. There was an endless supply of fish caught daily and as much water as each man could drink. Even the holds were aired and kept clean, but to no avail. As the disease was just as virulent in the tropics – if not more so – as in cold weather the chaplain could only conclude that a steam emanated from the ocean, and this steam, when mixed with the fresh air necessary for the support of life, in some mysterious way polluted the atmosphere. This might seem a strange notion to us but one must remember that most people believed, among other things, that the world was flat.

The trade winds eventually put in an appearance but because of the *Gloucester*'s stumpy main mast the two ships made extremely slow progress. Towards the end of July the wind increased and the *Gloucester* sustained further damage to her masts and yards. Gales turned to

storms and the ships hove to. The *Centurion* sprung a leak and all her men and officers were turned-to on the pumps. Meanwhile, the *Gloucester* lost her topmast and foremast, and then she too sprung a leak of such alarming proportions that she had to be abandoned. Seventy sick men were transferred to the flagship and the remaining few fit hands joined Anson's crew in sailing her towards land. Storms and calms harassed them constantly and the men continued to die. At last deliverance was at hand. They sighted an island and when a proa appeared, they captured the crew and extorted details of the island and its inhabitants from them. The island sounded like a paradise but in their weakened state it took the 70 men – the entire crew fit enough to stand up – five hours to furl the sails and get ashore.

Instead of the projected two months they had been at sea for six, and another 221 deaths had been recorded, both at sea and ashore. Anson himself had the disease by this time, although only mildly, as did most of his officers and their servants. But thanks to the abundance of fruit and vegetables on the islands (the same ones on which Magellan had landed a similarly disease-ridden company in 1521) all but the worst affected quickly recovered.

They suffered their fair share of excitement even on this small island, several hundred miles off the Chinese coast. At a time when Anson and the greater part of the crew were ashore the *Centurion* was struck by a violent storm. She broke free of her anchors and disappeared out to sea, much to the consternation of those left behind who envisaged themselves abandoned on the island forever or being made prisoners by the Spaniards and put to death for piracy. Anson soon dismissed such pessimism and directed the building of a vessel in which they would all sail to the safety of the mainland. This was no mean feat as most of the tools needed for the job were on the ship. Within a month, however, she was nearing completion. But the work was interrupted by the *Centurion*'s return.

The errant ship had had her share of adventures too. None of her port holes had been properly barred nor her guns lashed down at the moment of her untimely exit from the anchorage. Her yards had been lowered right to the deck to minimize windage at anchor so the only sail that could be set was the mizen. The night was completely black. The wind was hurricane force and directly to leeward was another island. The First Mate made a valiant attempt to raise the yards, but because half the depleted crew had to man the pumps to prevent the ship sinking and the other half were either inexperienced or still weak from illness, this manoeuvre was doomed to failure. After three hours the exhausted men gave up the struggle and prepared to meet their doom. Luckily for them the tide was so strong that it swept the ship past the island and out into the open sea. The storm ceased three days later and another effort was made to raise the yards but when a crewman was killed by falling tackle they again desisted. Instead, the anchor was brought up from its position hanging off the bows, a job that required all hands and two days to accomplish. Then a third, and this time successful, effort was made to set sail and for the next fortnight they plied back and forth into an adverse wind till, at last, they regained the anchorage.

The *Centurion* left the island finally in October to spend an uneventful 10 days on the crossing to Macao, near Canton. Here the ship was thoroughly overhauled, thanks to Anson's considerable expertise in dealing with Chinese bureaucracy, but the Chinese were very anxious to see the last of him, presumably because they were afraid of an attack by the Spanish.

Anson set sail from Macao in April bound, he had informed all but an initiated few, for England and Batavia. In fact, he had something very different in mind. He was determined to cross the Pacific again and ambush the Spanish galleon which he knew was about to depart on her delayed voyage to the Philippines. At the end of May he arrived at his station and waited. The waiting grew tedious but eventually the galleon appeared. Even though the Spanish ship was much larger than the *Centurion* and carried over 500 men Anson was able, with superior tactics and the lure of incredible riches aboard the galleon, to overwhelm her and capture her.

With his treasure and a great number of prisoners Anson sailed again for Macao. There he rid himself of the prisoners, now skeletal due to the conditions in the hold, and counted the money, which amounted to over a million pounds. Profoundly satisfied with his catch Anson weighed anchor and set his course for England, by way of the Cape of Good Hope. This last stage of the long circumnavigation was accomplished with the minimum of adversity and they were received with the utmost delight by the whole English nation, who deemed the expedition to have been the greatest success.

Anson himself was proclaimed a hero and he later set about improving ship design and the lot of the common seaman. Add to this the discovery of the correct cure for scurvy (stimulated by the chaplain's account of the voyage) which led to its elimination from the Royal Navy by the end of the century, and one has to conclude that Anson's journey had been worthwhile despite the appalling loss of life. The Navy duly made him a peer and later First Lord of the Admiralty. He continued in active service and achieved great success against the French in battle, doing much to raise the standard and morale of the Navy.

He was eventually made Admiral of the Fleet and from then on conducted various royal personages to and from the shores of England. On his last voyage he caught a violent cold which led to his death at his home in Hertfordshire, at the age of 65.

Commodore Anson attending King George II with an account of his voyage round the world

'Ice Bird's' Icy Voyage

Some people, in the pursuit of their goal, go through such purgatory, privation and physical hardship that one can but marvel at their strength of will and determination to carry on – not just to extricate themselves from their awful predicament but to go on trying to reach their ultimate objective. Sometimes they have to suffer a re-run of the same harrowing circumstances! One such adventurer was David Lewis, a New Zealander, who attempted to become the first man to circumnavigate the Antarctic single-handed.

David Lewis leaving Sydney in October 1972 to attempt an Antarctic circumnavigation

At the age of 17, Lewis returned home from school on his own in a canoe via 450 miles of rivers, lakes and seas. In so doing he experienced the excitement and independence and achievement which was to set the seal on any chance of his ever living a normal nine-to-five existence. While qualifying as a medical doctor he did some useful mountain climbing and then spent the end of the war as a medical officer in the parachute regiment. Unlike most people whose dreams surrender to the pressures of family and careers, Lewis struggled in vain to subdue his wanderlust. He eventually gave up the struggle on the break-up of his first marriage and went to sea. There followed many successful years of sailing: the first single-handed trans-Atlantic race alongside Chichester and Hasler; voyages to the Arctic; through the Magellan Strait; and later a circumnavigation of the world with his second wife and two small children. A lifelong fascination with the voyages and migrations of the Polynesians led to a four-year research fellowship at the Australian National University in Canberra for whom he conducted many voyages using the ageless methods of navigation by star paths, ocean swells and birds. His second marriage also failed around this time and he became responsible for the bringing up of his two small daughters.

The plan to circumnavigate the Antarctic had been in Lewis' mind for years and at last the opportunity – between two research projects – presented itself. Unfortunately the vessel he had intended to use sank as it was being returned to Australia. Lewis was only thankful that his son and crew escaped uninjured but it put a question mark on the viability of the forthcoming voyage. For a start, he had no boat. Secondly he had no money. Worse still, the vessel had sunk with all his equipment needed for the trip, and not one single item, including the boat, had been insured. Undaunted, he packed his few belongings, sent the children to live with their mother and set off for the coast to procure another boat. Within a week he had one, *Ice Bird*, paid for with an advance from his publishers and money begged from friends. A little sponsorship from a newspaper later came his way with which he

was able to purchase vital items of safety equipment and spares.

Lewis had a profound sense of self preservation and a very good idea of what was needed to furnish a vessel for such an undertaking. Certain items were vital for survival – steel plates to cover all the windows, new strong sails, arctic clothing – and were bought through the generosity of his supporters. As for food, he obviously gave far more credit to his powers of endurance than I would have done. The main items consisted of canned corned beef, ships' biscuits, potato powder, canned fruit juices, margarine, muesli and coffee. Vitamin C was provided in tablet form. Actually, he did have a few less mundane items of food on board in small quantities, but I would not have enjoyed existing on his rations. One omission which would have been unthinkable to most people (and certainly to me) when considering their comfort in the icy conditions was some form of heating. He was tough – he proved he was – but his experiences would not have been quite so dreadful given a little warmth below decks.

The day of departure from Sydney Harbour arrived. Well wishers, including television crews, overstayed their welcome, hanging around *Ice Bird* for hours, long enough to be heartily wished away by its skipper who by now was exhausted from weeks of preparation and already succumbing to the effects of seasickness. It was October, 1972, early spring in that part of the world; the departure date was timed to coincide with the best possible weather around the Antarctic Peninsula where Lewis aimed to make a landing at the American Palmer Base, or alternatively, 40 miles further on, at the British owned Argentine Island.

At first all went well but trouble with the radio soon forced him to make an unscheduled landing in New Zealand. He resented the need to disrupt his rapport with the seas that a week's rough sailing had re-established but the thought of his daughters' fears at his silence plagued his conscience. He stopped long enough to reassure his family and friends, sort out a bounced cheque and then departed. A week out of New Zealand the weather changed and afforded a

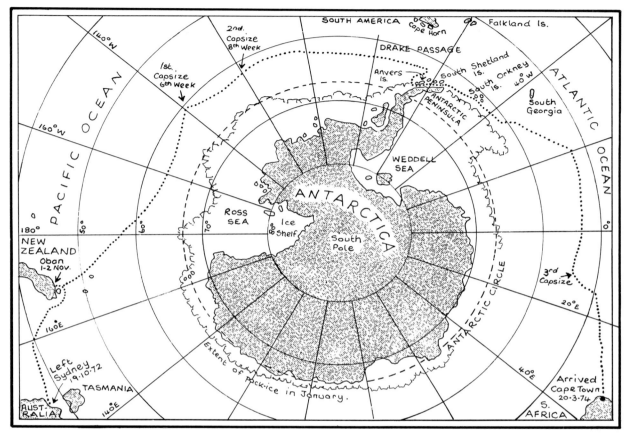

taste of things to come. Gales, combined with snow showers and frozen sleet, drove the temperature down to below freezing, while the occasional squall rolled the boat relentlessly on to her side, as though to give warning to those foolish enough to venture into the sea area of 50 degrees latitude which had been labelled centuries ago the 'Howling Fifties'.

Is it wise to take a small boat into such inhospitable regions, knowing that the risks of simply being wiped out are so high? Probably not. Again, the old question arises, why do it? David Lewis sets out his reasons in his own account of the journey: 'There seems to be a restless spirit inherent in the very nature of mankind that impels us across new frontiers. Without it, indeed, *homo sapiens* could hardly have developed his technology and thinking powers. The basic character of this exploring urge would appear to be always the same, regardless of the

particular way in which it is manifested. Thus it may equally be expressed in searching for truer forms of artistic expression; in the search for scientific truth; or in coming to grips with untamed nature. Thus each of us has his own dream – possesses the potential for his own personal kind of adventure. He then adds: "For myself, the need is to venture physically beyond familiar horizons or to enlarge by a little the accustomed limits of our vision ..."'

At least, that is what he thought in quiet reflective moments. As the weather got progressively worse, fears and doubts crowded in. Moral issues such as leaving his children behind to worry and possibly to be orphaned added to the mental anxiety caused by the threat of much worse conditions to come. The fresh water in the tank below the waterline froze, which meant he had to use the reserve supply in plastic cans. Ice had formed everywhere down below, his sleeping bag and clothes got wet and stayed that way – which was fine provided he did not take them off. Warming up a half-frozen sleeping bag with your body heat is a refined form of torture, in my opinion. I had a cabin heater going 24 hours a day in the Southern Ocean which kept my sleeping quarters warm and cosy, and above all relatively dry, so that coming down below frozen, wet, and stiff with salt was only a temporary state of affairs. For Lewis it was permanent.

He slowly worked his way south and east, through the Roaring Forties, the Howling Fifties and into the Screaming Sixties. The cold, combined with the continuous battering and bruising he suffered from being thrown about the boat in big seas, quickly used up his energy reserves. Any sort of comfort became impossible. The usual small tasks such as working out sun sights suddenly became enormously difficult. Exhaustion sapped his morale and led to depressing thoughts on the mess he considered he had made of his life. In this mental state he began to hear voices, happy voices from the past. He retreated gratefully into old memories, infinitely more preferable to the cruel reality outside.

One should not at this point think that Lewis was losing his grip or that his hallucinations were anything but normal. Most single handers hallucinate at some time or other, usually in moments of stress when the idea of having someone else around is very desirable. Slocum was rescued by the Pilot of the *Pinta* who took over the helm when he – Slocum – was unable to leave his bunk after an over-indulgence of unripe plums. I once experienced the phenomenon when I was stuck up the mast, incapable of going on or coming back down; my two mentors appeared on the foredeck and pointed out the probability, in a dispassionate sort of way, that I would not make it back to England if I did not continue up the mast first. I did, but it would have been impossible without their help.

Lewis was jerked rudely back into reality by noticing a sudden drop in barometric pressure. He had read of this portent; Russian fishermen had talked of 105-foot waves accompanying such a fall in the Screaming Sixties. This snippet of information stored in the back of his mind had caused the majority of his unease so far. A fresh wind howling in the rigging gave flesh to his fears. The howling changed to a high pitched wail and the waves increased rapidly in height. Lewis huddled behind the canvas dodger with tiller lines in his hands to assist the self steering gear should the yacht be thrown off course. A bigger than usual wave scooped up the vessel and slammed her on her side, smashing the self steering, tearing the dodger to shreds and causing havoc below. Lewis struggled to lower the torn stormsail and then crawled back down the deck on his stomach, to watch and wait. The wind continued to increase. It howled itself out of a storm into hurricane force by which time Lewis' terror had burnt itself out and he had retreated again into his other world of dreams. The waves he steered down became mountain slopes that he and the children had skied down in Australia. He returned to the present at the roar of an advancing wave. 'My heart stopped. My whole world reared up, plucked by an irresistible force, to spin through giddy darkness, then to smash down into daylight again.' *Ice Bird* had capsized through 360 degrees and finished the roll the right way up.

The scene that greeted Lewis' first horrified look was appalling; there was a great gap where the forehatch had been, the mast was broken off, and the water level in the saloon was already above his knees. As he fought his way to the main hatch through the multitude of objects floating about he noted irrelevantly, 'British charts float better than Chilean – one up to the Admiralty.' Once on deck a quick survey revealed a six-inch split in the cabin structure on the side that had smashed into the sea and a forehatch wrenched open at a drunken angle but still attached. He wedged it more or less back into place and stuffed rags into the cabin split. Then he baled for his life.

Like the luckless Caldwell I write about later he baled for hours till the boat was nearly empty only to be overwhelmed a second time by a wave. This time the liferaft broke free of its fastenings and disappeared. After a total of 10

The best picture I have ever seen of a man who has survived the ravages of the sea

hours bailing, the boat was dry and the wind had moderated to force nine. Rest was impossible though, as the mast was thumping against the hull and had to be cut loose. Seven and a half freezing hours later saw the mast free but at terrible expense. The following morning he noticed with horror that he had incurred frost-bite in his hands and had not noticed.

Three days after the capsize he got under way with a jury rig made of a spinnaker pole and storm sails with knots tied at their heads to fit the new 10-foot mast. Steering by means of tiller lines from down below was awkward but he was out of the worst of the weather – vitally important if his hands were to heal. Some of the time the boat would sail in more or less the direction he wanted to go but often he spent up to 14 hours at a time at the tiller lines, only stopping to grab food or use the loo bucket. After several days some agonising life returned to his hands which were swollen and still felt as cold as ice. He treated them with double doses of antibiotics to ward off infection.

Progress was approximately one knot: the Antarctic Peninsula was about 2,500 miles away. The temperature was minus 2 degrees Centigrade and a layer of ice coated the deck. Every few days the jury mast crumpled, which necessitated going up on deck to shorten the stays and re-rig. Each time the agony in his hands increased till he screamed with the pain. All this time he was without warm food and drink as the primus stove refused to work in the rough seas, but finally the weather eased and he managed lukewarm stew and coffee. Soon after the weather worsened again and he was forced on deck to tie the sails and mast down. Did he pray at this point, people afterwards asked him? He admits that he would have liked to but did not feel it right to ask for help that he normally scorned. He did express the hope, though, that a higher power, should it exist, might appreciate his attitude. The gale increased to a severe storm, not quite a hurricane but severe enough to build very steep opposing waves, whose crests were driven horizontally with the snow blizzard that accompanied them. At three in the afternoon the boat was capsized again, but with the precau-

Lewis' tough little ship Ice Bird *with her impressive jury rig approaching Cape Town, March 20, 1974*

At times Lewis had to force Ice Bird *through the loose ice with the aid of a boat hook*

tions Lewis had taken there was less damage.

For three days the storm buffeted the tiny vessel while Lewis cowered below, unable to summon the willpower to go on deck even though he was aware that his best new storm jib was being blown to ribbons. When it moderated he was in despair. This storm would surely be followed shortly by another, his progress was negligible, food and water would run out and he would perish from starvation if the sea did not get him first. The evening of December 20 was his darkest hour. But though he despaired of surviving his mind still applied itself to the question of how to make better progress. In the middle

of that forlorn night, the idea came to him.

At first light he began preparations to hoist the heavy wooden boom on to the mast step, using a system of tackles. After eight hours the new mast was ready to hoist. The system worked and an hour later a sail was drawing. Gone was despair, and the pus which was running out of his thumb no longer engrossed his thoughts. Some positive calculations reinforced his tentative hopes of sticking to the original rendezvous at Palmer Base, some 2,000 miles away. It was a bold decision. But fortune, apparently satisfied with the punishment she had dealt him so far, was now disposed to be kinder. The weather settled down to a more summer-like pattern, with longer periods of steady wind and relatively warm temperatures (zero to plus 3 degrees Centigrade).

Prudence dictated a strict water rationing in the case of further severe delays but, being a doctor, he could calculate exactly how much was required to avoid dehydration without unnecessary waste. Now boredom took over from anxiety to trouble his waking hours. Thirst became a tiresome preoccupation from which nothing could divert his thoughts for long. On the positive side, although two fingernails had fallen off, his hands were mending. Steering occupied the majority of his waking hours. Helming is a mindless occupation – unless one is in a race – and a particularly trying one to most single handers used to disposing of their time much more enjoyably, reading books or watching the world go by. (I would rather spend a hundred hopeful hours working on a system of self-steering that put in an hour at the tiller.)

The new rig performed well; so well that within a week enough distance had been covered to think of planning ahead for a landfall. The thought of seeing people again also caused him a few well-justified qualms regarding his appearance. A month earlier he had changed his underclothes when a much abused pair of sheepskin trousers had taken leave of him of their own accord. Since then, he had used the same clothes day and night, and he never removed his boots.

On January 18, he noted in the log: 'Cape Horn rounded 360 miles to the north.' A couple of days later he altered course due south for Palmer Base, 300 miles away. Soon icebergs appeared, only to be obliterated by a gale force blizzard. When it eased and the clouds opened up Lewis saw the forbidding ice-fields and mountains of the Antarctic Peninsula. To reach the base a rocky cape had to be negotiated. It was strewn with stranded bergs and moving chunks of ice through which Lewis threaded his way. The going was treacherous without an engine and there was only an occasional puff of wind to help counteract the currents that threatened to draw the boat on to the bergs. Many anxious hours later he was around the Cape and Palmer was only eight miles away. Alas, his troubles were not yet over.

The wind, which blew straight from the base, remained fitful for the rest of the day and half the night, after which it changed abruptly to gale force. The sight of the receding lights of civilization drove Lewis to letting off a flare but he knew the inhabitants would not see it, and he only succeeded in burning his fingers. There was nothing for it but to try to stay in one place and get some badly needed rest. He spent the remainder of the weary night reaching back and forth across clear water but even so narrowly missed hitting a rock skerry on the one occasion he went soundly to sleep. All the next day he inched forward to within three miles of the harbour. In the evening a drizzle obliterated the rocks and further progress was impossible. At dawn the visibility and wind were fair for the final run in but he again came close to ending the trip on a rocky shoal when just a mile from shelter. Breakers surged under the boat, picking her up and surfing her across the rocks just clear of her bottom. A mile further on she slipped into still water, eight and a half weeks after the capsize.

Battered and worn out though both skipper and boat were after their ordeal, Lewis was determined to continue with the attempt. It could not be done that year but the boat was repaired in readiness for the following summer, when Lewis returned from other commitments and set off again. Seven weeks into the journey and with only about a third of the circumnavigation left to go he ran into another

Lewis writing up his log after arrival at Palmer Base, January 29, 1973

hurricane. The vessel was capsized for the third time and once more lost her mast. Dejection and disappointment almost overwhelmed him but he had the willpower to set about the heartbreaking task of re-rigging and making for port. A month later he was in Cape Town. This time he had had enough.

It was not quite the end of the story though: Lewis' son took over the challenge and brought *Ice Bird* back to Australia, thus completing the circumnavigation.

Mutiny!

There are few Englishmen whose lives have been more talked about, written about, or filmed than William Bligh. Although some writers have tried to present him otherwise, he has been personified as the evil Navy captain of the eighteenth century; an insanely bad-tempered bully who oppressed and cheated the men under his command.

Bligh being cast adrift with 18 crewmen. Their survival was entirely due to Bligh's leadership

In his own account of the mutiny on the *Bounty* one gets a hint of the real man – of the just and able Naval officer, which he truly believed he was. If one then tries to sketch his character from the accounts of the mutineers there would be no resemblance between Bligh's view of himself and those of the mutineers.

Bligh's ill-deserved reputation was under-pinned by glaring omissions from official narratives of the time, which deprived him of much of the credit that was rightfully his. His suberb feats of navigation in the Bering Strait in the last vain attempt to discover the north-west passage, and his achievements as sailing master and hydrographer on Cook's ships – Cook had selected him, when Bligh was only 22, as sailing master on his last voyage – went largely unrecorded. Why?

According to a number of those involved in the fighting on the island of Hawaii, Cook's untimely end was a direct result of Bligh's orders to fire upon a native canoe, which resulted in the death of an important chief. The news of their chief's death was received just when hostile tension among the multitude gathered around Cook had been defused somewhat, and he had had great hopes of retiring unscathed from the shore. As the lament for their chief spread like fire through the mob, hysteria broke out: Cook was set upon and hacked to death.

Though he protested the rationale of his actions, and was never publically blamed for the death of one of world's most famous explorers, Bligh's reputation, at the age of 29, was soured. None of the charges brought against him over the years stuck (and there were a number) but his career was tainted by controversy and great personal dislike, particularly among valuable and close connections which his marriage had brought him. Only from his wife, a clever and talented woman, could he command complete loyalty throughout his turbulent life.

Bligh was an autocrat, like many of his fellow officers. According to an eminent contemporary, although he could command the respect of the men serving under him, he could not win their devotion. He lacked a sense of humour and imagination; more unfortunate still, he lacked the ability to make allowances for age, temperament or anything less than excellence. He felt it his right to abuse those beneath him – even, as with Fletcher Christian, those for whom he showed a great liking.

The fateful decision that made such an impact on his later life came early on in Bligh's career when he was sought after as a captain and navigator, due to his record with Cook. He responded to a request from a family connection to take a young man under his wing. To him Bligh extended unusual friendship and support; in fact he showed a partiality that was noticed and derided by others under his command who were receiving very different treatment. That young man was Fletcher Christian, who subsequently led against Bligh, his best friend and mentor, the most famous mutiny of all time.

In order to set the scene for the mutiny it will be necessary to sketch in the events leading up to it, as far back as August 16, 1787. On that date, William Bligh was given the command of a naval sailing ship, the *Bounty*, 90 feet long, with 46 crew, for the purpose of transporting breadfruit plants from the Society Islands in the South Pacific Ocean to the West Indies.

As their route was to take them around Cape Horn it was imperative to leave England in time to negotiate this notorious promontory before the winter storms. However, alterations which were made to the ship to accommodate the plants delayed their departure from Spithead till late December. As the season was now so far advanced Bligh was given permission from the Admiralty to alter his course, if the necessity arose, to go eastwards around the Cape of Good Hope.

The weather during the initial stages of the voyage was appalling. Storms carried away their spare yards and spars, stove in all the boats and the stern section where the breadfruit was to be stored suffered severe damage, causing the aft end of the ship to fill with water. Luckily, the Canary Islands were not far distant, and on his arrival there, Bligh gave a graphic example of his expectations of the respect due to him. He sent an officer to the Governor of the Islands to inform that gentlemen that he, Bligh, would wait

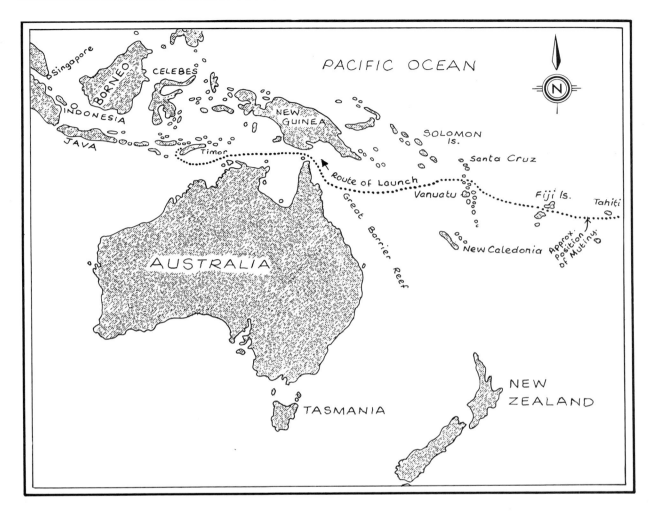

on him in due course – they had already received a polite invitation from him to avail themselves of whatever the islands had to offer in effecting their repairs. Bligh also instructed his envoy to announce that he would perform a 14-gun salute, providing an equal number of guns were returned. The Governor sent back the reply that he only returned an equal salute if the person was of a rank equal to himself. Bligh omitted the ceremony altogether.

On January 10 the *Bounty* left Tenerife and set sail for Tahiti, which Bligh hoped to reach without a halt. They spent a month battling with westerly storms around Cape Horn before giving up and going the long way, round the Cape of Good Hope. After some weeks in Cape Town, they sailed on, pausing twice more to secure wood and provisions along the route. The *Bounty* nearly ran into some unchartered islands off the south coast of New Zealand, which Bligh named the Bounty Islands, but finally arrived in Tahiti in October, 1788.

The *Bounty* remained many months in these islands which Bligh had visited some years before with Cook and where he was regarded by the natives as next in importance to the English God and King George. Although Bligh obviously did not feel much at home in the role of unproclaimed viceroy, he had gained valuable experience in dealing with the Polynesians through careful observation of Cook's strategies.

In great contrast to the manner he employed

with insubordinates, he was a sentimental man with those who showed him affection. The Tahitian King and his wife treated Bligh like a son (actually, they had been given to understand by Bligh's interpreter that he *was* Cook's son). Bligh cultivated their friendship with great earnestness and had no problem achieving his purpose of purchasing enough breadfruit to load the vessel fully. The crew were treated almost equally well, particularly by the women. Within a few weeks every crewman, including the officers, had been befriended by one or more amorous Tahitian girl and they then had to be harassed by the captain to continue their normal duties.

Bligh spent most of his time ashore dealing with the native hierarchy and making copious notes on their ways and customs. He appeared happy to let the men spend their time as they chose, provided the basic duties were carried out on the ship and the breadfruit plants were attended to. A plantation of these plants was immediately started and prospered so well that within four months Bligh could foresee their maturity. He envisaged a departure date by the end of another month and informed his officers accordingly.

When the men showed their reluctance to co-operate Bligh was at first astonished and then rapidly lost his temper. The spread of venereal disease gave him an excuse to humiliate publicly those affected by flogging them, which he imagined would bring them all their senses. Fletcher Christian, in particular, found himself singled out for disgrace, which inflicted severe blows to his pride and spirited character. When Bligh discovered mouldy and rotten sails which had been reported in good order his fury knew no bounds. He publicly accused Christian of criminal neglect of duty and his other officers of being liars and slackers.

Yet it was largely Bligh himself who was at fault for the state of his ship. Had he held proper inspections and gone to sea every few weeks, to chart the coastline and neighbouring islands, the decay would not have occurred. Instead, he had been indulging in his favourite pastime, observing the natives, and recording every minute detail of their habits and behaviour.

Shortly before departure three men deserted and this act represented a serious threat to Bligh's authority. In a fit of unreasonable fury he accused Christian of conspiring with the deserters and trying to incite mutiny. Christian denied it adamantly and, through lack of evidence, Bligh desisted in the charge. The men were rounded up and severely flogged.

They sailed on April 4, bound for other islands in the group. Bligh intended to replace any plants that died along the way and hoped to continue taking aboard fresh fruit and vegetables right up until their final departure from Polynesia.

The voyage began calmly enough. However, it appeared – not from Bligh's own account but from sworn statements made at the trial – that Bligh could not get over his humiliation at the way his officers had neglected the ship and their duties. His outbursts of abuse and tyranny became increasingly more strident. A few days before the crisis the ship called at an island to reprovision. There, everything ashore and on the ship that could possibly go wrong, went wrong. Many of the crew afterwards described their captain as beside himself with a resentment that bordered on madness. And yet, when the breaking point of Fletcher Christian's sanity came, Bligh professed himself to be completely taken by surprise.

It happened over an amazingly unimportant incident. Bligh discovered that his personal store of coconuts was being pilfered and Christian was the unfortunate one he picked on to suffer the consequences. An insulting and utterly humiliating scene took place with Bligh screaming in fury and shaking his fist, first in Christian's face and then at the assembled company. When he had run out of abusive terms they heard, to their dismay and disbelief, that he intended to stop their grog and reduce rations by half.

Christian retreated from the rebuke with tears running down his face. To a fellow officer he said, 'I would rather die a thousand deaths than bear this treatment any longer. I always do my duty as an officer and as a man ought to do, yet

I receive this scandalous usage'. Within hours nearly everyone on board knew that Christian intended either to desert or commit suicide. The sun set that evening on a ship wreathed in desperation and despair.

That night Christian resolved to put together a raft and make for a nearby island, although he was quite aware that such a plan was almost suicidal – the natives were only held from savagery by strength of arms. But he was prevented from putting this plan into action by the constant coming and going of people on deck. In desperation, he spoke of his plan to a junior officer, who pleaded with him to give up the idea. Instead he whispered that the men were ready for anything, they needed only a word from him. For a time Christian struggled to calm the hysteria that was pushing him towards a step which would mean the ruin of his life. But at last, he saw it as his only option, and acted.

He approached the eight men who had suffered severe punishment in Bligh's hands, plus others whom he knew to be recalcitrant. Their inducement to mutiny needed no more than a man to lead them; their resentment of Bligh was sufficient to render them heedless of the penalty of their actions, death by hanging.

They armed themselves, put guards on the officers' doors, then seized Bligh from his cabin and dragged him on deck. The accounts of Bligh's reactions at this point differ greatly, depending on whether one reads his own or the mutineers' accounts. At any rate, whatever he said to the deserters failed to impress them. His oaths or pleading merely served to increase their threats to kill him instantly if he did not do as they directed. A small boat was launched and all those who chose not to stay were roughly forced into it – except a few detained against their will to help work the ship.

Several seamen were allowed to collect together sails, ropes, casks of water, some bread, a small quantity of wine and rum, and a compass. The boat they were in was rotten and would have sunk as soon as all 19 were aboard. Seeing this, a few of the mutineers were prevailed upon to lower a sturdier one instead. The boat drifted astern of the *Bounty* where she was held

William Bligh, 34-years-old at the time of the mutiny. Brilliant leader though he was, he could not inspire loyalty in his men

on the end of a rope. A few pieces of meat, some items of clothes and four cutlasses were thrown at them, along with much laughter and derision. Then the rope was cut and Bligh was cast adrift.

Bligh's reflections during the first few hours in the 23-foot boat, while they rowed for the nearest island, soon caused him to feel almost light-hearted. He flattered himself that he had run a perfect ship: he had carried out his orders to the letter, the cargo of precious breadfruits was thriving and the men were well fed and particularly free from diseases. He thought carefully over his treatment of his men – of Fletcher Christian in particular, with whom he had believed himself to be on the friendliest of terms – and tried to remember any symptoms of discontent or words that pointed to a sense of ill-usage. On each count he felt entirely blameless. He did ask himself why the men had mutinied and could put it down to just one cause: the women of Tahiti.

The problems the 19 men faced – compared with modern castaways – were not only of starving to death at sea or being wrecked by storms; more hazardous still was the likelihood of being killed by natives. Up to then, Bligh had been well protected by arms and strength of numbers but he was well aware of, and prepared for, a very different reception from the same natives now they were almost defenceless and alone.

The nearest island was quite close; a day of rowing and a night of sailing and they were upon its shores. The heavy surf prevented a close approach and all but a few thought they would have to give up the idea of landing. Eventually, a few volunteers jumped into the sea and reached the shore, then aided the others to manoeuvre the vessel on to the beach. Only a few coconuts were found to reward their efforts. By the time these were gathered the weather had worsened and they were prevented from leaving.

They soon found themselves surrounded by interested and not altogether friendly natives, whose numbers increased by the hour. At sunset of the following day Bligh gave instructions to his men to go boldly into the boat while he attempted to divert the natives with talk. Enboldened by his great courage the men pushed their way through the menacing mob and reached the boat. Bligh's own formidable countenance and self command also enabled him to extricate himself from the crowded beach. As he climbed into the boat violence erupted. A hail of stones flew from the shore, many of which hit the men as they struggled to release the anchor. One seamen ran on to the shore in a rage to free the rope. He was immediately felled by stones and beaten to death.

Bligh cut the rope holding them down, slashed at the hands trying to pull them into the water and commanded the men to row for their lives. Canoes shot out from the shore and came in swift pursuit. While some natives paddled others picked up stones from the floor of the canoes and hurled them with deadly accuracy. Ignoring the bombardment and their injuries, the men rowed their hardest, but still it seemed the canoes would catch them. Then Bligh remembered a trick that Cook had used in a similar emergency: he threw some clothes into the water. The natives stopped to grab the garments from the water, fighting with each other for possession. The men rowed on into the gathering dusk. From the ever-widening gap it soon became obvious that the natives had given up the chase and were returning to the island.

The men were badly frightened by the experience. Going ashore had achieved nothing except the lightening of their boat by the loss of their largest companion. While this was to the general good of the others it increased their reluctance to look towards the islands for their deliverance. Bligh had already made up his own mind as to their future course but he believed the best way to get the men to support him was for the suggestion to come from them. After a little general discussion he was entreated by the *Bounty*'s Sailing Master to head for home – home being the island of Timor on which there was a Dutch settlement. From there they could obtain passage to England. The other men added their noisy approval to the plan. Bligh agreed that it was their only chance but emphasized that to survive the journey of several thousand miles they must be prepared to live on an ounce of bread and a quarter-pint of water a day. All promised to do so with an alacrity that surprised Bligh, who felt that their situation was considerably worse than before. The men could already see themselves among friendly European faces, each with a berth on an East Indiaman bound for England. The awesome dimensions of the task ahead was left to Bligh alone to acknowledge with realistic apprehension.

Not wishing to completely quash their great optimism Bligh merely delivered a solemn lecture on the hardships they would certainly

At the instigation of Fletcher Christian, the young man Bligh had befriended and supported, Bligh was seized from his cabin and dragged on deck

face and the absolute necessity of sticking to their rations no matter what the deprivation. He then set sail. Their immediate course was down wind, towards the Fiji Islands, which he recalled from Cook as being somewhere to the north–west. The islands would help their navigation, which had to be a matter of dead reckoning, based on the compass and the quadrant. After the Fiji Islands he would have to find the New Hebrides, Australia, and then negotiate the Great Barrier Reef.

A severe storm abruptly turned their euphoria to misery. All items such as spare sails and rope were thrown overboard to lighten the vessel which, Bligh noted gratefully, was behaving wonderfully considering her grossly overloaded state. The cold and wet penetrated to their bones as they fought to keep the boat afloat, surviving from one hour to the next on a teaspoonful of rum. Island after island crept by. Even in the worst weather Bligh studied the new, undiscovered lands avidly, often having to be held in an upright position by four men while he calculated distances and recorded every topographical detail.

After several days the weather improved and the sun appeared. Wet clothes were stripped off and dried and cramped limbs were eased in the warm sunshine. But the following day brought more stormy weather, more distant islands and the renewed menace of pursuing canoes. Aided by the sails they managed to keep the launch sufficiently far ahead to disappoint the hunters, who quickly wearied of the chase.

Day followed day of storms and bitter cold as they headed out into the open seas. So acute was the cold that the men dreaded the onset of night. Hardly a man could move by morning, unless he had to bale for his life. Some complained of severe bowel pains, others of such pain in their limbs that Bligh wondered how soon these illnesses would render the sufferers incapable of exertion. He forced them several times a day to strip off their clothes and rinse them in the sea, thereby ridding the garments of the accumulated salt from spray. When the clothes were put back on they felt warmer from contact with sea water.

After nearly a week, more islands appeared and were furtively skirted around, and a new course was set for the New Hebrides. Most days Bligh managed to write in his private journal, hunched under his protective clothing, carefully turning the damp pages of the log. The account is largely repetitive; heavy seas, cold, cramp, the doling out of food, interspersed with painstaking details of noon latitude positions and estimated longitude, size and appearance of the islands. Bligh was the first European to sail through the Fiji Islands and his charts are detailed enough for a careful navigator to follow his route, relying solely on his directions.

Going by his own account, Bligh's authority was absolute. He dictated their means of survival, from the course they steered to the meagre portions of food they ate – seemingly without serious dispute. Considering his insensitivity towards the officers and crew before the mutiny one wonders about the feelings of the men – what they felt towards him; what, if anything, they talked about. He does not say. He makes no mention of personal attitudes but wrote that the dreadful weather was probably better in the long run than hot sunshine, from which they would have all died of thirst. But there is no indication that he shared this view with anyone. To him the men had no individual personalities, only personal grievances. When the need arose to reduce their food and water rations still further he felt apprehensive as to how this would be received; some, obviously, were less tractable than others and he fully expected them to take it very badly. He prefaced his order with an explanation of the uncertainties they might yet face, but they all agreed to his proposals. What chance of survival could any rational man believe in without Bligh? No one else could navigate and to land on an island meant certain death. They may have found his dictatorship irksome but they needed him.

The days crept into weeks: hunger turned to starvation. Each morning dawned to reveal

No amount of pleading or threats could sway the mutineers from their desperate course of action

increasingly ravaged faces and hopeless eyes. The sight of each new island, its lush vegetation, coconut trees and camp fires, increased their misery, but as long as food remained Bligh was against taking any chances. Fishing was a total failure despite the abundance of fish swimming tantalisingly close to the boat. Occasionally, in the vicinity of land, they caught boobies and noddies, birds that got their names from their idiotic habit of sitting about on masts or yards where they could easily be grabbed. Bligh was as fastidious in his apportioning of these extra morsels of food as he was in their bread and water rations – even going to the lengths of devising a set of scales out of coconut shells and lead shot. No doubt it served to dispel some disharmony on that score; it also helped to fill in some of the surfeit of tedious time. Small quantities of the rations were stolen but when questioned by Bligh each man swore solemnly that he knew nothing about it.

A stretch of several hundred miles of empty sea lay between the New Hebrides and the Great Barrier Reef, near the topmost eastern corner of Australia. After this was crossed their way led into the Torres Strait between Cape York Peninsula, the most northerly point of Australia (then called New Holland), and New Guinea to the north.

Bligh had set a makeshift sail on each of the two masts to give greater speed – their progress in fact was remarkably good, more than 100 miles a day. But sailing into heavy seas brought even greater hardships. Everyone suffered from the constant spray and solid water shipped over the side, for by now the majority had painful salt-water boils. At least two men were constantly required to bale, but Bligh regarded this enforced exercise as less of an evil than the others as it kept them warmer than they would have been otherwise. He noted: 'When the nights are particularly distressing, I generally served a tea-spoon or two (of rum) to each person: and it was always joyful tidings when they heard of my intentions.' Notwithstanding this benevolence, complaints grew and the braver ones canvassed for a greater allowance of pork: they received an adamant negative from Bligh who kept the food more under his watchful eye than ever.

On Friday, April 22, more than three weeks after being cast adrift the weather reached its height of severity. Bligh recorded: 'The misery we suffered this night exceeded the preceding. The sea flew over us with great force, and kept us bailing with horror and anxiety. At the dawn of day I found every one. in a most distressed condition, and I began to fear that another such night would put an end to the lives of several, who seemed no longer to support their sufferings. I served an allowance of two teaspoonfuls of rum; after drinking which, having wrung our clothes, and taken our breakfast of bread and water, we became a little refreshed.'

On Tuesday, April 26, the sea became littered with branches of trees and driftwood, confirming Bligh's calculations that they were approaching land and the Great Barrier Reef. That welcome fact and a feast of two boobies (plus some flying fish found in their gullets) produced some optimism again among the men. In the middle of the night the helmsman woke Bligh at the sound of surf breaking close by. They hurriedly altered course and sailed in the opposite direction for the rest of the night, the anxiety at this added terror doing away with their recent confidence.

At daybreak Bligh headed once more for the Reef, coming upon it within a few hours. The sea appeared to be breaking heavily over every stretch of it, blocking their way through. As they edged closer the wind changed a few points, forcing them to sail along the line of coral. Suddenly they were hemmed in; the reef had taken a sharp turn towards the sea. The men were too weak to fight with the oars against the incoming breakers pushing them closer to the foaming barrier. Bligh had formed the rather desperate plan of attempting to sail over the reef when a gap opened up ahead, behind which a low-lying coastline could be seen. He shouted at the helmsman above the deafening roar of breakers to aim for the gap. At first it looked too narrow to allow an entry but as they closed with it a channel opened up. Assisted by the wind and tide the vessel lurched through and into the quiet lagoon beyond.

The men were overjoyed at the prospect of landing – which Bligh promised they could do – to hunt for food and sleep on solid ground. The first island they found was rocky and bleak, offering neither shelter nor prospect of food, but a little further on was another with a sandy shore, upon which they beached the boat. A party disembarked immediately and went off to forage for food but as it was nearly dark little was found. In case natives made an appearance Bligh allowed only half the crew to spend the night ashore but the extra space in the boat gave those on board a good night's rest. The next morning, duties were allotted to each man; some to hunt for food and water while others were detailed to clean the boat. In the fierce heat of the sun Bligh ordered everyone into the shade; likewise he forbade anyone to eat the many berries or fruit growing in abundance -- but in some things his orders were not obeyed. As soon as his back was turned the more self-willed members of the company tucked into whatever presented itself as edible. Severe stomach pains were the result of their gluttony, which frightened the sinners into believing they were about to die from poisoning. However the effects wore off and the berries proved to be harmless. An appetising dinner of oysters, clams and root vegetables (cooked by Bligh in a pan that someone had brought into the boat) restored some energy to the company. But by the next day those who had not had a bowel movement since leaving the *Bounty* were suffering from dizziness, extreme weakness and violent stomach cramps. As he suffered these pains himself, but found them bearable, Bligh believed they were not a danger to their lives.

There was no shortage of fresh water at their camp site, or of oysters. Old shelters and fireplaces furnished evidence that natives used the island occasionally – there were also foot prints of kangaroos. Thinking it probable that Cook had not come across the place Bligh named it Restoration Island. However, apart from the water and shellfish there was little else with which to supply their desperate wants. Bligh resolved, therefore, to move on. The morning food gathering produced another fine stew into which Bligh threw the last of the pork to cheat the pilferers; then he directed the company to attend prayers.

Just as they finished a noise on the opposite shore sent them scurrying for the boat. Dozens of Aborigines leapt and danced on the beach, waving spears and making signs for Bligh's company to go across to them. Stopping was out of the question but they sailed close enough to be able to record the appearance of the natives, while remaining a respectful distance from their weapons.

Seeing that some of the Aborigines were preparing to launch canoes, Bligh set sail to the north-west, passing many islands and seeing scores of natives running along the shores, apparently trying to attract their attention. Towards evening they came upon a deserted island and landed on a rocky shore. Bligh sent out food-gathering parties but several of the men became rebellious. The increased food, the temporary lessening of danger from the elements, and the austerity of Bligh's rule had emboldened the more cantankerous members of the company. They complained loudly of being forced to work harder than anyone else and refused to go off at Bligh's orders, stating that they would rather not eat at all. One man got particularly abusive and told the captain just what he thought of him. At that Bligh snatched up a cutlass and told the man to take one also and defend himself. He records that he was ready to fight to the death to maintain his authority and put an end to all such challenges in future. Seemingly cowed by this show of strength the fellow backed down.

While the men were employed in their various pursuits Bligh walked to the topmost point of the little island to ascertain their position. Seeing that the natives could easily have observed their landing he judged it wiser to go on to another shelter for the night. Accordingly, as soon as everyone had returned, they set sail for a small island to the north, further from the mainland.

Rocks prevented a landing in darkness so they were forced to anchor for the night and beach the boat at dawn. The usual forays for food turned up a few crabs and beans – enough for dinner but not to supplement rations. Defiance grew out of desperation; one seaman lit his own fire (Bligh had cautioned everyone against making their presence known to the natives) and set a part of the island alight. Another detached himself from the rest to capture his own noddies (he ate nine raw); at the same time he scared the birds away so that no more could be caught. This show of gross lack of consideration earned him a beating from the captain. Bligh observed bitterly in his diary that these scoundrels were happy enough to trust their lives to him in their greatest need but as soon as he had preserved them from want, they turned against him.

Because of the blaze they were again in danger of detection by the natives. They embarked at high tide and went on, threading their way through sand spits and islands inside the Great Barrier Reef. Several days later, Wednesday, June 3, 1789, they arrived on the west side of Prince of Wales Island – on the tip of the north-eastern corner of Australia. (Some of these islands Bligh named after the day of the week on which he found them, but only Thursday and Friday can be found on a modern atlas.) Ahead lay approximately 1,000 miles of open sea to the island of Timor. The six days spent in and around the islands had not produced the rejuvenation that Bligh had hoped but a remarkable change had come over the recalcitrant members of the crew, now they were faced again with their inability to cope without their captain. All harmony was restored; he was their undisputed leader. This confidence, he believed with naive gratification, was the key to the successful termination to the voyage.

The wind for the first two days was fair, generating good runs of 108 miles and 117 miles, but the weather deteriorated on the third night. Cold rain and salt spray speedily brought a return of former complaints. Two of their number, an elderly seaman and the surgeon, were fading fast. Bligh fed them wine, saved against such a contingency, and offered what encouragement he could. In a few more days, he promised, they would all be safe in Timor.

One of the accusations afterwards directed against Bligh by some of those in the ship's boat

was that by his strict withholding of food he enforced greater suffering than was absolutely necessary; when they arrived at Timor there were still 11 days' meagre supply of food. But he seems wholly justified in this. He husbanded supplies in case of serious delays – a wise move. On the passage from the Torres Straight to Timor, strong winds blew them very quickly across the last thousand miles of ocean but it might have been otherwise. There was also the possibility of missing Timor and having had to continue on to Java, another 500 miles further west.

Strong winds on the 8th and 9th produced more excellent runs. The weather moderated a little and they caught a small dolphin, their only fish of the voyage besides the regurgitated flying fish, but Bligh suffered a severe stomach upset from the piece that fell to him. Yet another gale on June 10 resulted in a 107-mile run but brought a rapid deterioration in many of the company; swollen limbs, extreme exhaustion and a marked inability to think clearly seemed to indicate that two at least would not last much longer. Bligh was informed by a young boatswain that he, Bligh, looked worse than anyone else in the boat. Bligh was amused by the naive words and 'paid him a better compliment.' On Thursday, after the noon position indicated a run of 111 miles, Bligh was sure they were past the eastern end of Timor and warned those on watch to beware of the approaching coastline. Many hours of anxious peering ahead was rewarded, at three in the morning, with the sight of Timor hardening up on the horizon ahead.

To quote Bligh: 'It is not possible for me to describe the pleasure which the blessing of the sight of this land diffused among us. It appeared scarce credible to ourselves, that in an open boat, and so poorly provided, we should have been able to reach the coast of Timor in forty-one days after leaving Tofoa, having in that time run, by our log, a distance of 3,618 miles; and that, notwithstanding our extreme distress, no one should have perished in the voyage.'

Two days later they entered the harbour off the town of Coupang and were received by the Governor of the island who offered them

Bligh and his crew being received by the Governor of Timor. Only one man died on the voyage, at the hands of savages

friendship and every assistance.

At this point, when one would have anticipated their troubles to be over, a fever claimed the life of the botanist (the only man with whom Bligh had felt an affinity), followed in steady succession by five others. Bligh was spared the same fate only by the diligent care of a doctor in a healthier part of the island.

After two months on Timor, Bligh bought a 34-foot schooner (he does not say by what means) to transport himself and the crew to a Dutch settlement at Jakarta on the western end of Java, from which port a fleet sailed for Europe each October. En route to Jakarta he experienced further disciplinary problems from some of the crew, for which two were arrested and left in Surabaya. The surgeon, to whom Bligh had administered the wine in his great need, was the last to die but not before writing a letter to an uncle in England blaming Bligh for putting difficulties in the way of his claiming a sum of money due to him.

Bligh himself reached England on March 14, 1790 and published a book on the mutiny shortly after the event. This account caused a considerable stir but the result was his official acquittal of the charge of losing the *Bounty* and his elevation to the rank of post-captain. It was not until some years later, when the testimonies of 14 mutineers, who were finally rounded up and brought to trial in England, were heard, that the tide of public opinion turned against Bligh. Strangely, the court did not concern itself with the causes of the mutiny, but only with the part each individual had played in the insubordination. Many stones were left unturned, accounts were confused, opinions differed. This left a good deal of speculation as to the causes of the violent emotions that had driven Fletcher Christian and the others to such violent revolt. Of the 14 brought to trial, three were hanged, some received less drastic punishments and three were pardoned. Fletcher Christian, along with several fellow mutineers, escaped possible hanging as they had been slaughtered by natives on the island of Pitcairn.

Shackleton's Perilous Rescue Mission

In 1914, Shackleton led an expedition in his ship, the *Endurance,* to attempt the last of the great Antarctic journeys – a crossing of the South Polar continent from sea to sea. His plan was to land 14 men on the Weddell Sea coast to mount an assault from 78 degrees south. Another six men would proceed south from Ross Island on the other side of the continent and hope to intercept the larger party.

The Endurance, *beset in the Weddell Sea, drifted northwards with the ice pack for ten months*

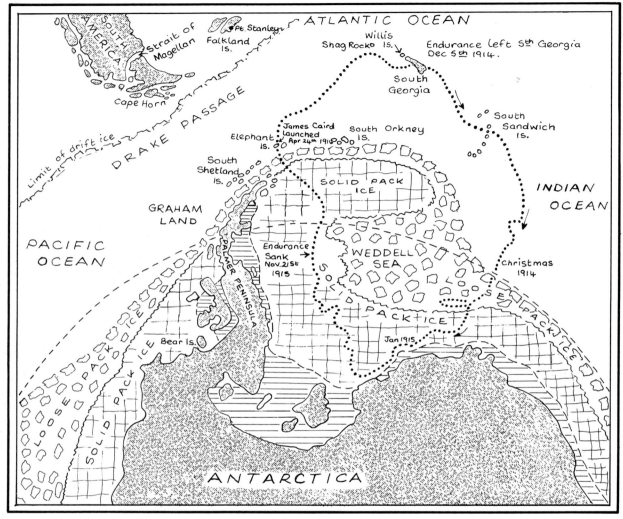

In January of the following year, before the *Endurance* could reach the Antarctic, she was beset by ice in the Weddell Sea in what were exceptionally severe weather conditions even for that icy region. For 10 months the *Endurance* and her crew were trapped in the northbound ice pack. They drifted slowly, living aboard the ship, until the gigantic pressure against the hull crushed her and she sank.

No radio contact had been established with the outside world during the time they were trapped, so no outside help could be expected. For five months the 28-man crew endured a perilous existence on the slowly melting ice, bat-tered by storms and haunted by killer whales circling constantly around the floes. Shackleton knew that sooner or later they would have to leave their floe and take to the ship's boats though he knew that an ocean passage in open boats in the Antarctic represented a negligible chance of success, even to men used to extreme hardships. Shackleton was compelled by a deep anxiety for the welfare of his men. It char-acterized his type of leadership and had earned

The gigantic pressure of the ice slowly forced the ship upwards and at last crushed her like an egg

him the respect and loyalty of every one of his team – they would follow him anywhere.

The melting ice floe eventually cracked right under one of their tents and a crewman fell through the fissure into the sea, encased in his sleeping bag. Shackleton located him in the darkness and with one superhuman heave hauled him back on to the ice. The crack closed a few seconds later with a thousand-ton snap. It was too dangerous to remain any longer on the ice. Boarding their small boats and heading for land, 60 miles to the north east, became preferable to certain death on the floes. The land was Elephant Island, one of the South Shetland group, a barren, icebound rock 480 miles from Cape Horn.

Hardened though the men were by their long exposure to the elements and prolonged inactivity on the ice cap, the first stage of the journey was punishing. Four days of virtually no sleep in sub-zero temperatures, continual fear of being battered to pieces by the grinding ice floes, tortured by thirst and frostbite, assaulted by blizzards – all drew heavily on their physical and mental reserves. After seven days they reached an uncertain haven on the island coast but, with only a brief rest, they again boarded the boats and continued along the coast for another seven miles. This last stretch was the worst of all in terms of sheer physical exertion. Ferocious gusts coming off the ice threatened to drive the boats out to sea, where they would undoubtedly have perished. They fought the oars against the wild seas with a strength born of desperation, and eventually reached the relative safety of firm land.

Not that they were better off in their new situation. It was April, winter was fast approaching and there was no shelter to be had other than their own tents which soon disintegrated in the wind. From then on they lived underneath the overturned boats which served as bedroom, smoke room, dining room, operating theatre and hospital. (To save the life of the youngest expedition member the doctor had to amputate several of his toes.) Shackleton now came to the conclusion that their only chance of survival was to risk the lives of a few men to save the whole party. He resolved that he and five others would take the largest of the three boats and go for help.

The nearest inhabited land was Cape Horn and the Falkland Islands but they were in the teeth of the prevailing westerly gales which blew almost ceaselessly at 60 degrees south, an impossible prospect for their 22-foot wooden boat, *James Caird,* in the middle of winter. There was no option but to go for South Georgia in the opposite direction.

I've seen the *James Caird* – grey, weather beaten, battle scarred. She looks like a day boat really, short and squat, with an open cockpit in the middle and decking, made of canvas and box lids, at either end. Fully loaded she would sit two feet above the water. Six men steered that tiny vessel 800 miles in the most appalling conditions saving not only themselves but also their fellow explorers on Elephant Island from certain death. It must have required the greatest courage and fortitude imaginable.

Everyone set to to make what improvements they could to the *James Caird*. The carpenter fixed one of the other boat's masts inside her keel to strengthen her against the heavy seas and a further mast and sail were reduced in size to make a mizen. A deck of sorts was contrived with painful labour which resulted in more frostbitten fingers, but it was to save their lives. In a few days the boat was ready and loaded with four weeks meagre food supplies. Broken-up floes streamed past their island and would soon become an impenetrable barrier, but a narrow channel remained clear and into this they launched the *James Caird*.

On that day, April 24, 1916, the sun came out for the first time in many weeks and the navigator was able to correct his chronometer: the precise time was vitally important for accurate navigation. As two water containers were dragged through the heavy surf one was punctured, though this was not discovered until much later. Those left on the shore shouted good luck and retreated to their boat shelters to await an uncertain deliverance. The boat sailed north for the open sea, passing penguins and seals upon which the shore party would soon have to live.

Several hours later they ran into a sea of ice — fragments of icebergs carved into monstrous and wonderful shapes by the continuous buffeting of the heaving sea. Death would have come in seconds had they been caught and crushed between the ice castles. The way through it was mercifully short, despite having to row as their speed under sail was too fast in such confined waters and would have led to collisions with the ice floes. (One such incident had holed a boat on the trip to Elephant Island.) By 10pm they were completely clear of ice.

Throughout that first night Frank Worsley, the skipper and navigator of the *Endurance*, steered north by the stars while the others slept. He was kept company by Shackleton, basically a non-sailing man, on whom the uncertainty of the future weighed heavily. He was their undisputed leader and carried the responsibility for them all with an unwavering strength that filled his men with admiration. It is a source of wonder and inspiration to me that he never failed to command that necessary respect and obedience from his men when the dangers were so overwhelming, when the miseries of discomfort were seemingly never-ending, and the chances of survival so appallingly small.

At one time the expedition had boasted oilskins and sea boots, but they had long since disintegrated. Clothes and boots were no longer waterproof and every sea that came overboard — a very frequent occurrence due to the low freeboard — drenched them to the skin with icy water. Even those sleeping below in their reindeer-skin sleeping bags had water washing over them; the canvas decking was anything but watertight. The cook managed in most conditions to heat up what they called 'hoosh' — which I think is a sort of stew made of seal meat — which was eaten extremely hot so that it warmed the body as well as nourishing it. They ate in a space too small to sit up in and sea water regularly slopped down their necks. 'Hoosh' was followed by biscuits, a few lumps of sugar and a cigarette. What routine the men followed when nature called the story does not relate: a pity, it would have been interesting to know.

There was a gale on the third day with a high cross-sea. Most of the men were seasick but swiftly recovered as the additional punishment of icy seas interrupted their vomiting and taught them to hang on to it. Certainly no one would have welcomed that extra hazard 'down below', the black cavern into which they wriggled on elbows and stomach. Once right forward in the sleeping compartment a certain amount of body heat was generated and only the heaviest seas penetrated its sanctuary. Worsley describes the conditions: 'Here we were lifted up and hurled down. With her bows and our bodies we whipped, swept, flailed, and stamped on the seas ... we leaped on the swells, danced on them, flew over them, and dived into them. We wagged

Sir Ernest Shackleton (right) and Frank Hurley. The 28-man crew lived for five months in tents on the slowly melting ice pack

like a dog's tail, shook like a flag in a gale, and switchbacked over hills and dales. We were sore all over.'

The weather on the third and fourth days was miserable. Conditions on board were grim yet their spirits were high for they were making good progress; it was only when the wind turned against them that disappointment and frustration made the same conditions almost unbearable. The wind moderated a little on the fifth day and Wolsley managed a position line – only to be bitterly disappointed in the result. He had hoped for a little progress despite the adverse wind but they turned out to be worse off than their fix two days before.

One crewman was suffering with rheumatism in his legs and feet as a result of wet clothes and cold. The remedy – warmth and dry conditions – was obvious, but impossible. Shackleton had a lot of pain from sciatica for a few days but made no complaint.

A gale blew the next day but in the right direction. All were elated by their excellent progress, but not for long. The following evening a

When the ice gave way beneath them they endured a perilous seven-day journey in small boats and landed on the inhospitable shores of Elephant Island

severe gale put a stop to all further attempts at sailing. The sea anchor was paid out and the boat drifted back down wind in the direction they had come. The sails had to be brought down into their cramped quarters to prevent them icing up and making the boat top heavy. Nothing, however, could prevent the arctic chill from freezing the water sweeping over the deck and forming ice on the hull. Eventually, the vessel became so thickly encrusted with ice that she was sluggish in the sea and threatening to capsize. The ice had to be chopped away, and quickly. One at a time for as long as he could bear it – usually about five minutes – each of them ventured out with the axe and worked at it; a miserable task with the boat leaping about all over the place and waves crashing over the luckless and struggling man. The ice was 15 inches thick in places but somehow they got rid of it. Three times in the next 48 hours this grim

task had to be repeated. They all agreed it was the worst job they had ever done.

At this stage conditions below were taking a decided turn for the worse. In Worsley's own words: 'The reindeer bags were now so miserable to get into that when we had finished our watch and it was time to turn in, we had serious doubts as to whether it was worthwhile. The smell of cured skin constantly soaked and slept in was appalling. First you undressed; that is, you took off your boots, and throwing back the flap of the bag thrust your legs in hurriedly. It felt like getting between frozen rawhide – which it was. You kicked your feet violently together for two minutes to warm them and the bag, then slid in to the waist. Again you kicked your feet and knocked your knees together and then like a little hero made a sudden brave plunge right inside. At first, while you knocked your feet together, it felt like an icehouse, and then it began to thaw out and you wished it hadn't – it smelt so, and the moulting hairs got into eyes, mouth, and nose. So coughing, sneezing, and spluttering, you kicked your feet valiantly

After the tents disintegrated in the wind, they lived under the upturned boats. Even on Elephant Island they were marooned, hundreds of miles from help

together till there was enough warmth in them to allow you to sleep for perhaps an hour. When you awoke you kicked again till you fell asleep, and so on.'

Long spells at the helm called for drastic treatment just to remove the man from his position and replace him with another. He had to be man-handled below, massaged and then opened out like a jackknife before he could be inserted into a smelly sleeping bag.

That day culminated in a nasty scare and near catastrophe. Shackleton, on the helm, shouted to those on watch that the weather was clearing, but immediately after shouted again 'For God's sake, hold on! It's got us!' Instead of a clear line of pale sky on the horizon signalling the end of a turbulent weather front, he was looking instead at a great wall of white water which loomed out of the darkness and buried them in its breaking crest. The five men desperately baled with any container that came to hand to keep themselves afloat. For a while it seemed a hopeless task but slowly the water level began to subside. Afterwards, they reckoned that an iceberg must have capsized in the area to have created a wave of such tidal proportions.

At last the weather did moderate and was followed by two days of wonderful sunshine and swift progress. By noon on the 10th day they were halfway to South Georgia. The following day's run was 96 miles, their best 24 hours' run, bringing them within 155 miles of an island off the west end of Georgia. The men were in high spirits despite the miseries of frostbite, burns from the primus stove and skin inflamed by the chafing of wet clothes. Thirst became almost intolerable. There was no fresh water and only the damaged container remained. Although the polluted water was brackish and unpleasant they were forced to drink it, but it was limited to the bare minimum of one gill a day per man. Still, land was near; they felt they could endure anything.

At dawn on day 15, pieces of seaweed were spotted, followed later in the morning by a shag, supposedly never known to venture more than about 15 miles off shore. (I once saw one more than 50 miles off shore and had to choose between the shag, the pilot book, and my navigation as to who was right and therefore where I was. It turned out to be me but I charitably assumed that the bird had been blown off course.)

Happily for the crew of the *James Caird* this bird was in its rightful place, a fact confirmed a few hours later by the sight of a towering black crag through a rift in the flying scud. The effect on their morale was electrifying. They congratulated each other and discussed what they would drink ashore that evening. Their fellow crewmen on Elephant Island, they said, would be rescued within the week. Their hopes, alas, were drastically ill founded, as they were shortly to discover.

By mid-afternoon King Haakon Sound was dead ahead and Wilson Harbour off to the north, but neither was accessible to them. One was open to the west and it would have been disastrous to approach in the dark with a heavy sea running; the other was to windward. The wind was rapidly strengthening to gale force again, forcing them to heave-to 18 miles off shore to wait for an improvement. All that night and the next day they wallowed in the heavy cross-seas, shipping quantities of water. They were in the worst possible position, caught on a lee shore and unable to sail out of danger.

In the afternoon the wind increased to hurricane force and shifted a couple of points, making their position even more desperate. They were driven inshore, pushed in front of a roaring line of crashing combers hell-bent for the opposing cliffs and glaciers on to which they would soon be dashed. The men watched, appalled, as every dizzy rise to the top of a breaking wave brought the cliffs closer. Each felt that their situation was hopeless.

But suddenly Shackleton yelled above the turmoil to bring up the sail from below. With great difficulty they hoisted it and pointed the bow away from the land. Worsley recounts: 'She gathered way, then crash! She struck an onrushing sea that swept her fore and aft even to the mastheads. While all bailed and pumped for dear life, she seemed to stop, then again charged a galloping wall of water, slam! like striking a stone wall with such force that the bow planks opened and lines of water spurted in from every seam, as she halted, trembling, and then leapt forward again. The strains, shocks, and blows were tremendous, threatening every minute to start her planking, while the bow seams opened and closed on every sea. Good boat! but how she stood it was a miracle of God's mercy.'

For three hours they battled grimly on, not believing they were saving themselves but just fighting off certain death for as long as possible, and to do nothing would have been suicide. Thirst and fatigue were forgotten as the coast receded slightly, giving them a little more sea room, only to be immediately robbed of this small hope when they saw an island directly in their path. In the darkness the cliffs towered over their heads; with hearts in their mouths they baled furiously and tried to reassure each other that they would make it, though each felt it impossible. Inch by inch the boat moved forward, buffeted by the backwash from the cliffs. With bated breath they edged past and beyond the point, and then, as if frustrated at their escape, the hurricane abruptly abated.

Now that the danger was over the men noticed their parched throats and swollen tongues but there was no water left. Some of their party were more exhausted than others; those who could, rowed, as their progress was slow in the dying breeze. King Haaken Sound was still nine miles away. During the morning the wind began to increase again from the direction of the sound until they found themselves once more being set onshore. Setting as much sail as the mast would bear and rowing up to windward, they made grudging headway towards the sound entrance. As evening fell it became obvious that they would not make it. Just a little to the south a cove with a possible landing area became visible. They bore away towards it. Although there was no obvious landing spot immediately apparent they squeezed through the narrow entrance between rocks and rowed to the beach. The beach was strewn with boulders but they

brought the boat in as close as they dared and leapt ashore to drink the water lying in pools at their feet.

Once their thirst was appeased everyone began to unload the vessel of her stores and gear. The men were almost dead on their feet with exhaustion. Shackleton got the stove working and made everyone hot milk and 'hoosh'. Then an enormous effort was required to hand everything out and carry it over the rocky ground, above the reach of the waves. Shackleton later confided to Worsley that he thought two of their number would have died had they had to remain another 24 hours on board. As it was, these two were nearly all in, and could scarcely make their own way up the beach to a shallow cave where they collapsed.

Shackleton took the first watch by the boat as she could not be moored with safety nor, in their present state of weakness, dragged across the boulders. Instead of the hour allocated to

Shackleton eventually decided to risk the lives of a few to save the rest. He and five others took the James Caird *and went for help*

each man on watch he stood three. Soon after the watch changed a wave ripped out the boulder the boat was tethered to and carried it further up the beach. Then the wave surged backwards, taking the boat with it, nearly carrying off the man trying to hold the boat down. That was the end of their sleep for the night for the boat now needed three men to attend to her and even then she threatened to stove in her planks on the boulders. Dawn coincided with high water and they set to to work the vessel up the beach. By lunch-time it was clear of high water and after a meal, they found the energy to get it right off the beach. By the end of the day it was settled on to the grass.

I find it wonderful that the men could carry out this task in their exhausted state and after all they had gone through. It must have been tempting to believe that they would not need the boat again; they were on an inhabited island and other vessels would be used to rescue the others. On the other hand the idea of abandoning the gallant boat to her fate after all she had done for them must have been unacceptable. As it turned out, they could not proceed overland from their cove because the way was blocked by glaciers. This was a possibility Shackleton must have taken into account when deciding to save the boat. It is lucky for us that they did so and later returned her to England enabling people to marvel at both boat and crew for generations to come.

The story does not end there, of course. The men remained in their cave for a few days, feasting on young albatross and making sorties into the interior while their two unfit companions recovered their strength. In the course of one of these expeditions they discovered sea elephants and driftwood, two essential ingredients to their survival if they should be forced to spend the winter there. One morning they awoke to find ice filling the entrance of their cave, pushed there by the sea. Next day a gale blew but the day after that was fine. The view of the routes into the interior from the vicinity of their camp looked unpromising enough to prompt Shackleton to relaunch the *James Caird,* not such a difficult task this time as it was downhill – and

they were much fitter – to search for a more suitable place to begin the overland march. With their gear aboard once more and the weather fine they set sail, full of optimism, for another part of the island. A few miles down the coast they landed again on a sloping shingle beach. Their new harbour was littered with a great amount of driftwood, including ship's flotsam and jetsam, blown here from vessels that had foundered off the Horn: carved figureheads, binnacle stands, brass-topped stanchions, all tossed up on to the shingle by an uncaring sea and left to rot. Among the sad debris they made a shelter of their upturned boat and blessed the Providence that had brought them safely thus far.

The next day it blew yet again so while the others made their new quarters more snug Shackleton and Worsley searched for a way over a hugh glacier at their back. From the top they could see their way into the saddle by which route they hoped to cross South Georgia.

It was coming up to full moon and Shackleton was anxious for the weather to moderate so that they could make a start. Across their path lay a considerable mountain range, averaging 5,000 feet in height, with peaks up to 9,200 feet. Huge lateral ranges struck off at right angles to it. The interior was ice and snow hundreds of feet thick with cliffs and peaks piercing the surface in places. It was a country ravaged by the severest storms and blizzards; its ice fields were continually bombarded by avalanches, and hidden crevasses and precipices lay in wait for the unwary. They had to be able to see where they were going by night as well as day. At last, after interminable delay – wearing to every one's nerves – the weather settled. It was May 19 at 3am, when Shackleton decided to make the move. He, Worsley and one other set off, leaving two behind who, he felt, were not strong enough to withstand the ordeal ahead.

A sledge had been prepared with provisions and gear for the journey but after only four miles it had to be abandoned; it had already become necessary to rope themselves together. Ahead lay a great ridge, spiked with peaks with passes in between. They chose the lowest and proceeded to its summit. It was impassable – as was the second, and the third. At each failure they retraced those hard-won steps and tried another route. They arrived at the fourth gap as darkness was falling. Ahead, the way could not be ascertained properly but to go back a fourth time was a sickening prospect. Shackleton decided to risk it.

They started the descent. After 200 yards Shackleton sat down on the ice, instructed the two others to sit close behind him, and let go. They shot down the slope into the darkness, travelling a mile in a couple of minutes and more than 2,000 feet in altitude. It was a frightening experience but they were none the worse for wear – except for the holes in the seats of their trousers. However, Shackleton decided not to try it again. After a quick meal of hot 'hoosh' the march continued. All about them were bluffs, seracs and icefalls, making the going extremely hazardous. At 7pm, the moon came out and they could see where they were going.

By midnight they had climbed to the top of the range and were looking down upon a large open bay. Because Shackleton feared they might overshoot Stromness Bay whaling station they took a north-east line. When, after several hours, they came upon the breaking-off edge of a glacier it became obvious that they had turned towards the sea too early. Back they trudged again. This time they struck out on a more gradual curve which brought them to another rocky ridge. There was just one gap in it, up to which they must climb. It was now 5am. A short rest and more 'hoosh' restored some of their flagging energy and they felt ready to attack the rock buttress. At last they could see what they were heading for; a valley, half filled with a mighty glacier, stretched away under their feet to another ridge, beyond which was Stromness Bay. Carried softly on the still morning air came the sound of the whaling station's 7am whistle. They shook hands and threw away the primus stove – the oil was finished so there was no point in retaining it.

The path they chose to follow worked well for half a mile but then became dangerously steep. Shackleton cut steps across a 100-yard ice

slope while the others, roped together, followed. If any one had slipped he would have taken the others with him to their deaths. They came to an even steeper face but the ice was slightly softer and they were able to kick a foothold while lying flat on their backs. In this manner they progressed downwards, afraid to lift their heads off the ice for fear of toppling forward. After about 1,000 feet the incline grew easier until they were in rocky hills below the ice face and could look up to see their incredible route etched upon it. They had reached the head of Fortuna Bay.

The going was good along the beach skirting the glacier and soon they were inland and looking for a way into Stromness Bay. At 1:15pm they stood on a 3,000 foot summit with the bay stretched out before them. Instead of taking a steep slope to the station, Shackleton decided on a circuitous route – which, they later discovered, added a considerable distance and many obstacles to this final stage. Their path involved walking along a stream of freezing water at the bottom of a ravine, at the end of which they found their way blocked by a precipice and a waterfall: it was either go down or go back. As none could face the second option, they tied a long rope around the smooth rock at the top of the waterfall, and then slid about 50 feet down it. They covered another mile of hills and frozen marsh before reaching the station.

The first man they met, a Norwegian, just looked at them in amazement and carried on. The next two, also Norwegians, fled at the sight of them. The fourth was the captain of the station who, once he had identified them, told the entire station of their arrival, and their plight. In a short space of time they were transformed into recognizable human beings again and were plied with food and questions. The first problem, rescuing the three men from King Haakon Sound, was completed in a day with a borrowed whaler. The problem of the men on Elephant Island was more perplexing and was to take them the entire winter to solve. On May 23, Shackleton, Worsley and one other took another borrowed whaler to find the men. They fought the elements for 100 days but failed to reach the island.

In four attempts with four different vessels Shackleton struggled desperately to reach his men, going grey with the strain and almost out of his mind with anxiety. On one occasion they came within 18 miles of the camp but were driven back by pack ice. One of the attempts was made with a 70-foot schooner but her engine broke down. At last the Chilean Government came to their assistance with the loan of a small steamer, and this time they made it. Through his binoculars Shackleton anxiously counted the men emerging from under the boat. They were all there. His relief and delight stripped years from his face.

The First World War had raged in their absence and some of the men later lost their lives fighting in it. Shackleton returned to South Georgia six years later on a new Antarctic expedition. His ship, the *Quest*, encountered a violent storm during which Shackleton remained

on the bridge, soaked to the skin. He had no rest or sleep for two days and retired finally to his cabin, worn out by anxiety. On arrival at South Georgia on January 4, he went ashore and arranged for the crew to celebrate Christmas – the storm had prevented a celebration on December 25. In the early hours of the following morning he was taken seriously ill and died very soon after of heart failure.

At the announcement of his death next morning the crew stood bare-headed in the rain, stunned at the news. It was hard to believe that the greatest man they had ever known had gone. Immediately afterwards came the announcement that the expedition was to carry on: Shackleton would not have wished it any other way. He was buried on January 5, 1922, at the whaling station, Grytviken.

The men left on Elephant Island watching the arrival of their rescuers. They had existed on the ice for 22 months: no lives were lost

The Poet and the Practitioner

'Why did you do it?' is the question I am still most often
asked about my circumnavigation. Straight away I get the
feeling that no answer I give is going to be very satisfactory.
Stock replies like 'for the challenge', or 'because it was
there', sound fine but they do not convey much to people
whose environment has not prepared them for such ideas.
I have tried explaining that the answer lies in circumstance,
opportunity, and a vast variety of personal motives. The
answer that appeals most widely, however, is – 'I must be
a bit mad'. It is easy to relate to madness; it explains our
differences if not much else.

Frenchman Bernard Moitessier before the first single-handed round the world race

Englishman Robin Knox-Johnston on arrival in the UK after the race

The aim of this chapter is not so much to tell a story of courage in adversity as it is an attempt to shed light on the curious impulse that prompts some individuals to go in for the kind of experiences that most people would not contemplate. I would also like to illustrate further the effect the combined forces of the elements and solitude can have on some people over a long period of time, and how others are able to resist being effected.

In 1967, Francis Chichester sailed halfway around the world, stopped and then went on the rest of the way. He was followed shortly by Alec Rose. The next thing on the agenda, so to speak, was for someone to go the whole way non-stop. Such a challenge had to be taken up: among those who showed interest were six Britons, two Frenchmen, an Australian and an Italian. Of the ones who finally set out, only one, Robin Knox-Johnston, returned to England after rounding the three great capes; Good Hope,

Leeuwin and the Horn. Some dropped out for the usual reasons – boats which proved unsuitable for the Southern ocean, gear damage or illness. Several became disillusioned early on and decided they had better ways of spending their time. One of the most interesting competitors, Donald Crowhurst, died at sea. He deserves a chapter of his own and I will return to him later.

For my purposes, in this chapter, I shall concentrate on two individuals, Bernard Moitessier, a Frenchman, and Robin Knox-Johnston, an Englishman. Both men were fit, experienced seamen and possessed justifiable confidence in their ability to survive at sea. Both were of sound mind – or at least as sound as anyone wanting to do such a thing can be judged to be.

Moitessier had already decided on a solo circumnavigation before 'The Sunday Times' race was announced: he was going, he said, for the good of his soul and when asked if he would

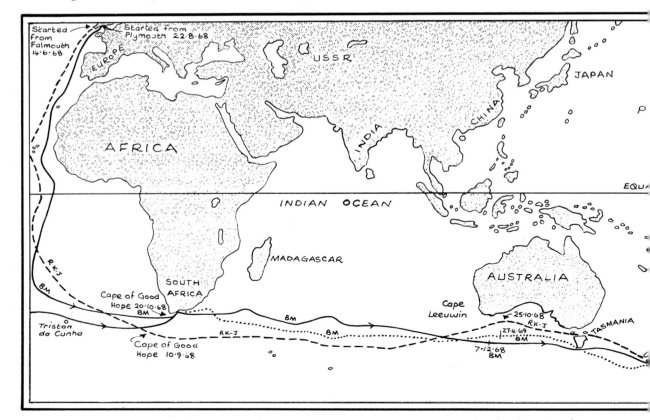

join in the race, made it clear that he had no intention of becoming involved in the hype and publicity of a sponsored event. In the end though, he decided to comply with the rules and start from Plymouth. It meant the chance of carrying off the £5,000 first prize, and since the rules did not specify the need to say 'thank you' he felt his personal freedom was not at risk. He was a romantic, with somewhat mystical notions about the sea – a modern-day Slocum who roamed the oceans like a vagabond.

In sharp contrast to him in almost every respect was Robin Knox-Johnston, a 28-year-old Merchant Navy Officer. Someone described him at the time as having 'very right-wing and blimpish views for one so young'. He was like many other British heroes of the past, staunchly conservative and patriotic. One thing was very clear in his mind: no Frenchman was going to be the first to circumnavigate the world single-handed non stop. Britons had always led the

way in these matters and by rights a Briton should do so now.

As one of those self-elected Britons, Knox-Johnston made his plans. Plan number one was to have a fast, 53-foot lightweight monohull designed and built. It would be big enough to rival the speed of any competitor and built into it would be some novel ideas to keep the cost down. Unfortunately, none of the many firms applied to for support could be persuaded to part with even the modest amount required for the vessel. Knox-Johnston was forced to abandon those ideas and turn his thoughts instead to his 32-foot *Suhaili*, a sound little ocean cruiser he had had built in Bombay and in which he had recently sailed back to the UK. That she could do a round-the-world marathon he had no doubts but he was not so sanguine about his chances of beating vessels like Moitessier's or the various multihulls taking shape in the boatyards of other competitors. His best

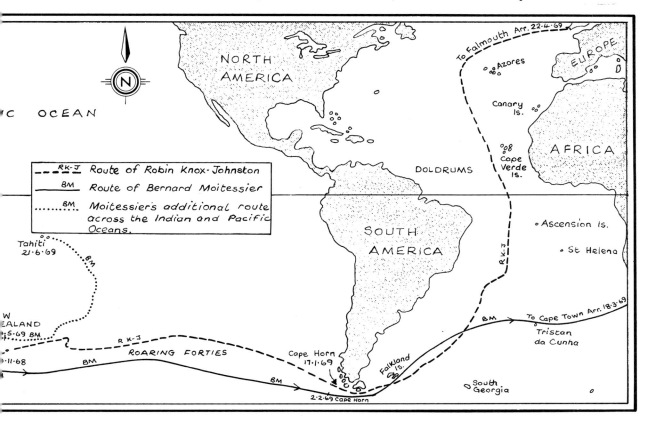

chance, he reasoned, was to leave months before the faster boats so that he could not be caught.

Contestants were invited to start any time between June 1 and October 31, 1968, on the understanding that it would be irresponsible to encourage them to take on the Roaring Forties outside the 'summer' season. (At the time, too, the 'Race' organizers knew that most of the sailors wanted to set off when they were ready and would not agree to start together. These days, there is just one start.) Knox-Johnston left in June about the same time as ex-paratroopers John Ridgway and Chay Blyth. These two had rowed across the Atlantic together so they knew something about the sea although neither had done a lot of sailing. By September they had both retired, having found out the hard way that their boats were totally unsuited to the harsh Southern Ocean conditions. On August 22 Bernard Moitessier set off from Plymouth, by which time Knox-Johnston was already 1,500 miles west of Cape Town.

The sight of his wife trying vainly not to cry upset Moitessier. He was anxious to be gone and nothing but the sea counted at that moment. He wanted to be alone with it. He likened himself to a tame seagull that had to get away sometimes to the open sea: no one questions its motives. Once clear of the Channel Approaches and heading south he shrugged off all thoughts of land and immersed himself in the business of sailing and getting used to being at sea again. He was not, apparently, intent on pursuing Knox-Johnston with the thought of overtaking him: he was merely living each moment to the full and attuning his mind to the spell of the elements – which greatly influenced his thoughts. He loved the sea, and this, I have come to the conclusion, was the most important factor in the later betrayal of his (admittedly rather loose) commitment to an official circum-navigation.

I, on the other hand, do not love the sea. I enjoyed being at sea, but without my particular challenge it would have soon lost its appeal. Presumably, if I liked sailing (which I do not) I would go to sea now. Neither Knox-Johnston nor I were particularly enthralled at the prospect of spending nine or 10 months at sea. If he had been in different circumstances and had seen the chance to be the first to climb a mountain, say, then I expect he would have done so. So would I (well, perhaps not a mountain as I am not very fond of heights, but certainly something else).

Knox-Johnston soon discovered that spending a long time at sea was not much to his liking. At first he pursued his steady way south with no problems other than a leaky plank, which he repaired by diving over the side. He frequently went swimming – a pastime fraught with the risks of sharks, capricious puffs of wind and the like – and occasionally he commented on the beauty of a sunset. But as the weeks went by most of the entries in his log contained complaints (mine was the same): too much wind, too little wind, squalls, unruly winch handles, bronze shackles that worked themselves loose, and so on. He did not spare too many thoughts for the mystical powers of the elements. When there was nothing much to do on board he found the enforced idleness irksome and time hung rather heavily on his hands. Thinking about what to eat bored him and prompted this comment in his log: 'I had some difficulty deciding what to have for dinner. If one had to put as much mental effort and imagination into the reproduction of the human race, it would have died out long ago.' A period of self-discipline and adjustment was necessary, he realized, to accept the fact that the next nine months or so would be boring if he was to see the journey through to the end. As the flagship of British aspirations he did not think that *Suhaili* and he presented a very heroic picture. Imagining the Drakes and Nelsons looking down on his modest efforts gave him some encouragement, but also he could imagine them groaning at times at his progress.

On the plus side though, after 43 days at sea, he safely concluded that solitude was not going to drive him insane. Only once had he heard voices and experienced the eerie sensation of his hair beginning to stand on end. Being an eminently down-to-earth sort of person and not superstitious, the notion of voices hundreds of miles from the nearest land produced in him only a momentary question about the supernatural, to be followed almost immediately by the conviction that there must be a reasonable answer to this phenomenon. There was, of course. He had inadvertently reconnected his tape player and was hearing the introduction to a concert. According to a psychiatrist who had interviewed him before and after the trip, his mental health was described as 'distressingly normal'.

Moitessier's feelings after a month at sea was quite different. Time had stopped (a common occurrence associated with solitude). His whole being was suffused with the wonder of being at sea with his boat, Joshua. He was filled with peace and wanted only to go on forever in the same way. He said: 'I think the previous trip was to see and to feel; I would like this one to go further.' Several days of poor progress moved him to remark: 'I do not lose my head but I meditate on the vanity of things ...'

Near Cape Town, Moitessier succumbed to an urge to leave a message reassuring his wife and children that all was well. Instinctively, he wanted to press on and keep away from land and people but for once he ignored the urge and hailed a passing freighter. With his slingshot he delivered the package on to the ship's deck but curiosity compelled the freighter's captain to come back for a closer look at Moitessier. The large ship passed by too close and caught the yacht's main mast, ripping out Joshua's shrouds and twisting her bowsprit 25 degrees to port. The mast was bent and the bowsprit looked irreparable, it seemed like the end of his nonstop circumnavigation. The numb reaction to calamity settled over Moitessier for a while but a night's rest and closer inspection next morning provided a solution to both mast and bowsprit problems. By the end of the following day Joshua was in one piece and heading for the Southern ocean again, her skipper buoyed up by his success and its portent for the future.

Not even grappling with the problems of heavy seas and iceberg limits off the Cape of Good Hope could depress Moitessier's spiritual communication with the elements for long. After three sleepless nights he noted in his log:

'I wonder if my apparent lack of fatigue could be a kind of hypnotic trance born of contact with this great sea, giving off so many pure forces, rustling with the ghosts of all the beautiful sailing ships that died around here and now escort us. I am full of life, like the sea I contemplate so intensely. I feel it watching me as well, and that we are nonetheless friends.'

Two knockdowns in the same day did no damage to the boat although his carelessness with the sextant, which he had inadvertently left in a vulnerable place, caused him some concern. He tended to forget himself, not to eat properly and to take only catnaps, while he revelled in the play of the boat on the sea. At the same time certain remarks make it obvious that he was well aware of the effect this was having on him. 'One has to be careful though, not to go further than necessary to the depths of the game. And that is the hard part ... not going too far.' The following few days produced such marvellous weather and good runs that he decided to have one of the three bottles of champagne he had been given to drink at each of the great capes. When the bottle was empty he went on deck to find a passenger on board. This, he admits, was also cause for concern, but after a brief chat the fellow left and Moitessier went below to sleep off the effect of the champagne.

I can well understand Moitessier's feelings regarding time. It loses significance and events become very difficult to pinpoint. But I cannot relate so easily to the way he allowed himself to be influenced by such things. Like Knox-Johnston, I am a more equable type. These were unknown areas into which I feared to tread in case they distracted me from my objective – as they did Moitessier. Not that he minded altering his plans if circumstances dictated. He was receptive to changes which were, to his mind, an improvement on an earlier point of view. Actually, he came quite close to quitting the long route back to Plymouth and stopping off for a while in Mauritius. He was tired, his back

Overleaf: The 32-foot wooden ketch, Suhaili, sailed by Robin Knox-Johnston, photographed just off the coast of the Scilly Isles

was hurting him and he was losing weight, due, he thought, to an ulcer which had troubled him for 10 years. His confidence had for a time been replaced by a feeling of emptiness, an unsureness about where to go. However, some vitamin tablets, increased interest in food and a few daily yoga exercises soon revitalized him, and the feeling passed.

By Christmas, Moitessier was halfway round the globe and had retreated a long way into his 'real' self. In the same way that outside influences no longer had the power to affect Crowhurst's inner self after four months alone at sea, Moitessier had fully succumbed to his fertile imagination and stepped beyond 'normality' – although, unlike Crowhurst, he was never in danger of losing his powers of rationality. On the occasion of the second bottle of champagne, passing Cape Leeuwin, he 'encountered' a rat which he had killed on another voyage. I wonder if most people's consciences, like mine, give them a slight twinge when they squash a spider or trap a mouse, knowing they have absolute power of life or death over the victim: live and let live, or rid yourself of a pest? Such twinges of conscience occur when one is faced with inanimate and powerful forces beyond our control. At any rate, the rat had looked Moitessier in the eye before he had killed it, giving him a choice, which he ignored. But the question returned many times to haunt him at vulnerable moments. All the books he now read exercised a power and profundity over him, and caused him to examine his innermost thoughts. In similar circumstances Crowhurst succumbed to Einstein's theory of Relativity and made that the basis of his (insane) salvation. For Moitessier, what he read was a confirmation of his inner peace of mind, built up of freedom from, as he puts it, 'the modern artificial world where man has been turned into a money-making machine to satisfy false needs, false joys' – and a rediscovery of the values of his native Asia through yoga. He lived every day for itself, with no plans beyond that of the present.

Knox-Johnston was, in comparison, unemotional and placid, and although he sometimes got depressed and fed up he could not be swayed for long from the primary objective of the voyage. He, too, was occasionally philosophical: 'It is perhaps as well that I am more of an optimist, or perhaps fatalist would be a better word, than a realist, as if I were to be the latter I would give up today. On thinking about it though, perhaps I am a realist optimist – it's all speculative anyway.' Actually, this was during a rough patch when gear had started to break after only one week of heavy weather in the Roaring Forties. He longed for a hot bath, a large steak with fresh vegetables and hours of uninterrupted sleep. The knowledge that these things were lost in the future almost made him despair. Fortunately, one cannot just get off when one has had enough – and, after a time, a change of mood and weather restored his sensibility and optimism.

By the time he had reached Australia his difficulties had become more serious; a broken tiller with a very makeshift repair, no self-steering at all, no engine and no radio. The idea of giving up was very tempting, the knowledge of Cape Horn still to come most unappealing. Still, he had come this far in a little boat, why not at least try to get further. It would be a shame to waste all that work done so far, only to achieve what had already been done by Chichester who had sailed non-stop to Australia. So he reasoned and decided to do what he thought most people in his situation would have done; i.e., carry on as long as possible. The weeks of adverse winds, slow progress due to lack of self-steering and countless other usual frustrations, combined with the most boring of all tasks for the single hander, steering, often had him swearing and ranting at the unfairness of things, but he continued to make slow, steady progress towards his objective.

A spate of uneasy dreams inspired some thought on the subject of dream interpretation. There was a great deal of idle time on the helm for him to speculate on the reappearance of long forgotten characters from the past and to wonder vaguely if they were a portent. Reading and steering at the same time was almost impossible so he hit on the idea of memorizing Gray's Elegy as a means of alleviating boredom,

Moitessier's 39-foot ketch Joshua *in rough seas in the southern ocean. Moitessier had already circumnavigated in this vessel*

and thought that the mental discipline involved would be good for his mind. Sooner or later though, when the weather abated and the compass heading improved, thoughts of such scholastic endeavours would dissipate without leaving disturbing effects on his inner self.

Slowly, but surely, he crept around the bottom of the South Pacific and neared Cape Horn. Frustrations increased in proportion to the adverse wind and sea conditions which slowed the boat down, at times to a crawl. Christmas and the New Year passed almost unnoticed in the grim struggle to keep *Suhaili* hammering through the heavy and wintry conditions of the Southern Ocean and far enough ahead of his competitors to win the race. Because he, like most sailors, regarded the Horn as the 'Holy Grail' of the course, reaching it and getting round it produced the greatest feeling of achievement – after which he just wanted to have done with the whole performance and get home. Alas, there were still about 9,000 miles to

go, a lot of it still in the cold, iceberg-infested Southern Ocean.

On January 18 his log read: 'My first impulse on rounding the Horn was to keep on going east. The feeling of having got past the worst was terrific and I suppose this impulse was a way of cocking a snook at the Southern Ocean itself, almost as if to say "I've beaten you and now I'll go around again to prove it".' Fortunately, he said, this phase passed very quickly. Thoughts of hot baths, pints of beer and other equally precious things put the matter into the right perspective and he turned for home.

Soon after the Horn he was able to establish through a radio report the whereabouts of the others. Of those left in the race only Moitessier posed a real threat and it seemed that he was steadily closing the gap. Later still he was to discover that Moitessier passed the Falkland Islands 18 days after *Suhaili*. Taking into account their relative speed differences this would have given Knox-Johnston only a few miles to spare coming up the English Channel. As it was, of course, Moitessier had something more interesting up his sleeve.

He, too, was progressing – somewhat more swiftly though – through the South Pacific, at this time neither happy nor sad, just watching the days go by and hypnotized by the persistent rush of water past the hull, the rhythm of inexorable progress and uneasiness about the future. The Horn was his objective but beyond was a blank. The sight of often massive waves and the sound – eclipsing all others – of their crests breaking like the roar of an avalanche added to and intensified his feelings. He was in a train rushing onwards towards an unknown destination.

As the Horn drew closer he focused on it with furious intensity, staying up on deck through the night to watch *Joshua* surfing in the gale force wind and heavy seas. The yacht drove towards the Horn at breakneck speed, controlled by the self steering, her passenger oblivious to everything around him, intent only on experiencing the exhilaration of the moment. In a wilder than usual surf the whole bow was buried deep in a cascade of spray. Suddenly alive to the danger of losing control of both his boat and his senses Moitessier reduced sail and went below. The wind slowly abated and Cape Horn slid by in the darkness. In the gloom of the cabin, hands around a mug of hot coffee, he pondered and wondered at the prospect of 9,000 miles to Plymouth. It seemed to him then that leaving from Plymouth to return to Plymouth was leaving from nowhere to go nowhere.

Almost invariably, after such a high, one experiences a state of depression of similar proportions. Moitessier was exhausted from lack of sleep and decent food and yet, once round the Horn, he had to push himself on for another nine days to the Falklands, where he hoped to let his family know his position. There he failed to make contact with the shore and suddenly could not contemplate attempting 16 miles of

fjord to reach Port Stanley. In a flash of lucidity he became aware of his extreme fatigue and the folly of attempting anything at all in his state. He hove to near the lighthouse and thought calmly for 15 minutes. After that he sailed away in the opposite direction and slept.

The next few days were full of emptiness and uncertainty. He needed time for the cure, time to sleep, eat, read and think. After 10 days the question of where to go was answered. Once clear of the ice zone around the tip of South America he turned *Joshua*'s bows again to the Cape of Good Hope. To begin with, as the days sped by, his only worry was a potential water shortage. But then the question of letting other people know of his new plans began to intrude. He pushed it aside. There was plenty to do to keep the boat sailing quickly in order to get past Australia and New Zealand while the weather was still good. The only real question now was, Tahiti or the Galapagos Islands? Tahiti afforded friends and easy mooring, whereas the Galapagos offered peace, a communication with nature and not much else.

It was during this indecisive mood that Moitessier picked up a piece of clay, part of a package of cement and plaster of Paris for underwater repairs, and began kneading it. The smell of the clay immediately brought back memories of his Chinese nurse who had raised him on tales of the Far East laced with her own oriental wisdom. Her philosophies concerned the ground, the earth, the giver of strength and peace to those who can feel and appreciate it. The clay brought it all back. The sea, solitude and communication with the living ocean confirmed it. He knew that he had at long last grasped the meaning of real peace. His only concern now was that others, when faced with his explanations of new found grace, would wonder whether or not he had lost his mind.

A week later, though, everything went wrong. Fatigue and the thought of his friends' incomprehension combined to cause deep uncertainty. Another four months of gales and cold in the Southern Ocean seemed, all of a sudden, to be going too far. He felt an overwhelming need to see his mother again. On February 28 he wrote:

'I am giving up'. (An odd way of putting it I thought.) He would take the course that was the happiest for all concerned; i.e., go back to Europe, collect all the gear necessary to overhaul *Joshua,* and then, having reassured the family that he was not mad, head for Tahiti. But the next day he had altered course for the Pacific again.

The changes within Moitessier were obviously profound and not to be altered by momentary fright at the thought of what other people would think. They might accuse him of turning his back on the commercial world and the useful contacts which had made it possible for him to be sailing a good boat with all the modern gear. But so what? They could say that had the real

Moitessier, a true mystic of the sea. He allowed the spirit of the ocean to penetrate his heart and reason and made his decisions accordingly

workers and innovators of progress in the past listened to vagabonds like him who often opted out of the real world, would they have got very far? No, but they would have been a lot better off, in his opinion. Modern life had become inhuman and those who wanted to rediscover the lost truth had to take to the roads or go to sea. And having done so, they had to attempt to recreate what had been lost; plant more trees – real living things – so that the cities and their people could find their souls again.

Thankful of having averted the tragedy of a wrong decision he was now able to settle down and sail on calmly towards the Cape of Good Hope. Three weeks later he reached it and handed over reels of movie film, stills and his log to a passing launch. He still had doubts about the reaction to his news but it was no longer his problem; those concerned with his welfare would have to deal with it in their own way.

On went the train journey; a journey for its own sake, going nowhere in particular but generating its own excitement and therefore its justification. The weeks went by, sometimes filled with the sheer joy of living but sometimes also with tiredness and lack of comprehension. He nearly did not stop. After New Zealand the Horn beckoned once more and there did not seem sufficient reason to alter course. *Joshua* was getting tired though and increasingly in need of maintenance – especially her rigging and sails. Sense again prevailed; he altered course and many weeks later steered the boat through the reefs off Tahiti and finally dropped anchor.

That is not quite the end of the story. Robin Knox-Johnston sailed on home and accomplished what he set out to do. He was the only one to finish the course which makes his achievement even greater. Were he to be accused of rating steadfastness, a sense of purpose and commitment higher than exploring the theoretical depths of his soul, I dare say he would not mind. After all, he did not set out with that in mind. Besides, not every one wants to be a poet.

As recent history relates, Knox-Johnston went on to compete in and win many prestigious yacht races. He became quite progressive in his choice of yacht design, specializing in the multihull field where he consistently opted for a catamaran. At this stage, they are proving to be the fastest and most successful off-shore racing vessels.

Moitessier remained tied up to a concrete quay for a while until his disgust with the cars roaring by a few yards away prompted him to move, along with a small bunch of like-minded travellers, to the last patch of bare earth in the harbour. Here, he and his friends planted a few banana trees and a six-foot-square piece of turf and sat each evening on their tiny oasis trying in vain to ignore the building going on around them. They were shifted off and more concrete was laid down. His friends all sailed off to find a less sullied part of the world but Moitessier stayed put and despaired.

Eventually, he got wind of a new movement in Europe, 'Friends of the Earth', and realized that there were Ralph Naders in the world who felt the same way as he did and who were willing to shout their views loudly to those who did not seem to care about the destruction of our planet. At the same time people around him were agitating to have trees, gardens and grass replanted among the concrete of the harbour. Before long banana trees were flourishing and there was talk of putting in pandanus palms.

Hope and optimism were restored to him. He was prepared to put faith in the coming of a hippy president and the influence of the Pope to whom he gave the proceeds from the sales of his book. In this way he hoped to be contributing towards the spiritual rebuilding of the world and help to halt the progress of the monster, civilization.

To go back to the first sentence of this chapter: 'Why did you do it'. I had been married for just a year when I did my circumnavigation. The sailing environment into which I had been precipitated offered opportunities for doing exciting things. Chay Blyth and Robin Knox-Johnston impressed me by their exploits but even more, on meeting them, by their apparent normality.

I had always yearned for adventure, irrespective of its form, and I had known for years that domesticity or even a normal career would not satisfy me. When the idea of a circumnavigation came to me (having sailed for a few months by then) I weighed all the pros and cons and came out after a few months deliberation on the side of the pros. I was not particularly fond of sailing (who likes being seasick, cold and wet, or getting up at all hours of the day and night?). Neither do I believe that I desperately wanted to show the world, myself or any other individual, that I could achieve

something that no woman had ever done before. Somehow, this was just something I felt capable of and I wanted to try it. Being alone held no terrors and I knew the actual sailing would be feasible with all the time in the world to set about it, once I actually got to sea. Oddly enough, those closest to me did not think it was a daft thing to try either. So I went ahead with it and was lucky enough to succeed.

Would I do it again? No, but nothing, barring disaster, would have stopped me then. Perhaps

Knox-Johnston stepping ashore in Falmouth, 10 months after setting off. He was the only one of the nine contestants to complete the course

it is the competitive drive that compels people to pursue similar exploits, like climbing another mountain or winning another race: if so, I am not competitive. But I still feel compelled to find the limits of my capabilities and to seek knowledge through experience, if in much less extravagant ways. That is what life is all about.

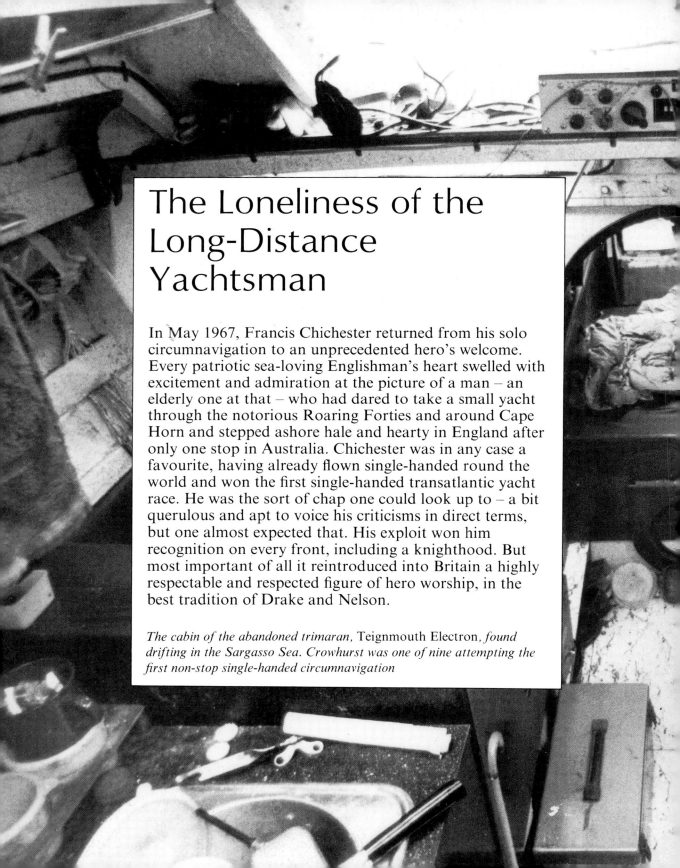

The Loneliness of the Long-Distance Yachtsman

In May 1967, Francis Chichester returned from his solo circumnavigation to an unprecedented hero's welcome. Every patriotic sea-loving Englishman's heart swelled with excitement and admiration at the picture of a man – an elderly one at that – who had dared to take a small yacht through the notorious Roaring Forties and around Cape Horn and stepped ashore hale and hearty in England after only one stop in Australia. Chichester was in any case a favourite, having already flown single-handed round the world and won the first single-handed transatlantic yacht race. He was the sort of chap one could look up to – a bit querulous and apt to voice his criticisms in direct terms, but one almost expected that. His exploit won him recognition on every front, including a knighthood. But most important of all it reintroduced into Britain a highly respectable and respected figure of hero worship, in the best tradition of Drake and Nelson.

The cabin of the abandoned trimaran, Teignmouth Electron, *found drifting in the Sargasso Sea. Crowhurst was one of nine attempting the first non-stop single-handed circumnavigation*

Chichester was not the first man to sail alone round the world: Joshua Slocum had circumnavigated the globe in 1895 and a number of others had followed suit, but there was not much publicity about their adventures. In Chichester's time, things were very different. The media was ready to proclaim his unique non-stop passage to Australia to the world, and a small fortune in endorsements, commercial royalties, lecturing and book sales awaited him. Chichester might have preferred it otherwise but he had to submit to the publicity to satisfy sponsors and an adoring public. His obvious financial rewards gave this type of adventuring a new, and lucrative, dimension, a trap for the unwary.

Within months of his return others were contemplating how to top Chichester's voyage by sailing around the world non-stop and faster. Several have had their stories told in the previous chapter. Another, particularly known to most people interested in the sea, was Donald Crowhurst. His biographers, Nicholas Tomalin and Ron Hall, put together an account of his voyage using material found on Crowhurst's boat. He did not live to tell the tale himself.

Donald Crowhurst was born in India in 1932, into a social class between the military and white administrators, and the native Indians. If his later 'paranoid grandiosity' sprang from an early sense of inferiority it mitted by his parents as a result of their social circumstances. They apparently felt that they were considered inferior to the military; in their turn they looked down upon the Indians. Because his mother had wanted a girl, she kept Donald's hair long until he was eight, after which it was cut off and he was sent away to school. To judge from his letters home and scribblings in his catechism he had a preoccupation with God and sin which indicated a powerful sensitivity to his environment and early life. At the age of eight he wrote, 'If we have done wrong or harm to anyone, we must confess to the party concerned first, and then God. No other confession is ever necessary'. Any boy capable of writing about or feeling deeply on such matters strikes me as possessing an unusual degree of intelligence and precocity.

At school he was considered by his mates as excessively brave; a leader, particularly of fainter-hearted boys into daredevil scrapes. He could do everything and was derisive of those who could not. At home, when on the odd occasion his father returned drunk and Donald was hustled out of the house by neighbours, he would entertain them with stories and jokes, apparently impervious to the turmoil going on within his family.

In 1947, the Crowhursts returned to England to live. Financially, they were badly off, a situation that slowly worsened until, at the age of 16, Donald was forced to leave his private school and forgo his ambitions of taking an aeronautical engineering course. Instead, he joined the RAF and studied electronic engineering. His father died suddenly, bowed down by circumstances, when only just beginning – for the first time in his life – to communicate with his son. Donald's greatest regret, he later told his wife, was that he did not get to know his father soon enough.

Life in the RAF followed in the same vein as his unruly school life: pranks, showing off, stunts and excessive risk taking. For years he would call on old friends in the unsociable small hours of the morning; they would give him coffee and marvel at the way he behaved. He had charm, a great deal of wit, and he brightened up their comparatively dull lives.

For unknown reasons Crowhurst was asked to leave the RAF, presumably because of some escapade that went awry, and he immediately joined the Army, obtained a commission and took another course in electronics. This second career did not last long either. He was hauled up in court for 'borrowing' a car to return home one night. When asked by an officer what he was up to he jumped into a river to escape, was captured and ended up being fined and photographed for the Scotland Yard Criminal Records Office. It was an insignificant sort of offence, but it was too much for the Army. He was asked to leave.

It was now 1956. Crowhurst was 24 and had not yet found an outlet for his intellectual talents – other than being an entertainer, and an

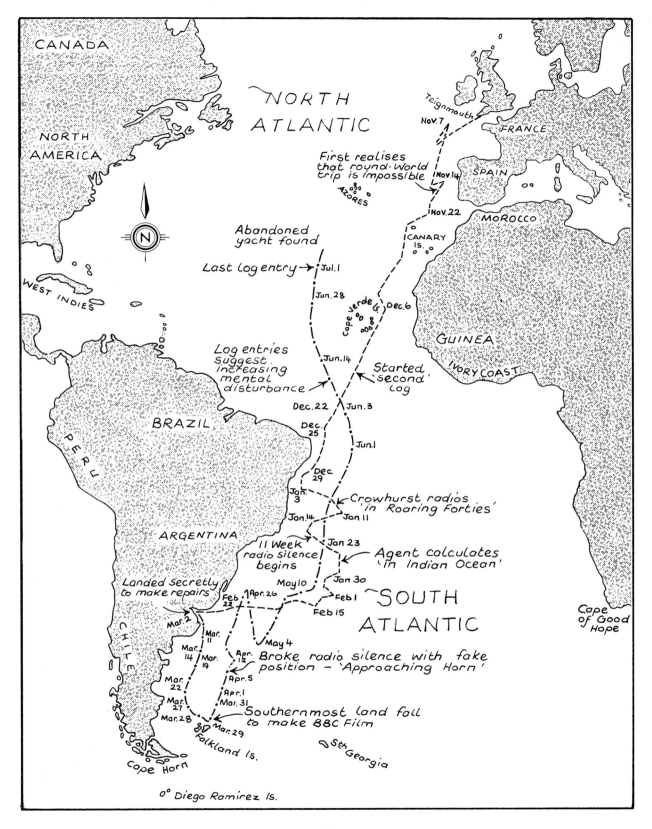

CANADA

NORTH AMERICA

NORTH ATLANTIC

Teignmouth
Nov. 7

FRANCE

First realises that round-World trip is impossible
Nov. 14

SPAIN

AZORES

Nov. 22

MOROCCO

CANARY IS.

WEST INDIES

Abandoned yacht found

Last log entry → Jul. 1

Jun. 28

Cape Verde Is.
Dec. 6

GUINEA

IVORY COAST

Log entries suggest increasing mental disturbance

Jun. 14

Started 'second' log

BRAZIL

PERU

Dec. 22   Jun. 3

Dec. 25

Jun. 1

Dec. 29

Jan. 3

Crowhurst radios 'in Roaring Forties'

Jan. 14   Jan. 11

ARGENTINA

Jan. 23

Agent calculates 'in Indian Ocean'

11 Week radio silence begins

May 10   Jan. 30

SOUTH ATLANTIC

Landed secretly to make repairs

Feb. 22   Apr. 26   Feb. 1

Feb. 15

Cape of Good Hope

CHILE

Mar. 2

Mar. 11

May 4

Mar. 14   Mar. 19

Apr. 12   Broke radio silence with fake position – 'Approaching Horn'

Apr. 5

Mar. 22

Apr. 1

Mar. 27   Mar. 31

Mar. 28   Mar. 29   Southernmost land fall to make BBC Film

Falkland Is.   Sth Georgia

Cape Horn

0° Diego Ramirez Is.

enigma to his friends. He was told at Cambridge that he had only to pass Latin to be given a place there. Presumably, he must have studied for it (he could easily have achieved it from an academic point of view and I imagine that socially it was a situation he must have aspired to), but he never sat the exam. Perhaps it was the continuing gaiety and riotous living with his wild group of friends that went against the effort required. At any rate, he earned a bit of money doing research work for Reading University laboratories, and lived it up.

At the age of 26, Crowhurst married an Irish girl of his set, socially superior in her background but with a very sincere regard for him which never wavered throughout their married life. A year later they had a child. Crowhurst had started sailing and began a job with good prospects in an electronics firm. Unfortunately, Donald and the job did not suit each other. He disliked the travelling and working routine, not to mention the customers and his superiors. He chucked in the job after a year and took on another, equally uninteresting, to while away the time until he could figure out how to go about what he really wanted to do, which was to design a piece of equipment and market it himself. He was very clever with electronics, at designing and solving problems – and he particularly liked to work alone, shut up in a small room away from the rest of the world. Already he seems to have reached the point in his life where he was in retreat from his failures. To his friends he was desirous of presenting himself as an intellectual and a bit of a recluse. It was a role he played to them and to himself.

With his small group of friends he indulged in theories of God and the mind, and life as a great game to be played. They humoured him, enjoyed his company and admired his cleverness and vivacity. In their opinion (which was given later), Crowhurst considered himself the most intelligent person around. Undoubtedly he was very bright, but he felt his talents were unrecognized. He needed to become a big important person and his failure to do so produced a deep sense of frustration and dissatisfaction.

He tried his hand at local politics by standing

as a councillor and won by convincing sufficient people that he had the successful businessman's ability to solve all their problems.

By now he and Clare had four children, although it is hard to see how he supported them all. He had started a small factory to market his own radio direction finder (a navigational aid for yachtsmen). Apparently, there was nothing unique about the design, there were others similar to it on sale, but if he had succeeded in marketing it properly it should have done as well as its competitors. Crowhurst had great faith in himself which he could communicate to others and in this way he attracted a Taunton businessman as a sponsor for the new venture. Stanley Best had invested quite some money and time into the project before coming to the conclusion that Crowhurst, although a brilliant innovator, was no businessman and unlikely to make both their fortunes.

Although his business was failing, Crowhurst's ingenuity, always poised and ready to recognize interesting possibilities, came up with a very novel way to prove to the world that *he* was no failure. Chichester had just returned from his circumnavigation. Crowhurst scoffed at all the fuss and made out that Chichester had achieved nothing that had not already been done. He, Crowhurst, claimed that he had had the idea of a non-stop circumnavigation years earlier but the time had not been ripe to get on with it until now. He soon discovered that several other yachtsmen had the same intentions. As soon as the race was announced Crowhurst declared himself an entrant.

The boat he really wanted to sail in the race was Chichester's own *Gipsy Moth*. But she was destined for a concrete berth at Greenwich, and no amount of persuasion on Crowhurst's part could convince the committee involved in the embalming to hand her over to him. Only after several months did he give up the idea of *Gipsy Moth* and decide instead to have his own boat built. Although he had maintained all along that

Donald Crowhurst, 37-years-old, frustrated by his inability to make his mark in the world, before departing on his precarious voyage

Chichester's yacht was the ideal one for the undertaking, he suddenly opted instead for a trimaran – a totally different concept in safety and sailing performance. Multihulls were then – and basically still are – generally considered unsuitable for sailing in deep sea conditions, particularly short-handed.

A deadline of October, 1968 had been set as the last possible departure date to qualify as a competitor and it was already May. Crowhurst as yet had no boat and no money with which to finance the project. However, his optimism and powers of persuasion managed to convince Stanley Best, who was on the point of pulling out of Crowhurst's doomed company, to put up the money for the proposed trimaran.

Crowhurst was now in his element, turning over ideas and solutions to problems at a terrific rate, arguing the suitability and integrity of his craft over his competitors and inventing new equipment to cope with the serious safety drawbacks attached to multihulls. His biographers ask us at this point to ignore the ultimate disaster, to forget that he left with his boat in the utmost state of disarray, with all the electrical equipment incomplete and useless, and to believe that these early setbacks would have looked like evidence of determination and integrity had the end result been a happy one. 'Almost every account of a successful adventure contains in its early chapters instances of over-optimism, confusion, and pushing salesmanship'. I do not think such a statement is justifiable in Crowhurst's case. To suggest that he could have succeeded in his objectives – so ill-founded and unreasonable – in such a state of disorder is unrealistic. Indeed, such a project ought not to prosper. To succeed for the right reasons is hard enough; to succeed through the wrong ones would make a mockery of achievement.

The trimaran, *Teignmouth Electron,* was basically a 'Victress' design (her designer Arthur Piver lost his life at sea in the same year – it is assumed as the result of a capsize), but Crowhurst had some major changes incorporated. For instance, watertight bulkheads between all eight compartments and a much smaller, and therefore more seaworthy, super-

structure – all very commendable modifications.

The building programme was very rushed. Because the building yard was unable, in the time allowed, to obtain the correct type of materials necessary for certain construction work it had to make do with inferior materials – decisions which later showed up as grave errors. As the pressure mounted Crowhurst became fully immersed in the electronic side of the project, the part that he felt at home with. There were serious delays over sails and rigging which Crowhurst was supposed to have organized himself and the launch date was pushed further and further back. The day arrived when Crowhurst exploded in anger and frustration at the potentially disastrous short cuts having to be made in order to complete the hull in time. That evening his wife pleaded with him to give up the whole venture. To her surprise he seriously considered the possibility but then told her that it had become too important to him and he had to see it through. Clare Crowhurst had the greatest faith in her husband's ability to make a seemingly improbable event happen. It had happened often enough in the past.

Teignmouth Electron set off on her maiden voyage, from Norfolk to Devon, just over a month before the deadline for the start of the race. It soon became apparent to Crowhurst that all was not well. The vessel would not sail efficiently into the wind, so in a head wind he could expect to make almost no progress at all. None of the hatches on the float compartments fitted well and were already letting in considerable amounts of water. The self-steering gear was designed for a monohull's relatively slow speeds and could not cope with the vibration set up by a faster-moving trimaran – the screws shook themselves loose every few hours.

All in all, the discoveries on that first trip (which took two weeks and not three days as expected) were not of the sort to inspire confidence. On the contrary, Crowhurst must have done some mental calculations and begun to feel very frightened. It is essential to have at least some faith in the vessel on which your life will depend. It is hard enough having to wrestle with doubts about yourself and whether you will cope with being alone, the only navigator, sailing master, maintainance crew, etc, without having to question your boat's actual ability to stay afloat. These were my feelings in the same situation and I cannot imagine he felt otherwise – especially as the preparations had been so chaotic.

When they finally arrived in Teignmouth the builders got to work again while other helpers rushed about buying food, spare parts, electrical components and innumerable valuable items of equipment. It was not surprising, given the utter disorder, that some indispensable items never arrived on board, the most disastrous omission being a long length of pipe needed to pump sea water out of the compartments. Crowhurst did not discover its absence until he had been at sea over a week.

On the day before departure Crowhurst was in a deplorable state, shaking from lack of food, sleep and probably with terror. It was obvious to everyone that he did not want to go. He kept murmuring, 'It's no good. It's no good.' At 2am Donald said to his wife: 'Darling, I'm very disappointed in the boat. She's not right. I'm not prepared. If I leave with things in this hopeless state will you go out of your mind with worry?' Alas, she did not realize until so much later that this was an appeal to her to do what he could not do himself, call the whole thing off. Instead she replied with another question: 'If you give up now will you be unhappy for the rest of your life?' He spent the rest of the night weeping.

The following day, with only a few hours to go to the deadline, he set off, only to return almost immediately for help in untangling the halyards and foresails which someone had rigged incorrectly. Once that was sorted out he departed, this time for good. It was the last they ever saw of him.

The next week at sea must have been enough to convince him that no man in his right senses would take such a vessel into the Roaring Forties. Some of the screws had already disappeared from the self-steering gear and he had no spares. The floats had to be bailed out with a bucket, a dangerous and arduous task with no likelihood of a solution unless he put in for repairs. Light and contrary winds made the going extremely slow – he even went backwards at times because he could not summon up the energy to correct the course. Lack of sleep, the strain of being in the shipping lanes, preoccupation with the vessel's integrity, all these things combined to make him lethargic and depressed. Every day brought fresh evidence of the folly of a rushed preparation: the wrong book of radio signals, not enough methylated spirit for the stove, the missing hose for the pump, and so on.

Crowhurst's biographers tended to be critical of what they called his 'slapdash' methods of navigation; they mentioned that he rarely took simultaneous sights of stars or of planets. But from this accusation I believe he should be exempted. Many long-distance sailors (myself included) must subsequently have proved that there was nothing wrong with employing the simple methods that he followed (the meridian altitude and a morning or afternoon sight every few days). They are quite sufficient for reliable navigation. In confined waters extra sun-sights, radio direction finding, common sense and caution are far more essential than text book expertise. Actually, I doubt if any of the 'experts' would undertake such voyages; they would consider them far too foolhardy.

Crowhurst's log books and tapes, even at this early stage, were in two styles: one portrayed the way he really felt and the other the way in which he wanted to be seen by his admirers. For them he rhapsodized about the porpoises, the delights of making toast in a force seven gale and his relief that no serious damage had ensued from banging his head on the side of the cockpit. In the real log he wrote: 'This bloody boat is just falling to pieces due to lack of attention to engineering detail!!!'

Nearly two weeks of erratic progress had brought him past Cape Finisterre and some way down the coast of Portugal. There, to his way of thinking, the greatest catastrophe of all happened. In a heavy sea the cockpit hatch had leaked vast amounts of water over the electrics

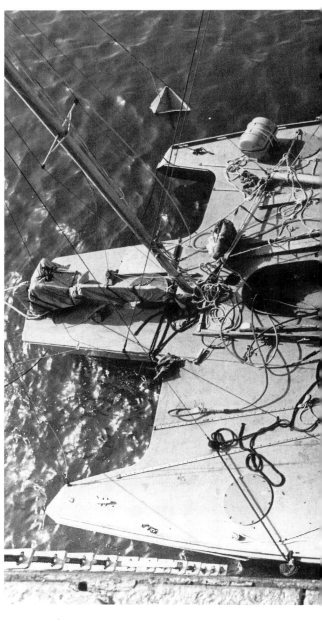

Above: *Crowhurst sorting out tangled lines on the day of departure. The boat was in a state of chaos and Crowhurst's mental state was in equal disorder*
Right: *The distance sailed by the potentially unseaworthy trimaran was impressive; despite early damage she was still in one piece when found*

and his very precious generator, without which all his electronic gadgets were useless (none were connected and most not even built yet, but that was not the point). To exist without electricity was unthinkable, it was his lifeline, without which he felt hopeless.

There follows a long and heartfelt assessment on his predicament as he now saw it. As usual there were two versions, one for the public, on heroic and stoical lines, and a real one which was simply an honest and realistic summing up. The real one listed the reasons why it was not possible to take the boat into the Southern Ocean. The self-steering allowed the boat to broach at speed and with big seas anything could happen: he would be arriving far later than orig-

inally had been intended so he could expect severe weather which the self-steering gear could not cope with. No electrics meant no time signals and his chronometer had already packed up. There was no way to pump out other than exposing himself to the distinct possibility of being thrown overboard, etc. The list went on and on. Included in it were rational solutions to each problem but they mostly involved giving up. That was the only logical thing to do.

He sailed slowly south, working on the generator and trying to come to terms with the situation. No matter how he juggled his options on paper, he could not make them add up to anything acceptable. Once the generator was again in working order and the radio could be used, he thought of discussing the dilemma with his wife and passing the onus of responsibility for giving up on to her. However, when he finally did speak to her, he gave not so much as a hint of the real hopelessness he felt. They talked mostly about the problems with the pump and although Crowhurst complained about his lack of fast progress so far, he merely reported that he was in good health. The possibility of giving up was never even raised.

Wracked by indecision, depressed by failure, and with the fear of death clouding every thought, he came to a virtual stop near Madeira. The effects of isolation were taking their toll. Crowhurst would probably have had no precise idea – as probably none of us have – how solitude would affect him in the long run. For those with a solid belief in their convictions solitude strengthens resolve and creates an atmosphere in which self-sufficiency flourishes. For those who are aware, if only subconsciously, that what they have undertaken is wrong for them, they become vulnerable to profound fears and doubts, to feeling alienated from safety and all outside help.

There is evidence in his logs that Crowhurst struggled to convince himself that he should stop at Madeira but failed to find the strength of will. At length, he carried on south and cabled home to say that he would not be using the radio any more as generator problems were forcing him to conserve energy. This was the first indication that he was embarking on another course of action, one that he had laughingly hinted about to a friend some weeks before departure. He began sending cables that were ambiguous as to his exact position. The wording was such that almost anything could be read into them. His agent of course interpreted them in the best possible light, thereby compounding the misconception regarding his progress. Although the deception was not coldly deliberate at first, the weight of yet another wrong must have added heavily to a mind already over-burdened by dishonesty. With the faking of a journey round the world came curious and very complicated logistical problems that had to be assessed for credibility and feasibility. It meant something

positive to think about but it also contributed to the perturbation of his mind.

Crowhurst now pursued a deliberate course south into the trade winds and over the equator. Daily he fabricated the sun-sights and position lines of his faked route and painstakingly copied them from rough draughts into a log book, while his real positions were entered into another log book. Both these accounts were later retrieved from the trimaran along with a mass of other written material and dozens of recorded tapes. These records, true and faked, provided the testimony to his mounting dilemma and its eventual solution.

Once he had reached the equator sailing occupied more of his time, as the fretful comments in his log showed. Disasters kept occurring to the boat in the form of flooded floats or broken equipment and although he did not, or could not, do much towards rectifying the problems he wrote copious lists of jobs that needed to be done in order to put the boat right. Time, at this stage, must to him have assumed awesome proportions. In a sense we have manipulated time to our convenience, getting up at 7 am, going to bed at midnight, with the day time well regulated to suit our purposes. This orderliness disappears at sea and the passing of time becomes either something you are not really conscious of or, in moments of low spirits or trouble, an oppressive focus of attention. Crowhurst had taken no literature with him other than a few sailing stories, some volumes of mathematics, and Einstein's Theory of Relativity. With only those he could not escape into another world and forget the present, neither could he find the sort of stimulation that might have directed his thoughts into a healthier channel.

By Christmas he had been at sea for nearly two months. The strain of being alone and in distress at such a time was obvious in a tape he made in his 'public' voice. His emotions swung constantly between melancholy and bravado. Among the material later retrieved from the boat was a map that he had drawn of Rio de Janeiro which showed that, again, he had tried to give up. Instead, he went right inshore (only he was not near Rio but 1,000 miles to the north)

Left: Rob and myself. We were one of several husband - and - wife teams competing in the Round Britain Race

Below: A 1585 map of Magellan's voyage including the Strait

Anson's flagship, the
Centurion, captures the
Spanish galleon off the
Philippines

Captain Bligh and some of his crew being cast adrift from the *Bounty*

Ernest Shackleton's boat, the *James Caird*, depicted during her perilous voyage in Antarctic waters

Bernard Moitessier on the ketch *Joshua*

Suhaili, sailed by Robin Knox-Johnston, the only yacht to complete the first non-stop single-handed race around the world

Donald Crowhurst's trimaran, *Teignmouth Electron*, found abandoned in the Atlantic in July 1969. He had also aspired to being the first man to race alone around the world

A yacht sailing hard at the start of the ill-fated 1979 Fastnet Race

The grim conditions encountered by David Lewis on his attempted Antarctic circumnavigation

to get a closer look at people and normality. His role-playing so distorted his real perspective that he was having difficulty distinguishing between his public image and his real self. At that point he seemed to believe that he really was near Rio. The distinction became rapidly more blurred as his real situation became more intolerable. Seeing the land may have made him feel better for a while but was otherwise of no avail. He had gone beyond the point of seeking assistance. All single handers experience a reluctance to mix again with the outside world once they have known the 'purifying' atmosphere of the sea; at the notion of going ashore again one experiences that feeling of inertia – but in a more intense form – that long train journeys can produce, when you wish the train would go on forever. I recognized it in myself as a negative emotion which had to be overcome. In Crowhurst's state of mind, just seeing people on the shore and knowing that he was incapable of simply sailing into the harbour, must have done further damage to his powers of reasoning.

For the next month or so he headed vaguely out into the empty ocean where detection by a passing ship would be least likely. He spent his time trying to minimize the effects of bad weather on the boat by running off or lying a-hull; otherwise, he occupied himself with calculations for his false course and sending progress reports to the press. The messages were banal and high spirited but carefully worded so that much had to be read between the lines. In this way he was able to avoid telling an outright falsehood. He hoped, almost to the end, to find a way of extricating himself from the deception.

After some weeks he decided to maintain radio silence, as his signals would be coming from the wrong place. In the following three months he never acknowledged the many telegrams which Cape Town Radio transmitted to him, but he wrote them all down. By March, despite his caution, the trimaran had suffered sufficient damage to make it imperative to call in somewhere for repairs. Crowhurst chose a very small port on the Argentinian coast and after much hesitation made a landing there. Of the people he met during the next two days

one later described him as 'mercurial', the other thought he seemed in good spirits and 'completely normal'. He drew charts for them of the racing yachts' route around the world to explain why he was there but he also drew them a chart of his real course around the Atlantic. They were puzzled but as language difficulties prevented any but the most basic communication they failed to understand what he was getting at. Crowhurst became very agitated when the port official announced that he must contact the authorities in Buenos Aires for instructions but soon afterwards seemed to relax. This was so nearly the moment of his salvation but, due to odd quirks of fate, the message did not get through to the right level of authority. While waiting to be denounced he set about repairing one of the floats with materials that were provided for him. The repairs were completed within two days, and as there had been no word from the authorities, he departed.

Instead of heading north towards the better weather he went south, as far as the Falkland Islands, where he paused for a look. He obviously wanted to taste something of the kind of experiences that the other competitors were facing. Considering the sort of boat he had, he was lucky not to have got it. I am astonished that he made so little of the mundane sailing problems that the rest of us had to complain about. His self-steering gear had ceased to function so he would have done a lot of helming. The cold must also have been considerable yet he did not spend much time complaining about such things. He apparently considered them insignificant compared to his real difficulties.

Eventually he broke radio silence with a cryptic message about nearing the Horn and slowly headed north again. Euphoric cables poured in from everyone; he was already a hero and if he kept up his remarkable performance he might even win the race.

Weeks passed while he meandered north over the equator and into the Variables. He continued to report on his progress but at home they were wondering at his erratic course and speed. In fact, what he was now trying to do was to lose the race. The thought of braving out his deception at home was becoming unendurable; the only chance of minimizing the scrutiny of his logs on return was to come in second. Then came the blow that put an end to his last option of escape. The only other boat left in the race with a chance of finishing before him, Nigel Tetley's *Victress*, sank shortly before reaching England. The irony of his situation could not have been lost on Crowhurst: if he had not forced Tetley to push his boat so hard in order to keep in front, Tetley would have won and Crowhurst would probably have been able to sail home quietly into second place.

For the next few weeks Crowhurst continued to act like a rational person but, to anyone reading his logs, the deep disturbance of his mind becomes rapidly more apparent. He sent cables to his wife about dwindling food supplies and talked a lot into his tape recorder (still in his 'public' voice) about the strange creatures in the Sargasso Sea, where he now drifted aimlessly. He was trying desperately to maintain his personal identity. He projected himself as others saw him; struggling on, despite the odds, witty and philosophical. The need to speak directly to his wife obsessed him more and more, and he spent whole days and nights soldering electronic components together in a last desperate attempt to get the transmitter working. It failed. After that, he went to pieces.

Leaving the boat to look after herself he began to write down a great new truth that was rapidly taking shape in his mind. Highly intelligent minds like his have reached a degree of sophistication which enable them, by an act of will, to free themselves from the normal physical restraints and enter another dimension, that of abstract existence. At last, Crowhurst had found a way to escape from his predicament.

It took seven days of fierce deliberation before his mind was sufficiently divorced from reality to accept the fact that, in order to reach this dimension, he must quit his bodily form. Time played a last, vital, role in his release. On the seventh day he counted down the hours, minutes and seconds to the end of his self-appointed time and, chronometer in hand, he stepped over the side.

Crowhurst's story confirms a theory that I have, one which I first heard from a contemporary single hander: it does not do to be too intelligent if you intend to spend a lot of time alone at sea. To be simple (meaning uncomplicated), not overly imaginative, and single-minded is the best recipe for the successful outcome of such a venture – or at least the way to achieve the outcome you wanted in the first place. In an extraordinary way, Crowhurst's did end successfully: it was just not the one he chose at the outset. I admired his cleverness and courage, not in the way he trapped himself into an impossible situation, but the way he got out of it. I have not explained the machinations of his wonderful theory, one must read the book by Tomalin and Hall to understand that, but I trust that he concluded his voyage in peace.

The last entry in Crowhurst's private log

98

I am what I am and and I
see the nature of my offence

I will only resign this game
if you will agree that if
the next occasion that this
game is played it will be
played according to the
rules that are decreed by
my great god who has
revealed at least to his son
not only the exact nature
of the reason for games but
has also revealed the truth of
the way of the ending of the
next game that

It is finished —

It is finished

IT IS THE MERCY

11 15 00   It is the end of my
          any game the truth

has been revealed and it will
by done so my familly require me
To do it

11 17 00   It is the time for your
          move to begin

I have not need to prolong
the game

        It has been a good game that
must be ended at   the
I can   will play this game when
        I will resign the
game 11 20 so   There is
no reason for hurry.

A Bad Luck Story

The following is a bad luck story. Any of us, under similar circumstances, might be capable of the sort of mistakes the Davisons made in their desperate move to escape intolerable circumstances. They were not motivated by criminal intent but were simply following a path dictated by faith in their own beliefs as I was when I set out on my solo circumnavigation. The outcome of their voyage showed up their errors in the worst possible light but any break in the chain of ill fortune would have resulted in a different ending, with their blunders being tolerated. Such is life. In the end it was the sea that eliminated that margin for error where most of us, with luck on our side, would have scraped through.

Frank Davison, it seems, was one of those people born under an unlucky star. When he met Ann he was the owner and manager of an aerodrome, a fleet of aircraft, the director of several aviation companies and was closely involved in various non-flying concerns. Ann had answered an advertisement for a pilot and got the job. A year or so later Frank divorced his wife and married Ann and together they ran his businesses. Then the war intervened and the order came grounding all civilian aircraft. The aerodrome was requisitioned and compensation was paid but it did not take into account the non-flying activities carried on there, which had to be discontinued. Frank thought the organization he had built up might be of some use to the war effort but after endless talking and wasted time nothing concrete materialized. His aeroplanes, along with the rest of the civilian gear, were put into a disused grandstand, where they were shortly after destroyed by fire when a passer-by started one of the engines. Their house was also requisitioned and their offer to be pilots was declined (Frank because of defective sight in one eye and Ann because no one was interested in female pilots.) They felt rejected and Frank was bitterly wounded by events over which he had had no control.

Realizing that flying was over for them, they turned their energies and capital into developing a small quarry which Frank owned and had administered alongside his other businesses. The next few years of hard work were happy ones for them both. The smallholding they had bought prospered and the quarry expanded. They missed the adventure of flying, though, and if this present phase of their lives had not also come to an abrupt end it seems unlikely that they would have remained content for very much longer. In retrospect Ann Davison certainly felt that they were the sort of people for whom the call of adventure and excitement was irresistible. She was right – at any rate for herself – for even the dreadful experiences of their final voyage did nothing to quench her spirit of wanderlust. She later became the first woman to cross the Atlantic single-handed.

Because of a very bad winter production from the quarry came to a halt and there was no output for a number of weeks. Mortgage repayments became overdue but when the weather improved a period of unremitting hard work saw them back to full production. Despite back payments their mortgages were unaccountably foreclosed. Frank Davison was badly hit; in the past his unstinting efforts and considerable abilities had always been sufficient to ensure the success of whatever project he had set himself. Since the war began he had been hustled out of aviation, turned down as a pilot, and had now lost his quarry for reasons once again beyond his control. He began to lose his self respect and the bitterness of rejection led to a period of withdrawal. Only after a long personal struggle was he able to rationalize and accept his present circumstances – a struggle which nevertheless left an indelible mark.

Their lives now took a very different turning. They decided to get away from it all and farm an island in Loch Lomond. For a few months all went well till the bank claimed their remaining cash to cover outstanding debts from the quarry business. The geese they were planning to rear trampled to death all the young goslings and the goats died from some mysterious island parasite.

They left that island and bought another, more workable, one. Now, at last, it seemed that they had found their feet. The work was relentless and not always enjoyable but they prospered. There was a wide variety of interests in connection with working the island – in forestry, farming, control of livestock, and working on and around boats. Frank Davison adored sailing and was very competent. Ann had been introduced to the water when they first met and had not liked it at all. An island life demands a great deal of getting about by boat so perforce Ann had to learn to work ship in all conditions and in all weathers.

Despite her husband's confidence that she would be a natural, based on her prowess at handling horses and aircraft, Ann never really learnt to sail. She blindly struggled through the many hair-raising operations their sailing life demanded but without gaining any real insight

NORTH SEA

IRISH SEA

Belfast

Isle of Man

Dublin

Wicklow

Waterford

Rosslare

May 20th

St. George's Channel

Anglesey

May 17th

Blackpool

Newcastle

Carlisle

Lancaster

Preston

Liverpool

Scarborough

Hull

Lowestoft

Aberystwyth

Fishguard

Cardiff

Bristol

BRISTOL CHANNEL

Lundy

LONDON

Bournemouth

Brighton

Boulogne

Penzance

Falmouth

Plymouth

Start Pt.

Portland Bill

June 6th

June 3rd

ENGLISH CHANNEL

Cherbourg

Dieppe

Isles of Scilly

Lizard Pt.

Eddystone Lighthouse

CHANNEL IS.

Le Havre

N

Brest

FRANCE

103

or understanding into what was happening. Her husband's misplaced confidence made him impatient of her shortcomings, until, not unnaturally, she worked up quite a hatred for the sailing part of her life.

After a while they began to get restless again. Finding their feet and making a go of something which they would not, under normal circumstances, have chosen was all very well. But too much was missing in their lives. The lure of the unknown was beginning to reassert itself. While mulling over the vague hopes, dreams and ambitions which they had often entertained Frank spoke with increasing earnestness of selling up, buying a suitable boat, and sailing around the world until they found the right place to live. At first Ann was dubious about committing themselves to a lifestyle she was not sure she would like, but when she saw the depths of Frank's enthusiasm she buried her own misgivings and entered into the plan wholeheartedly.

Due to inflation and a woeful understanding of the value of boats the Davisons found themselves paying far more for a vessel than they had estimated. What is more the boat they finally chose needed a great deal of work done on her. She was a fishing boat built in 1903 on the lines of a yacht, and had originally been a ketch. At the time they bought her she was just a hull, in a frightful mess but with the unmistakable marks of quality in the materials and in her lines. The work became one of those insidious jobs which begins modestly and then mushrooms; each modification led to another and finally *Reliance* was not being refitted so much as rebuilt. The boat had a reputation in the area for she had been fast and had won races; she was generally much admired. This influenced their own feelings for her and the old adage of spoiling the ship for a hap'orth of tar took on a very real significance. Nothing could be skimped in the fittings or furniture. Frank was supremely happy and unperturbed by the increasing demands of the ship and their dwindling capital. He was caught in the spiral that many of us have experienced at one time or another; the job must be finished properly, the future was vague, and

somehow, everything would turn out all right.

When the work was sufficiently advanced they moved aboard, and that night Ann had a nightmare. Water was pouring in through a hole in the side of the hull, rushing and roaring. As the ship filled and water swirled over her she fought and tried to shout for Frank. Later she told Frank of her dream but could not explain it. The nightmare recurred again and again. They tried to rationalize it as a possible deep-seated fear of the sea, but Ann was not convinced. It did not occur to them to look on the dream as premonition of disaster. It was a mystery to be tolerated in the hopes that it would one day go away. In any case, what could they have done? It is difficult to treat dreams seriously if they interfere with the sort of future the Davisons had in mind.

When at last they reached the stage of being almost ready for sea a horrible tangle of financial complications tied them to the shore. Inexorably they had allowed themselves to be carried along on a tide of enthusiasm for the boat. Furthermore, misplaced emphasis on less important points – woodwork and French polishing in the stateroom, the bathroom with hot and cold running water and full-sized bath, and the beautifully equipped galley – had left other areas neglected. The sails, for example, received scant attention. They had managed to obtain a jib, main and mizen but for various reasons only the jib was bent on. The engine room was a most incredible affair, occupying the largest part of the boat, and equipped with an engine that required two people to start it and constant attention to keep it running. The engine was a major contributor to their eventual downfall.

By now their financial difficulties were so acute that the whole project was in jeopardy. Ann had recognized the path they were following and had reluctantly voiced her doubts about going on with the venture. But the idea of selling was an anathema to Frank. 'We'll make out, we must.' And he went on, 'I can't start again. I'm sick of starting things. This is the last. I have put everything of myself into *Reliance* . . . she is more to me than just a ship –

there will never be another.' Ann, naturally, backed him up. She instinctively felt that in order to maintain faith in himself he could not admit defeat. It is easy to be wise with hindsight.

Desperate efforts were made to salvage the project with ideas of fishing, chartering or leasing the boat out to whoever would take her for money. The downward spiral gathered momentum but, never quite believing in the crash that had to come, they clutched vainly at straws, always with some solution to their problems just out of reach. Idea after idea was mooted, any of which could have, indeed, should have, worked. But it seemed they were the wrong people with the wrong ideas, and with the wrong boat at the wrong time. Finally the mortgagees threatened to foreclose. The Davisons asked if they could sell her themselves but they did not get so much as a bid.

Frank was stricken at the thought of losing the vessel without even having had a sail in her. They could not sleep and spent every day pursuing endless propositions and every night discussing them, going to bed at 4 or 5am, exhausted but unable to sleep. Then, with creditors, mortgagees and writs snapping at their heels, they stepped over the brink and decided just to slip out of Morecambe Bay and leave all their problems behind them. After two weeks of feverish but furtive activity they slipped away, watched only by an open-mouthed boy on a bicycle.

It was the end of May, 1948. The weather looked ominous but for the first few days and nights it was sufficiently calm to allow a period of shake down. Ann could not eat, which worried Frank, and they both suffered excessive fears for each other's safety. On the second day out in roughening seas the cooker broke free and started a fire. It was brought under control with the loss of their fruit and vegetables, some burnt-out wiring and a lot of charred wood.

Slowly, as the weather worsened, the boat became harder to handle under power alone. The Davisons were physically unfit and mentally tired from the anxious months ashore. They had both suffered from chronic lack of sleep before setting off and now rest was virtually impossible

Ann Davison who became the first woman to sail single-handed across the Atlantic

with the sea so rough. Thoughts of putting up the sails were discarded due to the physical and mental inertia so common to those who suffer seasickness in severe weather. As the gale reached its height the wheel suddenly jammed – the link chain had fallen off. As Frank struggled to repair it a great sea threw the boat on to her beam ends carrying Frank to the very end of the counter where Ann thought he had gone over the side. He was unhurt but she was nearly hysterical with fear. The realization that she was exhausted dawned on her, but not the seriousness of it. She had neither eaten nor drunk for nearly five days, not even a glass of water.

Frank, although not much better off himself, seemed to see their situation rather more clearly and thought they had better head for a port to rest. No attempt had been made to navigate and both their clocks had stopped, but a course was set 'with a bit of east in it' to take them back from where they had come.

Shortly after, a passing ship hove to – on seeing them broach dramatically – in case they needed assistance. Somewhat unnerved by the past few days Frank had earlier suggested stopping a ship but Ann was dead against the idea. They passed slowly astern of the vessel, unable to signal as there had not been enough money to buy flags. As the ship disappeared from sight a voice in Ann's head distinctly said, 'There goes your last chance'.

Drinking hot tea and struggling to keep awake they headed, they hoped, for land and a quiet haven. Frank suddenly noticed that the sea, which had eased considerably, was beginning to whip up again. They were approaching a light, which became several lights as they drew nearer, and which eventually manifested itself as a light-vessel at anchor. Before any action could be decided they plunged into seething white water which broke over the shrouds and crashed down on to the decks. 'Shoal, by God!' said Frank, and the next second a resounding crash shook the boat. For a moment she wavered, then lifted her stern and raced on into the darkness. Unable to stop and not knowing which way to turn for safety they tore on and on, crashing and jarring over the bottom, in an attempt to get away from the light-vessel which they assumed marked the centre of the hazard. Ann went below to look at the charts but shortly returned none the wiser to find the boat heading straight for the lightship, the wheel jammed again. Frank leapt below to replace the chain while *Reliance* plunged wildly towards the light-vessel. Within minutes the wheel was freed and the boat slid past. Ann searched the charts again, hardly able to keep awake from reaction, but from the Lune Light to the Bay of Biscay there was nothing to give them a clue of their position. Then, abruptly, they were back among lights and buoys, which ever way they turned.

Unable to face any more problems Ann's mind shut down and she was overwhelmed by the desire to sleep. As if from far away she heard Frank say he would find a way out. Some time later the buoys disappeared and they were miraculously clear.

That night they each managed a few hours sleep and the next day felt wonderfully refreshed in the warm sunshine and calm seas. Thoughts of giving up and going into port were abandoned. Instead they spent the day trying to mend the engine, which had unaccountably stopped, putting up a couple of sails, one very ill fitting, and generally tidying the ravages of the weather. That afternoon gave them a taste of contentment which they had not known for months, and would never know again. By nightfall lights had appeared all along their lee side, lights that made no sense whatsoever. They eventually concluded, with reservations, that they might be off the Skerries again. They were, in reality, off Land's End several hundred miles away but it never occurred to them to look that far south.

At dawn the lights went out and there was no land to be seen. The whole day was spent mending the engine and by nightfall it was working. Darkness showed up more lights to leeward, some of which corresponded to lights on the Welsh coast, and others did not. After an interminable night of confusion at dawn Frank headed determinedly towards the land. On the way the mizen sail fell down leaving only the headsail. They closed a long rocky point with a white lighthouse on it. After a cursory glance at the chart Frank pronounced it to be Holyhead. He had departed from his normal exacting procedure of taking bearings and double checking, a serious indication that his state of mind was such that he was prone to unbelievable errors. They looked indecisively into a bay, without quite knowing whether to risk an entry or not, but then were frightened away by a motor vessel which sped over to them and seemed to want to make contact. It gave chase but on the point of drawing level inexplicably gave up and went back to the coastline.

The incident was unsettling and they gave up

the notion of finding a quiet bay in which to rest. Frank set a course for Ireland and decided to try their luck in Waterford. They blundered on, bewildered, through another wild night, seeing coastlines that did not match their charts, lights that made no sense and searching for lightships which were not there. The loom of a bluff appeared dead ahead, and they clawed away from it only to meet the blinding flash of a lighthouse in their path. Disaster confronted them when the wheel jammed again, and then the engine stopped. They dashed to heave the anchor over the side, saw it roar out, there was a splash and silence. Thinking the chain had not been secured to the boat, the last chance was the staysail but heave as they might on the halyard it would not hoist. Investigation showed that the anchor chain was holding it down. They had anchored within yards of a treacherous shoreline of cliffs with a huge rock just astern of them.

As water crashed over the decks they sat amid the chaos drinking rum and discussing the incident with hilarious exaggeraton, until sleep overtook them. They were awakened by footsteps on deck. It was the crew of a lifeboat who had answered to a report of a ship in distress. The men were surprised to see Frank, having assumed the vessel was abandoned, but left when they were assured their help was not needed. As all such incidents are reported by lifeboats to Lloyds, Frank knew they must leave to escape detection.

While Frank fixed the engine Ann spent some fruitless time searching the charts for Newlyn where the lifeboat had offered to tow them. She gave up after a while and together they endeavoured to pull up the anchor, an immense task in their state of exhaustion. An aeroplane circled overhead – photographers, Frank thought. They motored over the anchor held fast on the bottom, until the chain gave way at the deck and the whole lot was lost over the side. They returned along the coast to the point of the previous night and peeped timidly into a bay, longing for rest and shelter, but not daring to go in. They were overwhelmed by the feeling of being hunted and had no intention of giving in. On that they were in total agreement and such was their apprehensive state of mind that lesser matters were incapable of being resolved.

By nightfall they had reached the eastern end of a large bay and spent a weary night motoring back and forth across the mouth until dawn came and they could see the way in. At last, churning water told them they were in a tidal race, which finally gave Ann the clue to their real position, off Portland Bill. Frank was steering a course up Channel, going with the heavy seas; Ann was arguing against their present course and wanted to turn round and head back out to sea, but Frank patiently explained how impossible that would be with a full gale blowing and their fuel running low. Faced with such seemingly insuperable problems Ann felt engulfed in a tide of weariness into which she just longed to sink but Frank, with some sense left, asked her to work out a course for a French port where they could find shelter. Down below, while grappling with the daunting task of navigation and bending down to retrieve something, she blacked out. It was terrifying, uncontrollable, and happened again and again throughout the day. She finally gave Frank a course but could not tell how she had arrived at it; in any case, the problem was submerged by the greater one of survival. The weather conditions were appalling by midday as they were thrown about in a frightful sea raised by opposing wind and tide.

Much of Ann's time was spent in the engine room seeing to the many actions needed to keep the engine running. Temporary unconsciousness added considerably to her difficulties, as did the discovery that the boat was suddenly taking in water around the mizen step. The main bilge pump had chosen this time to choke and Ann found she was unable to work out how to clear it, or how to operate the auxiliary pump. On appealing to Frank for help he replied that he was too tired to explain, commenting only that they would 'have to put up with it and hope for the best'.

Suddenly aware that Frank was nearly all in she went below to try and make a hot drink. Though exhausted almost beyond reason she was still able to move surely about despite the violent motion. The stove, too, had ceased to work but a dogged determination forced her to spend an age setting it up and making Frank his coffee. Later, again, she stepped into the engine room where, struggling between bouts of unconsciousness, she refuelled, topped up the oil, and then returned to the galley to heat some soup. It was two hours before she returned on deck, only to have the mug spill in a lurch, necessitating another trip to the galley. Frank drank it then caught her arm and insisted on knowing what was wrong with her; with rain beating in his face and in a wild disjointed manner, he talked incessantly of yachts nearby until it dawned on her that he had driven himself beyond breaking point. Shocked beyond belief she did not know what to do. Saying loudly that the header tank needed topping up she dashed down to do it. On her return to the wheelhouse she saw him crouched in a corner. Striking a match she looked into his face and saw only blank unreason.

The following hours were a nightmare for them both. Frank raved and fought with Ann. Only his extreme physical weakness enabled her to prevent him going on deck and over the side (he was convinced they were tied up alongside). A light had appeared to leeward, the Eddystone in all probability thought Ann, and hoping to get help she tried to light the flares. Frank threw the whole lot over the side in a fury. While keeping an eye on him she tried to light anything that came to hand but the wind and motion defeated her. Finally, near dawn, Frank collapsed and she was able to get the Carley float, together with a pair of paddles and lifejackets, ready to abandon ship if need be. They had not been able to afford a proper liferaft, the one absolutely vital piece of equipment which would at least have meant a chance to escape with their lives.

At daylight Frank reappeared, still dazed, but at the sight of the Eddystone lighthouse just to leeward, he quickly regained his senses and set about controlling the ship. At this point Ann passed out, regaining consciousness again hours later to the sound of a voice from a nearby fishing vessel offering assistance and Frank refusing it. The sea was calmer now, the boat

was back in order with sails set, and they were heading out to sea again. Plymouth was on their doorstep but it was not mentioned between them. The choice was Ann's, for Frank was by this time looking to her for decisions. Unfortunately, more than ever, she believed that in giving themselves up Frank would be driven out of his mind. The wind deserted them as they tried to cross the Channel, leaving *Reliance* drifting helplessly in a steamer lane. All night Ann struggled with weariness till Frank had had eight hours' sleep. On being woken he proved to be delirious so she left him again and returned to the wheelhouse, wondering whether to turn back for Plymouth. Still she hestitated and decided to wait till morning when he had slept properly.

In the morning he blamed his behaviour during the night on a dream, and continued to sail the boat across to France. Ann had no sleep during the day. Instead she made them food and after each enormous meal Frank fell asleep. It blew hard all day and sailing was difficult with just the staysail but by nightfall the French coast was in sight. The staysail chose that moment to tear in half and with the engine seized they had no option but to drift back out to sea. At dawn they rehoisted the repaired staysail and drifted about. Fishermen twice offered assistance but each time Frank gave assurances of being in control. Lights turned up again at night, still the French coast, and they stood watch and watch about, Frank sleeping off watch but Ann spending her time in the galley listening to the radio.

They strove desperately to get out of the Channel, but progress was minimal with inefficient sails and a strong head wind. That night they were inundated with offers of assistance from vessels of every kind as they drifted back across the Channel but Frank fended them all off. The next day they were trapped by wind and tide in Lyme Bay and blew a jib to pieces. The next night produced another gale and more tossing about in furious seas within sight of the Devon coast until, at dawn, an ominously green sea foretold of shallow water and the need to get out. *Reliance* refused to turn through the wind and had to be gybed round, losing valuable sea-room; soon they were flogging up towards

Portland Bill once more. With another gale forecast it was imperative to fix the engine yet again, a task accomplished by nightfall. As it was tacitly agreed that Frank must have all the sleep he could get he turned in with the boat making steady progress past the Bill. Suddenly they were off course and heading down wind towards land. Their last sail blew at this moment and Ann called Frank to start the engine. It started on one cylinder only, not enough to counteract the sternway they were making towards the Bill. They slid past stern first to see huge waves breaking high and white on outlying pinnacles of rock, right in their path.

Somehow, *Reliance* scraped past the point and headed bows-on to the cliffs. Frank dropped the mizen and went below to see to the engine. The boat started to turn, was nearly round, when the engine stopped completely. They ran to the deck to try the remaining anchor but it was too late. She struck bottom, harder and harder, and then, before their horrified eyes, buried her bow into the cliff. Lifejackets on, they got the float over the side and leapt overboard, Ann catching her leg in a tangle of rope but managing to wrench it savagely free. Some hard paddling got them away from the boat and immediate rocks.

The float was a lozenge-shaped ring of cork, canvas bound and painted red and yellow. The ring was woven about with an intricate system of lifelines, and in the centre of the ring, suspended by a rope network, was a wooden box. They sat on the ring to paddle, with water up to their knees. Sometimes the water swept across their laps. They were very cold, for their woollen trousers and jackets were wet through. Frank had thrown off his shoes. Terrific activity burst out on the cliff-tops: rockets went up, and bicycle and car lights pierced the night as people watched the death throes of the *Reliance*. Soon the Davisons saw a lifeboat heading towards them but a strong current was carrying the float swiftly out to sea. Yelling at the top of their voices and waving a torch failed to alert the lifeboat which passed inshore of them.

When daylight came land could only be glimpsed from the tops of a steep vicious sea thrown up by the Portland Race. All at once they were in the water, capsized by a breaking wave crest. They struggled back only to be hurled out a minute later. They learnt how to keep the float from overturning as the seas grew worse but had to take the full force of the waves over themselves. Hours dragged by in misery and fear till Frank could take no more. Delirious and fading fast he tried to climb out but Ann held him down. Then a wave more massive than the others went sweeping down on them. When the float broke free of the water Frank had gone.

At that point Ann laid her head on her arms and waited for the end to come. But it was not to be. A wave broke over the float and woke her to angry despair. The thought occurred that the end could be hastened by the knife in her pocket but it had fallen out. The more obvious way did not occur to her until some days later but by then it was too late. So she waited. The world's accusations and suspicions went through her mind as the morning wore on and the sea moderated. She visualized the headlines and heard the rumours and speculation of the armchair sages ... Purposely wrecking the ship ... Shirking their responsibilities ... Suicide ... But she was able to turn against those thoughts and refute them. Their way of doing things may have been unorthodox but their principles had been sound – of this she was convinced. To follow an aim to the end is a fundamental necessity; to give up without fighting to the finish would nullify all that had gone before and admit to a worthlessness of all they had tried to achieve. She was the one left and in rage she shouted at the sea that she would go back to carry on what she and Frank had both begun.

The tide turned, taking her back towards the land. Then about two miles offshore the current eased the float across the Bill and seaward again. Breaking off a wooden handhold to use as a paddle Ann managed to steer sufficiently to bring the raft on an intercepting course with the very end of the Bill. The shore was a mass of rocks and giant boulders with the sea crashing over them like thunder. It was either that or the whole circuit over again. Paddling madly with the handhold brought her within the pull of the surf where the raft was picked up and swept towards the rocks. She ended up lying on her back with the float on top of her. When the next wave came crashing in it carried her further in and on to more rocks. Clinging to each one brought her slowly and painfully inshore till she found herself standing inside a cave with sheer cliffs behind.

Her pockets were empty except for a lucky photograph and a useless watch, not much with which to begin the fight back, she thought. Shouting for help until she was hoarse only brought the sound of seagulls and the thunder of surf in reply. After a while she began blacking out again and lay down to rest. At last, realizing that staying where she was would make her return to shore rather pointless, she crawled over to the boulder-blocked entrance to find a way along the coast to a place where the cliffs could be climbed. The climb was painful and slow; near the top she lost her grip and slid back several yards and looking down, saw a straight drop of 50 feet to the sea. This she somehow found profoundly irritating and it spurred her into making the final effort to reach the top. Geared up then for the final fight – although she did not know with whom – a grassy slope confronted her, leading to a radio mast. And beyond? She slowly walked to the top of the slope.

Ann started life again with little more than the clothes she stood in. First the creditors had to be satisfied and to this end she wrote two books. They made her enough money to pay off all her debts with some left over. One would have thought that having anything further to do with boats would be the last thing on her mind now that she was free. But Ann had a perceptive and intelligent grasp of the fundamental principles by which most right-minded people live, and she asked herself why she had allowed her values to have been so altered that she could have allowed the *Reliance* tragedy to have happened. Why had she suffered such fears and insecurities? Life at the moment represented little more than a monotonous passing of time. Her confidence in herself was severely shaken and she did not really care much about living,

but a persistent voice within her pressed for answers. Although she was not at all sure she was following the right lead, she began work at a boatyard, learnt how to sail properly and then bought a small yacht. She had formulated the idea, obscure even to herself, of sailing across the Atlantic, on her own, in an attempt to find the key to her life.

It was a punishing crossing, mostly unrewarding until the end, but it served the purpose. For days and days she drifted outside the entrance to Nassau, encountering minor adversities which loomed so large to her sleepless brain that she was unable to overcome them. All her insecurities and fears of the last years swept up in an overwhelming tide which engulfed her. In this state of mind she would not trust her navigation nor believe that the coastline she saw was the right one, nor that if she approached the channel she would not end up on the rocks. The spell was finally broken in a ludicrous interchange with a passing ship; she gathered her wits and crept timidly on her way. Exhausted and cross after days of virtually no sleep she dropped the anchor off Nassau. Then the clamour in her tired brain began. It insisted on knowing why she had behaved so ridiculously. She put up a defence to her own argument that she had shown a justifiable caution in not running into situations which could have landed her in serious trouble. Instead, she accused herself of running away from taking responsibilities, of mentally wringing her hands when confronted with possibilities that included danger, of being unable to face up to them. She lacked the courage of her convictions. If she had been in her right mind, the argument went on, she would have just gone ahead bravely and done what her reason dictated, and she would have reached the safety of the anchorage days earlier. But in not doing so she had found the key to the way forward: having the courage of her convictions.

In her words, 'What is courage? An understanding and acceptance; but an acceptance without resignation . . . for courage is a fighting quality. It is the ability to make mistakes and profit by them, to fail and start again, to take

The ketch Reliance *wrecked in Cave Hole, Portland Bill – June 3, 1949*

heartaches, setbacks, and disappointments in your stride, to face every day of your life and every humdrum trivial little detail of it and realize you don't amount to much, and accept the fact with equanimity, and not let it deter your efforts.'

She was the first woman to cross the Atlantic alone under sail. Whichever way she saw it, the general public viewed her venture with admiration and delight. Although she accepted their congratulations with a wry amusement, her confidence benefited by it and grew to the point where she could leave the mistakes of the past behind her and look to the future with a positive self-reliance.

'Pagan's' Pacific Voyage

John Caldwell's reason for crossing the Pacific from
Panama to Australia was like that of the chicken which
wanted to cross the road: because it wanted to get to the
other side. He had been demobbed from the Merchant
Navy after serving on a ship out of Australia, where he
had met and married Mary, a WAAAF officer.
Circumstances had contrived to separate him from his wife
after a three-day honeymoon, following which a failing
ship, then the caprice of the War Office, had combined to
keep him many months from his beloved.

One gleans very little impression of Mary, save that she must have been an exceptional sort of person to have so besotted our distraught hero that Caldwell was finally ready to clutch at any straw in order to be restored to her. After fruitless combing of the New York, San Francisco, New Orleans and Panama waterfronts for a ship, he pounced on someone's suggestion of sailing a boat back. The next day he purchased a 29-foot cutter for $1,000 – without even having looked at it. Someone had recommended it, and that was good enough for him.

It took only two weeks to get *Pagan* ready to sail and loaded up with food and spares. There were a number of other individuals very keen to get to Australia, but none were desperate enough to sign on as crew once they had seen the mode of transport. Two stray kittens were press-ganged aboard to fill the position of companions.

His initial destination was to be one of the outer islands of the Galapagos group, 1,000 miles south-west from Panama, but if he failed to find it – a reasonable expectation since he had not yet learnt to navigate – the next possibility were the Marquesas, some 3,000 miles further west.

As his preparations neared completion, thoughts of getting under way from the quay and moving safely into the steamer channel began to tax Caldwell's mind. He had only once before stepped aboard a small boat, so questions such as 'What does a boat do when you heave the sails aloft?' not unnaturally made him rather nervous. In order to prepare himself for the event he bought a book called 'How to Sail' and tried to memorize the names of the various pieces of equipment and the correct procedures for getting under way.

On Saturday, May 25, 1945, he decided that he and his boat were as ready as they would ever be for the departure from Panama. The idea of avoiding experienced eyes was uppermost in his mind and so 6 am was chosen for his first try at the tiller. With sails unfurled, halyards free and sheets out, and the engine gently turning over, he let the lines go from the quay. She moved slowly up channel. On the spur of the moment he decided against using the sails as the engine performed so well but bethought himself to ready the anchor in case it was needed. While engaged in picking up the anchor with both hands, the deck tilted slightly, and he slipped and went backwards over the side. Weighed by the anchor he went down, till he thought to drop it, and fought his way back to the surface. *Pagan*, meanwhile, was continuing on towards some moored yachts. A spurt of fast swimming failed to make much impression on the distance between them as the anchor was dragging with the tide. He broke out into a harder stroke, head down, and only looked up to see that *Pagan* was even further off. However, she suddenly struck a buoy, glanced off it and headed straight back towards him. He dived out of her way and surfaced to see the chain-plates above him; a quick grab, a swing up on to the deck and he was at the tiller again.

His next contretemps would have made me laugh except that I can see myself in my green state at the outset of my circumnavigation, and am forced to reflect, there but for the grace of God ... He pushed the tiller down and swerved towards a clear spot where he hoped to relax a minute and take stock; instead *Pagan* fetched up at the end of the anchor chain, twisted around, and doubled back towards the moored boats. In a panic he cut the engine, then wished he had not. The anchor dragged and the boats got closer. They had scraped past the first one when he remembered the sails. In a trice the main was dragged up and *Pagan* was off like a shot. Suddenly, the speed of the boat drove all he had learnt from the book out of his mind, leaving it blank and bereft of logical thought. With a jerk the boat found the end of the chain again and stopped, straining and swinging till the wind went ahead and she gybed. As the boom whipped across Caldwell had the sense to duck and then ran forward to pull up the anchor.

At last, a semblance of order was created but, instead of playing it safe and continuing at a sedate pace towards the main steamer channel, Caldwell displayed a trying bravado which is somehow the key to the predicaments in which he continually found himself. He felt a need to

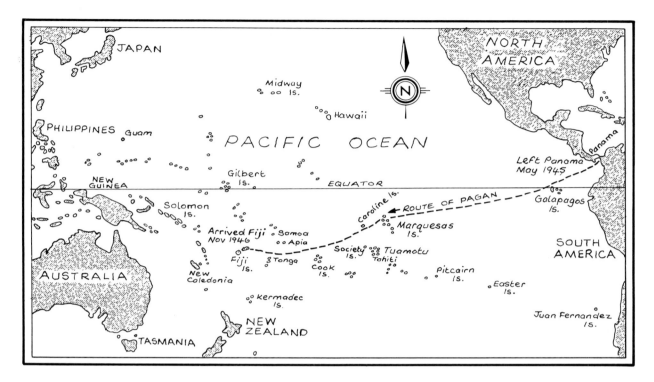

redeem himself in the eyes of those who had witnessed his amateurism so far. Hoisting both the staysail and jib and bombing along at a very credible five knots, he put the helm down to tack. She came up into the wind and then fell off again. Twice more, he repeated the manoeuvre, with the same results, and then ran aground on a sand bar. After useless efforts to refloat using the engine, and himself as a tug, he was finally able to enlist the help of a passing ship's wake to wash him free.

Now, at least, he seemed to think that enough was enough, and headed out through the channel and into the gulf of Panama, decks overflowing with sails, their sheets dragging in the water and halyards flying loose in the rigging. All that day he practised with the sails until hunger, tiredness and night overtook him – at which point he realized he was utterly lost. There was an island in the vicinity where he hoped to make a landfall and rest for the night. He found it by following the sound of surf till the air was full of spray and rocks appeared on all sides. Frantic shouts in the darkness warned

him of the dangers and almost without thinking he heaved out the anchor. Fishermen came aboard to tell him that he was safe enough, so he stayed.

Caldwell's experiences so far at least had the happy result of convincing him of the foolishness of setting forth on his long journey with so very little experience. Practice was what was needed, so to this end he remained in a small group of islands in the Gulf of Panama for a week and grappled with the baffling art of sailing and navigation. Every day he bounced off rocks, went aground on sandbanks, and even mowed down several members of a welcoming committee who got in the way of one of his more flamboyant exercises. That error cost him his anchor, which disappeared that night from the end of the chain. Thinking it better to keep what he had left intact, he departed the following day.

However, he did not feel quite ready to face the Pacific ocean. A longer cruise around the islands seemed like a good idea, especially to try spending a night at sea. All went smoothly until another one of those reckless moments when he decided to cut a corner by shooting past a point between growling rollers. The timing went wrong, *Pagan* was hit on the beam by two combers in quick succession which threw her so close to the rocks that he could see crabs clinging to them. The two cats were afloat on the deck with just their heads in view, swimming wild-eyed towards him. With the cats in hand, ready to be thrown ashore, Caldwell held the tiller hard over with a knee and waited petrified as the boat started to hit the first line of rocks. In the nick of time the bows came up into the wind and began to meet the waves full on. The sails now pulled hard and the boat gained headway away from the shore. That episode served to give Caldwell confidence; he had acted sensibly under duress and saved the boat. It was enough. He set off on the morning of June 7 for the crossing to Australia.

Some miles off shore, when the land behind him had virtually faded from view, it occurred to him that he needed a course to follow. The correct way to go about it taxed his ingenuity somewhat. He finally laid a ruler flat on the chart and drew a line between his point of departure to the Galapagos Islands. (Far be it for me to criticize this naivety, having myself once confused latitude and longitude over several thousand miles of Southern Ocean.) Confident that all he had to do was to sail straight down it, navigation was put aside for the more pressing problems of what to do with his first gale, already howling about him. The way he put in his first reef needs to be told in his own words.

'How to get the sail off? How to steady the spar in such a wild setting? The Indians say the best way to do a thing is to do it. But in a boat there is a proper way. One doesn't unbend the halyard, then needlessly allow the wind to whip it from one's hand ... as I did. Such negligence is dangerous because the sail spills the wind and flails wildly at loose ends. The sail can split right down the centre, the Marconi clips rip from the luff, and four or five seams strain and rent so quickly as to leave the sail in six shapeless parts in a matter of seconds. The reason I know that is that is just what happened.'

The mainsail, blown into spare parts, had to be retrieved, an operation best accomplished *from* the deck, *not* clinging to the boom whipping back and forth. In the 20 minutes it took to subdue the sail Caldwell reckoned he must have seen each side of the deck a thousand times.

In between heaving up over the side and trying to stretch out in the lee bunk, the lethargy so well known to motion-sickness sufferers crept over Caldwell's mind, so that it was with only mild surprise that he noted the jib disintegrating and throwing off bits into the wake. *Pagan* was now wallowing so alarmingly that he was forced to gather his wits and go on deck to grapple with hoisting the staysails. When they failed to steady her, he threw out an improvised anchor which was sufficient to bring her bows up into the wind. Seasickness, weariness and anxiety had chaffed at his reserves; he was asleep down below when the next disaster struck. A sledge-hammer blow on the keel had him stumbling out of his bunk, reeling as shock reverberated through the hull. He grabbed the cats, the thought 'Wrecked!' reeling through his mind, and made for the deck. Instead of jagged rocks confronting him, at first there was nothing. Another crash sent him to the side to see the massive bole of a tree larger than *Pagan's* hull. She had backed off the crest of a wave while making sternway in the storm, and landed athwart it, and now rocked from side to side, each rebound wracking the hull with blows. Desperate efforts to fend it off with the boathook, failed. Heavy rollers crashing on the trunk twisted it beneath the keel, exerting a shifting pressure against *Pagan's* timbers, till she 'groaned deep in her parts with the whole-souled complaint of a wounded man'. Eventually, the keel made its way down the length of the tree and *Pagan* floated free. A hasty search in the bilges turned up no immediate sign of damage but the presence of a live squid was an ominous sign. Soon, the water level in the bilges started to rise. At first, pumping out contained the flow, but it slowly worsened. It became imperative to get to land before the timbers opened up more and the boat foundered.

Land, in fact, was not far down wind. Despite the storm and his lack of navigational finesse

Caldwell's dead reckoning was exactly correct, for land appeared three miles away, and he was moving fast towards it. Not fast enough, however, for continuous furious pumping could not contain the rising water which soon drowned out the engine and rose up the sides of the saloon. The mournful howling of the cats told him that they had been washed off the bunks. Slowly the boat closed with the shore as he worked madly at the pump. *Pagan* began to settle and waves lapped against the gunwales. Expecting at any moment to see her dip her rail under and sink, Caldwell felt instead a gentle bump as the keel made contact with the bottom, and the boat lost way. The cats appeared swimming out of the hatchway followed by their cork blocks which he had attached to them at the onset of the storm. He tossed them towards the shore, pulled down the sails, and grabbed a rope which he tied round himself. Before long he had retrieved the cats from the water and tied his line to a mangrove stump.

Sitting, some hours later, on *Pagan*'s slanting deck invoked the melancholic reflection that he had so far spent almost as many sea hours with his boat in this condition as keel down in deep water. Still, as he saw it, his situation was serious, but not desperate. Although the island was uninhabited there was plenty of fruit and vegetables to supplement the ship's diet of canned food, and a survey soon showed the damage to the hull to be repairable. In fact, the next 10 days spent caulking seams, lead patching, resetting and hammering and resting after these labours on the sandy beach, gave him a feeling of 'brotherhood with life' such as he had never experienced before and thought would never experience again. Only one thing was missing ... Mary. That single factor drove him on with the repairs till the boat was again shipshape and ready for sea. The next difficulty was how to get her off the beach without an anchor. There were trees around so he felled one and exercised much ingenuity in fashioning a kedge-type anchor, with long and short wooden flukes. So that it would not float, he weighted it with bits of lead sawed off the keel. (Whether this poaching affected sailing performance in any way, the story does not relate.) Getting the boat afloat now presented no difficulties as he was well practised in this respect. Very soon the same 'wicked intuition' that had inspired him to sail alone from Panama now directed his bows once more towards the open sea.

During the crossing of the next bit of ocean to the Galapagos Islands the weather threw at him every contrary mood at its command; wind on the nose, flat calm or gales; glassy rollers sweeping in against him suddenly confronted by vicious crests of waves behind; and rip tides of steep, bouncing waves torn up by conflicting currents. Vague, fluky winds caused another accident that nearly put an end to him. Carelessness on the bowsprit, just when he was thinking that he had been out on it enough times to feel safe, pitched him spinning into the stormy night sea. He fought instantly for the surface only to be thrown behind the boat by a quick series of waves. The desperate strokes to reach the transom would have been to no avail, had not fortune in the shape of a pair of trousers hanging from the transom presented a handhold with which he could pull himself to the stern and climb on to the deck. Lying on the deck gazing at the wake (as I once did after a similar close shave), he reflected about his escape, and the risks and uncertainties, and wondered if he would have taken the voyage on, knowing what he then did. He concluded, yes; it was fun and despite the danger he loved it. 'There was an appeal that every man feels – the appeal to adventure.' And it was taking him back to Mary.

In spare moments, he taught himself celestial navigation. To the expert, this will no doubt sound like a travesty, but there are people (I am one) who believe that deep-sea navigation by the sun (measuring the sun's altitude with the use of a sextant and looking up tables to find out where you are in relation to it) is relatively simple and straightforward – not that I would have felt happy putting it into practice with such careless abandon as Caldwell. There is, I believe, an awful lot talked about the science of celestial navigation which the average, sensible sailor can do just as well without. To understand the theory requires many years' study and a pretty sharp intelligence, but one does not *need* to understand the theory – I never even attempted it. My errors were comical and embarrassing, but I was still able to find my way around the world with a lot of caution and head scratching.

Relatively simple though it may be, the ability to take good sun sights does not come to one in a flash. If one lacks the skill, the only other way to estimate progress and position is by dead reckoning. And, of course, there is a trap, waiting to engulf every amateur out of sight of land. Caldwell reckoned his speed was a 'modest seven knots'! Considering the difficulties he was having moving forward at all I imagine his speed would have been more like three knots – and not all of those in the right direction. At any rate *he* thought he was already halfway to the Galapogos, though he was most likely only just out of sight of Panama.

The next bit of excitement was a shark, half the size of *Pagan*, who was very keen to scratch itself on the hull. Caldwell could see its two rows of unbelievably large, twisted teeth and of course he had to have them to show Mary. In no time at all he had it on the end of a line. A mighty struggle ensued in the next half-hour or so, a struggle to the death, or so thought Caldwell. At last, alongside the rail was the shark, showing only the feeblest resistance to being pulled along by the hook firmly embedded in its jaw. The teeth gleamed tantilizingly near, but how to get them? A shark weighing hundreds of pounds is not something many would care to have as a passenger but Caldwell was not the sort of chap to dwell on such niceties. His 'wicked intuition' that all was well soon decided him that the simplest course of action would be to pull the shark aboard and dispatch it by removing its head with the axe. Having first leant over the side and punched it in the nose to show who was boss, Caldwell hoisted the beast inch by inch over the transom with the aid of a gaff hook and the main halyard. There it lay, head in the cockpit and tail over the side, but a quick swipe with the hatchet into its spine to put an end to further resistance did not have the desired effect. At the stroke of the axe the shark came to life,

sending the kittens scuttling for the foredeck and sweeping its opponent off his feet. As the great body twisted about the tail pounded the cockpit and smashed everything it made contact with, the main hatch cover, tanks and cockpit combings. After that, it broke its way down below and set about demolishing the engine. All the while, Caldwell hacked at it with the hatchet, until at last he was too exhausted to plant another stroke. Fortunately, by then it had expired.

It took the next two weeks to repair the damaged stern and remove all traces of blood and bits of flesh from the boat. The teeth, of course, were kept and later cleaned and polished and, presumably, presented to Mary.

Despite falling overboard a second time, (he saved himself by catching hold of a lifeline rigged for the purpose) Caldwell reached the end of nine days' sailing without serious mishap. By dead reckoning he had covered some 900 odd miles, which meant he ought to have been close to the Galapagos. The appearance of sea birds seemed to confirm the proximity of the land. To make sure, he took a number of sun-sights, the first of which put him somewhere ashore in central Panama. The next two days' readings put him unmistakably about 350 miles from Panama. He refused to believe them. The readings indicated that a barren isolated rock was somewhere in the immediate vicinity. He climbed the mast to confirm that he was correct in his previous calculations and that no such island existed. There was an island, exactly like the one described. Far from being dismayed at this obvious insult to his intelligence, he was positively delighted at the discovery of how easy navigation was proving to be. This is a feeling I can well understand, remembering what a miracle I felt I had performed when land appeared for the first time. I felt as though I had created it.

It takes all sorts to make adventurers: as somebody once said, if people were all the same there would be no need for assorted biscuits. What exasperated me so much about Caldwell was this propensity for inviting disorder, which a man in his position – in his words 'desperate to get back to Mary' – should have been doing everything to avoid. When he saw a pack of cavorting whales on the horizon he was reminded of a desire to approach them which he had often experienced as a merchant seaman. Naturally, he headed straight for them and gently nudged a sleeping whale with *Pagan*'s bow. The poor creature woke in such a fright that the ton or so of water it deposited on the deck in its haste to get away nearly sank the vessel. Caldwell gave them a wide berth from then on.

On the next occasion diversion presented itself in the form of a tropical waterspout. Caldwell had always said that, once captain of his own ship, he would investigate this phenomenon. Instead of giving any credit to the old mariners' tales of solid water being sucked up into the clouds or of great whirlpools powerful enough to drag a ship under, he had a hankering to prove that they were harmless. Now, I am a conservative, in some things even a coward. It is true, I was foolhardy enough to sail alone around the world, but if I had seen a waterspout coming I would have sailed for all I was worth in another direction. And as for inviting a fully grown shark into the cockpit ... So I was quite amazed, although not really surprised, to read that this extraordinary fellow had the temerity to disregard all the old wives' tales to prove this very unimportant point to himself. Upon closer inspection, he did have a moment of uncertainty, but as at that moment the spout changed course in his direction there was no time for second thoughts. The wind howled and the decks rocked as spray from a chilled, wet wind plucked at him clinging to the mast; the air was black as night but nothing dreadful occurred. In less than a minute he emerged into bright sunlight on the other side. According to *my* sources, he was lucky.

Passengers are not easy to come by out of sight of land or ships. All the same, Caldwell managed to acquire them. A bird, some kind of gannet, joined for several weeks and allowed himself to be petted and fed – another thing I never managed to do – but most odd of all was a large rat. It apparently came aboard when the boat ran aground on the deserted island and accommodated itself in a crate of cheese, pork and prunes. Also in attendance was a school of dolphin led by a battle-scarred veteran which Caldwell called 'Old Death'.

So, complete with menagerie, Caldwell sailed on and made a landing as planned at an island in the Galapagos group, for scraping, painting, and a general overhaul. Twice, on the approach, he courted disaster by making insufficient offing and had to rely on oars to extricate himself from the currents which all but set him onto the lava escarpment. He managed to post a letter to Mary though, 60 pages written on both sides. The post-box was a white barrel attached to a stake, planted on a deserted beach. He put five dollars with the letter to ensure delivery. It was posted in July and Mary received it in the first week of October; his projected time of arrival was the last week in September.

The next 3,000 miles to the Marquesas were dispatched in uncharacteristically trouble-free style. There was nothing much to do on the sailing side as *Pagan* seemed to steer herself wonderfully well with the wind on the quarter, in much the same manner as Joshua Slocum's *Spray*. Needless to say, there were minor scrapes along the way, like falling off the top of the mast into the sea, and hooking a giant devilfish which resulted in the loss of a traveller and rail; nothing serious enough to require elaboration though. He made a brief stop at Caroline Island to augment dwindling food supplies, having discovered earlier that all the cans stowed in the forward compartment had rusted away in the damp. There was no processed food to be had on the island but he was able to exchange an assortment of clothes, tools and odd jars for coconuts, breadfruit, water, two pigs and two chickens. The children on the island made such friends of the two kittens that he felt obliged to offer them as gifts, too. With reluctance he took leave of the friendly company and put to sea for the last 4,000 miles of ocean.

Caldwell noted that the day was Thursday, September 5, 1946 – a day he never forgot. The hurricane season was not strictly supposed to start for another month yet, but like a lot of things, hurricanes do not always go by the rule book. Six days out of Caroline Island an ominous swell appeared from the north, and when heavy skies and near gale force conditions set in it was obvious that the centre of a cyclonic disturbance was quite near. There was nothing to do but batten everything down and wait. Hours later the first of the hurricane winds struck the vessel, blasting away the storm sail. She was now under bare poles, riding into the waves reasonably well with the help of a sea anchor. Soon, though, she was pounding and pitching so wildly that Caldwell, lashed to the bunk, listened intently for any different sounds from the hull which would signal a structural defect in the 26-year-old planking. The first damage was a broken shroud which had to be replaced as the mast was vulnerable without it. So fierce was the wind over the deck that standing, or even sitting, was quite impossible.

By inching his way forward using the lifelines for support, Caldwell managed to attach the forestay to the chainplates on the damaged side. Unfortunately he made the mistake of sitting up to examine his workmanship at a moment when green water was sweeping the deck; it picked him up bodily and threw him against the deckhouse and then into the sea. There was a rope tied around his waist which held him to the vessel but even so it seemed that he could not survive being smashed against the hull, or avoid being choked by the waves pushing him under. He saw the boat a few feet away but could not move towards it. Luck intervened: as a wave washed him towards the rail, it dipped and he was suddenly aboard again. He vomited up water and then staggered below.

It was daylight when he next surfaced and the wind was still, but not, he soon realized, because the hurricane had passed, but because he was in its vortex. Six hours of tortuous, windless movement later the assault began from the south.

Hour after anxious hour passed, waiting, wondering, and finally being galvanized into action when the expected happened. The line holding the sea anchor parted, *Pagan* broached and refused to come up into the wind. She lay broadside on to the mountainous seas which drove her over at an increasing incline. In a remarkably short time Caldwell had brought his handmade anchor up on to the deck, attached it to the stemhead and got himself back down below. But the boat in those few minutes was too vulnerable for the sea not to take advantage. A succession of heavy breakers burst on to her exposed side and drove her under, tearing loose the mast from its step. Simultaneously, the water broached the two doors protecting the main hatchway, and poured down below. Caldwell fought his way through the torrent of water and surging objects that kept knocking him down, and climbed up into the cockpit. Across the deck was the broken mast, crashing about with every wild movement of the boat and threatening to damage the hull. He chopped it away with a hatchet and *Pagan* rode more easily, but she was very close to sinking. There were gaps where three portholes had been and the front of the deckhouse was stove in; water was washing in the hatchway with every roll and already it had nearly filled the saloon. He baled for hours with a bucket. Just when the water was down to the floorboards *Pagan* was spun around like a top and was once more inundated by an incoming wave. This time in his utter desperation Caldwell baled out everything; all the floating objects that got in the way of the bucket were tossed out in a frenzy to lighten the boat. There was no thought of what he was doing save baling for his life. Many hours later, he collapsed.

When he awoke the hurricane had passed. There was water in the boat as she had sprung a leak, and utter chaos reigned above and below decks. After pumping out, the first priority was to rig a jury mast and get moving, which took a day to accomplish. The next job was to take stock of food and water supplies. They were: a bottle of ketchup, two unlabelled cans of food which turned out to be sauerkraut, a coconut, and four gallons of water – plus a quart of battery fluid. He had not realized, in his panic, that he was throwing all his provisions away. But worse was to come. He soon learnt that he was totally without navigational instruments as the sextant and compass were smashed beyond repair. There were no charts left, or sailing directions, or light lists. All of these had washed out of the cabin when it was full of water.

I would dearly love to know exactly what was in his mind as the realization of his actions sank in. He talks only of practicalities, and not of the dreadful remorse that one would imagine must have sunk him to the depths of despair. From what he could remember of his position five days earlier he drew a map on the floor of the cockpit. A nail hammered in represented his estimated position yet he was grimly aware of the guesswork of the latitude and longitude of the various islands in the area. There was a coral reef, nearly barren and uninhabited, somewhere in the immediate vicinity. Upon reflection, the likelihood of finding it seemed remote. He opted instead for Samoa, 400 miles away and 16 to 18 days sailing. If he missed Samoa there was only Fiji, 600 miles further on. After that, nothing but ocean for thousands of miles.

He found two hooks and some line, and a small packet of fish bait. 'Old Death' was still around, which was a comfort as the small fish that accompanied the dolphin meant a mobile food supply. For some inexplicable reason, though, fish were now nearly impossible to catch. He found the bottle of ketchup empty the next morning, having drunk it in the night without thinking. That left only the cans and the coconut. Caldwell now displayed an extraordinary attitude towards food and his predicament. He simply could not ignore his already harrowing hunger pangs and ate both the sauerkraut and coconut in one sitting. That left only the water and the fish bait. He did very carefully ration the water, though, and never exceeded his allotted one pint a day.

For several days, between dipping himself in the ocean – he had read somewhere that it was a good remedy for thirst – and a regular pumping of the bilges, he concentrated on fishing. He did catch one after a long wait but as it was released from the hook Caldwell watched, stupefied, as it jumped off the deck and plopped back into the sea. He caught the same fish some while later and this time jumped on it with all his weight. There was nothing to cook it in

except Vaseline. Several days and no food later he licked out the jar of Vaseline. After a dreadful night of food dreams the medicine cabinet yielded up a jar of Vick and two tubes of boric acid; he ate them. The next night he woke up chewing his blanket. Hours of searching failed to produce the stowaway rat which must have been washed out with the charts; instead, he unearthed a chamois cloth, an army shoe, some pepper, a tube of lipstick and a jar of face cream. These last two had been intended for Mary. He also found a small box of tea, a bottle of shaving lotion, a bottle of hair oil, and a tiny jar of fish eggs for bait. What he did with this little treasure trove I will tell in his own words.

'I chopped the chamois cloth into tiny fragments, spilled them into a strong tea made from my ration of water and some of the tea I had found, and boiled them for ten minutes. This I seasoned heavily with pepper, a half-can of tooth powder and a generous dash of the shave lotion. To give it an interesting taste, I tossed in a fistful of salt water and a part of my can of machine oil. The result was a stew that made my eyes burn and my nose revolt when I ate it. Since the chamois had been used to strain gasoline, it gave the brew a distinctive zip.'

The next day he ate the lipstick, 'not too bad', and the jar of face cream, which left him with an oily taste in the mouth and feeling squeamish, but it temporarily banished the hunger pangs. The following morning he fared better; an eight inch long fish jumped into the liferaft trailing astern and before he could decide how it would taste fried in machine oil, he had eaten it raw.

Already, he was near the place where Samoa should have been sighted and the increased number of birds indicated that land was not too far distant. One of these birds he felled with an arrow made of bits of boat interior. The birds grew more numerous but land did not appear. Without a compass there was no reliable way of knowing where the wind was coming from if the sun was obscured, which it nearly always was. Even at a speed of one knot he realized he must have overshot Samoa by now, three weeks since the dismasting. A crucial decision had to be made; to go on searching in the immediate area for Samoa, or to go south-west to the Fiji Islands, which covered a much greater area. He decided to spend one more night searching and had awful dreams of being wrecked on a beach where a huge whale was stranded. He started to eat the whale at the tail end and awoke trying to get his teeth into the bunk boards. It was enough. There remained only two weeks supply of water at half-a-pint a day and Fiji was three weeks off.

Having made the decision to go south-west, his feelings about his predicament underwent a subtle change. He was no longer in a temporary state of hardship. There was the knowledge that he might not find the Fiji Islands or that the water would run out a long way before he did. Also, there was the threat of another hurricane. With these sober reflections in mind he altered course and then, on an understandable impulse, went down on his knees in desperate appeal to a source of help he had so far scorned. I imagine most atheists would have done the same.

Hunger became all engrossing. He had eaten the army boots, boiled and cut into thin strips. They were inedible, but he got them down. A wallet went the same way but a genuine hide belt conjured up such sentimental attachment that he put it back around his diminished waist. The hull had sprouted a growth of weed like grass, which, when soaked in hair oil, could be persuaded to resemble a salad to a willing palate. But it was soon all gone. A chance throw with a piece of cement from the bilge connected with an inquisitive bird and sent it plummeting into the sea. Before he had a chance to think what he was doing Caldwell had fished it out and torn it apart. Every morsel, except for a few large feathers, went down his throat, feet and beak included.

The next two days were foodless; the one after that produced a ship on the horizon. It passed quite close but did not see him, although Caldwell even lit a fire on deck to attract attention.

The effects of starvation were becoming very marked in his protruding bones and accentuated veins and, worst of all, in the swelling of his feet and ankles to twice their normal size. A gale happened along and the jury mast came down.

Caldwell was unable to get it inboard and even the exertion of tying it alongside was enough to cause him to pass out below. When he came to the boat was nearly full of water and only the realization that it was not another hurricane blowing gave him the heart to pump out. Then, land appeared.

It was a small island, topped by a volcano and lush with vegetation around its base. Although there was no sign of habitation Caldwell thought there must be mangoes and pineapples growing there, and probably fresh water. It was about four miles away. He had only to alter course to approach the reef, find a way through it and anchor in the lagoon beyond. Hour after hour passed and it was a long time before Caldwell realized that the current was carrying him away from the island, not towards it. The sail area was simply not big enough to make headway against it. By nightfall the island had gone.

It then dawned on him that it was the last island of the Fiji group. (In fact, he was wrong. He had incorrectly estimated his position and speed – no cause for wonder – and therefore could not have known that his position after his dismasting was not quite as desperate as he thought.) As the island disappeared, he was faced with the belief that ahead of him now was just empty sea. It would take weeks to reach the New Hebrides, and he had a quart and a half of water left, enough for eight or nine days. At the best possible speed he would be without water for a week. Impossible.

For the first time in his life, Caldwell took a long hard look at death. Notwithstanding a proper appreciation of his position, he concluded that, even when death was a real presence, it did not have the sense of finality that made one convinced it was going to happen. He never really believed he was going to die, although he had often wondered if he was going to perish out there alone on the sea. He toyed with the idea because it was a new one but it did not depress him. There was too much for him to live for, he believed, to succumb to such an idea. It is a fascinating reflection to ask ourselves how we would fare in his position, but it is one which will undoubtedly go untested for the majority of us, even for me. For, although I have put myself in potential danger by going to sea, I have never been faced with the dilemmas that Caldwell encountered.

The next morning the makeshift mast came down again. In Caldwell's weakened state such mishaps assumed calamitous proportions. On this occasion only the swilling down of a bottle of shaving lotion gave him the necessary impetus to restep the rig. He was never quite the same after that, whether due to the effort or the shaving lotion I am not sure.

The days went on, a sluggish progression westwards. One morning, another shark appeared and came in close to inspect the boat. It offered a chance of delivery, enough fresh and dried meat to last for weeks. I think even I would have given it some consideration by then. They eyed each other warily while Caldwell figured out how to go about catching it. A search of the boat produced a length of steel from which he fashioned a spear. It took two days to complete. The night before the battle, hunger pains kept the desperately needed sleep away. There was nothing left to eat on board, nothing but the engine oil. He drank it, it nearly made him ill, but it stayed down and he slept. The next day he finished the job on the harpoon and slept a few more hours. The shark was confident and moved in closer to eye what it obviously fancied for its own dinner. The spear went with deadly accuracy to its target. This time, in Caldwell's state of exhaustion, the fight took longer. Slowly, he drew it in. A few feet from the hull, there was a flurry and a jerk as the hooked shark was attacked by another shark, and then by half-a-dozen others. Caldwell watched the predators devour his last hopes of food, and gave himself up to despair. It was the lowest moment of the trip.

The day inevitably dawned when the drinking water was down to less than half a pint. When that was consumed there was nothing for several days, other than a few drops of evaporated steam from boiled salt water. Then came a squall and a gallon and a half of water. Despite the increased water ration, his brain, which had grown fuzzy since the fight with the shark, refused to work normally. When the water level rose to his bunk, he was compelled to do something about it, but he was never able to find the energy to pump out completely. Sleeping and pumping were almost his sole occupations, till the drinking water again had to be rationed to a half-pint a day. Calms settled upon the area. There can be nothing more soul-destroying than the sounds of a boat going nowhere on a glassy, rolling sea; everything creaks but nothing moves. Day after day, despite praying, not a breath ruffled the surface. A turtle rubbed itself against the keel and in his unsuccessful efforts to capture it Caldwell ran a piece of rusted iron half an inch under his knee cap.

On the 22nd day since his last morsel of food, the wind reappeared and with it the return of his unquenchable optimism. It was pushing him steadily onwards again, towards land, an estimated 10 days sailing away. How he was going to cope with the pumping out and an increasingly painful knee, he refused to consider. Four times during that night he woke from his place in the cockpit to work the pump and, in the morning, ended his usual morning prayers with the customary plea, 'let there be land'.

There was. It was another small island, much the same as the last. This time, though, it was closer. He ran down the length of the outer reef looking for an opening. None appeared and the end of the island loomed. The water in the bilges was rising as he had not bothered with pumping it out, could not in fact find the strength to do so. If he passed the point, he knew he was doomed. There was only one thing to do. He turned directly towards the reef and drove the yacht upon it. She hit, sprung a plank and sank by the bow. As she keeled over at an acute angle Caldwell was washed off the deck and into the sea, where a roller somersaulted him onto the coral. He got to his feet and staggered to the edge of the reef, till he could see the deep lagoon separating him from the shore. Knowing that to enter the water would be to sink to the bottom he sank to the coral instead and slept. He was wakened by the rising tide washing at his feet and made his way back to *Pagan* to find something to use as a raft, as the trailing liferaft had also been wrecked on the coral. He laboured instead with a knife to free the mast lashed alongside. It floated free as the boat was thrown over on to her side. He climbed on to it. It bumped over the reef and floated slowly across the lagoon. Caldwell awoke from his drowsing when he felt a jolt as the mast reached the shore. He crawled up the sand a small way and immediately fell asleep.

Rising water again aroused him, and he discovered he was in an alcove, surrounded by rocks, into which the tide surged. Somehow, he managed to climb the 20 feet of lava cliffs and collapsed at the top. He slept the rest of that day and the whole night, and awoke determined to find food. The rocks were razor sharp and it took an hour to cover just 10 yards. He had a rest and did another few yards. Some hours and 20 yards further on he found a lone coconut tree, just a short one, but its fruit was out of reach. After another rest he found an old nut on the ground and spent the next 24 hours trying to pierce it with the knife but he lacked the strength.

On the third day ashore, coral poisoning was making its presence felt in a dozen places, his knee was black, and his tongue swollen and sticky. There was no hope in what he was doing, he had to return to the water and try another way out. He made his way back to the shore and lay there. This time he was awakened by a different sound, voices, children who were excited at their finds on the beach, but with no idea of his presence. When they came upon him they fled in terror. An outrigger appeared some time later with native youths on board who gazed at him in amazement. Finally, they responded to his weak directions to enter the narrow opening of the cove. It turned out to be impossible; the wind was too strong and the waves kept pushing them out. After a time they went away, but indicated that they would return. It was night when he next awakened to see lights of three outriggers anchored off shore in the strong wind. They apparently still could not reach him. Other than shouting encouragement, they seemed prepared to wait. But Caldwell, cold now adding to his problems and feeling

that his end was nigh, set up such a wail that one of the boats detached itself from the rest and disappeared. Much later, noises above him heralded a rescuer from landward, who picked him up like a child and carried him down to the waiting boats. In a commotion of shouting and wild paddling they got him into the outrigger from the ledge on to which he had been carried, and laid him in the bottom of the boat. They covered him with a piece of cloth, and produced food and drink. He threw caution to the wind and gorged himself.

Not yet were his troubles quite over. If it had not been for the native woman who pumped the food and drink out of his stomach, he might have died soon after from his excesses and coral poisoning, not to mention a septic knee. He pulled through, and after a week was able to get about and agitate for a means to get on with his journey home.

On the morning of November 15, he and his rescuers flagged down a passing schooner bound for one of the larger Fiji Islands which boasted a radio station. Unfortunately, the radio was broken, so his impatience had to be contained till he reached Suva, another week or so. There he sent a few heartfelt words to Mary, who had already heard of his deliverance through some unknown source. After the telegrams, more fretful waiting, but at last the U.S. Army Air Corps took pity on him and arranged his flight home.

Adrift

A conviction commonly held by most sailors – especially when they hear of someone having to escape into a liferaft from a sinking yacht – is that it could not happen to them. It is a universal and – considering the statistics – rather irrational attitude to a lot of our daily hazards, such as crossing the road or driving on the motorway. One of the predominant reasons for this ostrich-like approach concerning safety at sea is not wishing to appear to others (or ourselves) overly anxious. The person who will go to the lengths of preparing himself adequately for the eventuality of spending some months in a raft would probably be considered too paranoic to go to sea – which would possibly be true.

Auralyn 40 minutes after she received a fatal blow from a whale. Maurice Bailey is in the foreground

Some years ago a very comprehensive survey was done on liferafts, based on first-hand experience. The resultant design would have produced a raft strong enough, light enough, big enough and sufficiently well equipped to provide an acceptable chance of survival, but so expensive that no one would buy it. In the end a few cheap improvements were made and the sailing fraternity was appeased. We take our chances or we do not go to sea. One does not hear from those unfortunates who set off on their modest world cruises and meet their fate at sea. The harrowing stories told to us by the few who lose their vessels but do live to tell the tale suggests that they might be in the minority.

The following account concerns an English couple, Maurice and Maralyn Bailey, 41- and 32-years-old respectively at the time of their experience. They sold their house and put all their resources into a 31-foot cruising boat, which they planned to sail to New Zealand. Early in February 1973, nearly a year after setting off from England, they prepared their yacht *Auralyn* for the Pacific ocean crossing from Panama. They were both fit and well. Maralyn had suffered from arthritic pains which had delayed their departure from the UK for a year but those were now gone. Six days out into the Pacific, and 10 from the Galapagos Islands, disaster struck. Maralyn was about to start cooking breakfast and Maurice was just waking up when the boat was shaken from an impact with a heavy object. They both leapt on deck and saw a large whale astern, threshing wildly in a sea of blood and foam. Maralyn's first concern was for the plight of the whale but Maurice leapt below again to see what damage the whale had inflicted on their boat. He found a hole about 18 inches long by a foot wide just below the waterline, aft of the galley. Their first action after the initial stunned shock was to attempt to fix a collision-mat to stem the flow of water. It is usual in such circumstances to stretch a jib out around the keel and fasten it on deck by the corners. It did not work in their case as the yacht had bilge keels which prevented the sail cloth lying flat over the hole. They next tried stuffing blankets into the gap, pumping out all

the while but the water level continued to rise. Some 40 minutes after the whale had hit them they realized the *Auralyn* was going to sink. The decision to abandon her was made without fuss or panic. While Maurice got the liferaft and inflatable dinghy ready Maralyn gathered together as many essentials as were to hand into several sail bags and threw them into the dinghy, along with the portable water containers and emergency kit. *Auralyn* settled in the water as they got into the raft. In stupefied silence they watched the yacht sink slowly beneath the waves.

For a long while neither spoke. The sudden absence of creaking hull and slatting halyards intensified their feelings of bewilderment and deprivation. Maralyn abstractedly began putting the contents of the raft in some sort of order while Maurice rowed slowly about picking up odd things that had escaped from the vessel as she went down. Both were numb with shock. After some time they began to speak about what had happened. Maurice blamed himself bitterly for his inability to save the yacht. Maralyn quietly mourned the loss of their best friend, companion and home. Waves of dejection and despair alternated with attempts at confidence. They would soon be picked up; they had many friends who knew where they were and would wonder why they did not arrive in the Galapagos Islands. This optimism was dashed by the realization that it could be months before they were seriously missed; their non-appearance would be put down to their having stopped off at another island somewhere.

At length Maralyn roused herself to make a survey of everything they had managed to salvage. The pile of food looked pitifully meagre, but they were a little encouraged to see the extent of their navigating equipment. With strict rationing the food and water supplies would last 20 days. Maurice calculated the distance to Galapagos. Knowing the prevailing winds and currents he realized they would have to row south to have any chance of intercepting the islands. He did not suggest this immediately to Maralyn though. His view of the gravity of their situation was more profound than hers.

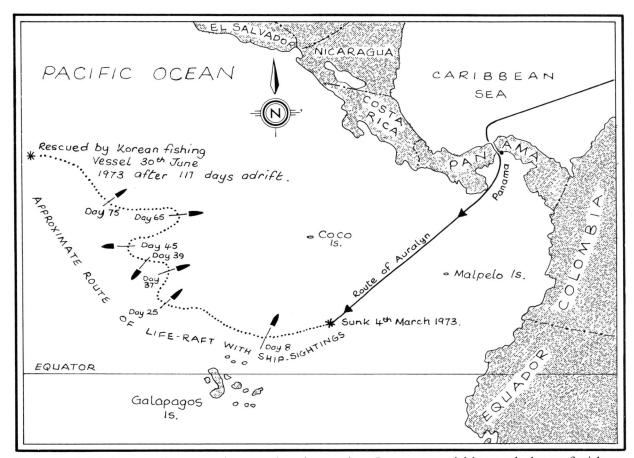

Because of this he was the more depressed and found it difficult to even pretend that he had control of their situation.

Maralyn had always had a flair for organizing and command which now came to the fore. She wanted at least to appear optimistic and positive in order to keep up their spirits. She decided that they should row at night and sleep when they could during the day as the fierce heat would make over-exertion dangerous. But she thought they ought just to drift that first night as they were heading for a shipping lane.

They could only lie down to sleep one at a time. The other would sit hunched up in the remaining space and keep watch. At dawn Maurice found contaminated water in four of their 10 gallons of fresh water.

They cowered under the raft canopy during the worst heat of the day and that evening began rowing. It was a punishing and almost fruitless task as the dinghy had to pull the raft which was badly designed for towing. Eight hours of hard labour took them only a few miles south but, more depressing than that was the fact that, although their consumption of water had almost doubled, it had brought no relief from thirst. They continued rowing for two more nights until Maurice had to tell Maralyn that he thought they were wasting their time. The currents were carrying them north faster than they could row. Maralyn agreed to head for the shipping lanes instead and busied herself with rigging a small sail on the dinghy to help them on. Maurice had not the heart to explain the pointlessness of hurrying their progress north: the idiosyncrasies of the counter winds and currents they would eventually meet would simply drive them south again.

From the dinghy Maralyn photographs Auralyn *as the stricken yacht settles slowly in the water*

The first week went quite quickly with the strangeness of their situation still being absorbed, and there was plenty of navigation and calculations to attend to. The next unwanted problem turned up in the shape of a large turtle. The raft bottom held some inexplicable fascination for these creatures, which the Baileys found alarming. There would be a gasp as one surfaced near the raft, followed by a series of bumps hard enough to lift objects off the floor. The prods became so numerous that the Baileys themselves occasionally received unceremonious blows to their backsides. They retaliated by swiping the creatures over the head with a paddle but that only occasioned short-lived surprise before the turtles' fatal fascination drew them back. Maralyn suggested dragging a smallish one into the dinghy and killing it to eat. As a suitable looking victim presented itself shortly afterwards they grabbed it and heaved

it aboard. But Maurice was loath to resort to killing the wretched creatures until absolutely necessary.

Just when it began to look as though that necessity had been reached a ship appeared. Their relief and delight that their ordeal was over after only eight days was intense. The ship was on course to pass within a mile of them. As she drew near Maurice fired off several flares. Time went by but there was no answering signal from the fishing boat. In sudden desperation Maurice lit one more flare and Maralyn waved her oilskin jacket frantically. But the boat was already moving away and in another few minutes was growing smaller in the distance.

Sadness and despair held them silent in the dinghy while they consumed the rest of their meagre lunch and readjusted their minds to the awfulness of their situation. Both food and water supplies were running low and if rain did not come soon their water would have to be restricted to dangerously low levels. There was little to alleviate their despondency.

The following morning they decided to kill the turtle still lying in the bottom of the dinghy. Maralyn had the job of cutting its throat while Maurice held it still. It was a gruesome, awkward business, made the more so by a lack of adequate tools and their reluctance to kill a harmless creature. At last it lay dead and bloody in the bottom of the dinghy. Together they carved it up and removed some large steaks from underneath the shell. Hoards of little fish crowded around the blood and meat tipped into the sea, some of which Maralyn caught on a hook she had fashioned from a safety pin (their emergency fish hooks had not been repacked into the survival kit in Panama). Besides the steaks they now had fillets of fish, various delicacies from inside the large heads of trigger fish – the most common one to take the hook – and eyeballs. The next hurdle was forcing themselves to eat this grisly-looking fare. Maurice rapidly overcame his revulsion and tucked in heartily but Maralyn needed several days to pluck up enough courage to eat properly.

Between the serious occupations of catching their food, and eating and sleeping, they endeavoured to keep their minds diverted by playing games such as 'Cat's Cradle' and dominoes, utilizing bits of string and blank pages torn from a log book. Maralyn had thrown in several books but bitterly regretted not having had the presence of mind to add their pocket chess set. Other distractions included the sight of killer and sperm whales cruising past a few yards away – which always made Maralyn very nervous. One day a sperm whale showed a decided interest in their presence. Most of the leviathans came by in pairs or threes but this one was alone and apparently looking them over with a speculative eye. It surfaced behind the dinghy and slowly came up alongside, until its blow hole was level with Maurice and Maralyn crouching timidly in the raft entrance. Ten agonizingly long minutes passed, during which the Baileys felt themselves to be in the greatest danger of a swipe from its massive tail fluke, then it decided to dive – obviously fed up with waiting for a response to its advances.

Soon after this incident the weather turned colder and a strong wind raised white caps on the tops of waves – conditions one would think nothing about on a yacht. In the raft life became infinitely more tiresome and exhausting with the need to sponge out the salt water spraying in through the entrance. Within a few hours wherever their skin came into contact with the moving rubber they developed sore patches and blisters. The cloud above, however, had a providential silver lining. Several days later they experienced their first rain storm. It was easy to collect a good quantity of water running off the canopy by holding up a bucket. However, their delight was tempered when the water turned out to have a foul taste, as the canopy was covered with a waterproof rubber coating which washed off in the rain. Even though the taste grew weaker as the canopy grew less waterproof the collected water was never pleasant to drink.

Another turtle went the way of the first and this time both Maralyn and Maurice were able to extract far more enjoyment from its delicacies, revealed beneath the shell and in other parts during closer scrutiny: liver, heart, kidneys and a delicious fatty substance which they found particularly palatable. No sooner was that turtle dispatched when a long series of rain storms kept them fully occupied collecting water and keeping the floor and contents of the raft dry. It was a wearying task and, once overtired, they found it much more difficult to keep up their spirits.

Maralyn noticed that Maurice was losing a lot of weight and looking gaunt and emaciated. After some persistent enquiries she got him to admit that she did not look much better. The pure fish diet was providing ample protein but obviously not the carbohydrate necessary to maintain flesh and muscle. Fishing had to be done before every meal as food would not keep long in the heat. As the fish diet palled they began to crave another turtle. When at last one appeared there was none of the former vacillation as to the animal's right to live: the turtle, a much bigger one, fought for its life with surprising violence, biting Maurice on the ankle and inflicting severe scratches on his arms and legs with its flippers, but this resistance just made the Baileys angry. The kill took a long time with the penknife but eventually they rested beside their gory victim, content in the knowledge that it was going to provide life-saving food.

That same evening, their 25th day adrift, they saw another ship. Maralyn waited until she could make out the vessel's navigation lights before wakening Maurice. Only two flares remained. The first one failed to light and without a word Maurice threw it away, and lit the second one. The whole area around them was illuminated by the intense white light. They waited in breathless suspense for the vessel to acknowledge them. It sailed on into the night.

A week of squally, cold weather crept by. Each night was as dismal as the last; each dawn heralded the same miserably damp conditions. On April 10, day 37, a ship came within half a mile of them. There were no flares left, nothing with which to attract attention but their yellow oilskin jackets. It seemed unbelievable that no one would see them, but this ship also sailed on.

After this Maralyn started pondering the problem of their apparent invisibility. Before leaving the yacht for the last time she had

This photograph shows how difficult it is to spot very small objects on the open ocean. In it is a liferaft and dinghy but, because of the patterns of the light and dark, they are virtually impossible to spot just 500 yards from the camera. A number of ships passed the Baileys at a distance of less than one mile

excitement, the ship began to turn. It went around 180 degrees and stopped. A few minutes later it turned another arc, apparently looking around. Maurice and Maralyn waved their jackets till their arms ached from the effort. Long minutes went by, then the ship, unbelievably, resumed its southerly direction and steamed off over the horizon. They were devastated.

There is a photograph in the Baileys' book which was taken in the English Channel on a bright sunny day. The sea sparkles silver on deep indigo and there is almost no swell. I searched for what the caption said was there, the raft and dinghy, but I failed to pick them out. The caption pinpoints their exact position just 500 yards from the camera. Even so, one has to look very hard to see the two objects in the pattern of shadows and light.

The weather turned rough again to depress their spirits further. On the 45th day the fifth ship passed by. The methylated spirit refused to light, due either to the strong wind or the damp. As the ship steamed past, portholes flooded with light, Maurice flashed the torch in its direction. No one appeared on her decks and she passed out of sight like the others. In silent desperation they continued their interrupted rest in the bottom of the wet raft.

In the morning both the kerosene and the matches were too wet to be of any further use. Even when dried out the matches would not strike. At this point in his log Maurice comments with some incredulity on Maralyn's unfailing optimism that they would be rescued. She continued to speak of the future as certain. There must be some reason, she claimed, for their having stayed alive this long. He described Maralyn's ideas as fatalistic; she believed that most of the things that happened to one were predestined – although she was reluctant to attribute the design of it to a god. Maurice was a profound sceptic and unable to take any comfort from such an argument. Maralyn strongly believed that people were capable of doing what they wished with their lives, provided they were prepared to use enough determination to achieve their goals.

This belief undoubtedly lent Maralyn strength

grabbed various articles of clothing still on their hangers. These she now ripped up into strips, tied the strips to the hangers and put the 'flare' into the container of kerosene that Maurice had saved from the sea. There was also some methylated spirit which could be poured over each to set them alight quickly. Two days later another ship hove into view and the Baileys went into action. This one was obviously going to pass even closer than the others; they could not fail to be seen. Maurice climbed into the dinghy and lit a bonfire of rags, kerosene and methylated spirit. He fanned it and smoke billowed up. After a few minutes, to their great

and enabled her to recover more quickly than Maurice from the crushing disappointments meted out by the incompetent watch-keepers aboard the ships. Undiminished, too, was her love of the sea. When they talked of the future Maurice became enthusiastic about a peaceful life in a country cottage with a large garden full of flowers and vegetables. Maralyn let him talk about it for a while but finally had to tell him this was not what she wanted. This unlikely Utopia had never worked for them in the past, why should it do so now just because of their present circumstances? It was most unlikely that this hardship would radically alter their fundamental way of thinking. To live a sedentary life ashore was what they had most wanted to avoid. They had done the ultimate – sold up everything and sailed off into the sunset to find adventure and excitement in foreign places. The urge to do so again would surely reassert itself once they were rescued and had recovered from their ordeal. It would be better to be realistic and start planning their future right now.

Once Maurice was convinced she did not hate the idea of ever going to sea again he joined her enthusiastically in designing their new yacht. It was a bold plan which had the benefit of giving them something new to think about. Endless time was now spent dreaming of the perfect boat, down to the minutest details of galley and provisions for long journeys. This led naturally into the other topic of absorbing interest: food. Although the Baileys' diet was quite plentiful they craved proper food. In every instance of shipwreck that I have researched the theme of food reigns above all else – hunger being our most basic survival instinct. Sooner or later it becomes an obsession which overrides every other desire or emotion.

Day followed day and week followed week. Maralyn marked special days like turtle days or ship days on her calendar; otherwise, there was nothing to differentiate one from the next. Desultory conversation occasionally turned to what Maurice, at least, considered to be the most likely conclusion to their predicament: how they could affect the swiftest and least painful end to themselves or each other when hope was completely lost. There was no gas left and any other kind of suffocation did not seem practical and as Maralyn did not like the idea of letting herself drown that left only the turtle knife or eating a poisoned fish. Maralyn always turned Maurice's thoughts away from such gloomy reflections as soon as she could and tried to convince him instead that they would be rescued.

Early in May they began their third month in the raft. During the first week the weather deteriorated and living conditions became grim in the extreme. Because of a split in the tape joining the two circular tubes at the front of the raft, movement within had to be restricted to a minimum or the tubes might have broken away and then the raft would have had to be abandoned. Slow punctures which defied mending meant that the chambers could no longer be properly inflated. Each time the sea became rough the water slopped in over the sides. The best they could do was to pump air into the chambers every half-hour day and night, and bale out. Then it transpired that even the previous week's sunshine had done them an ill service in contaminating most of their water supply. They were down to two one-gallon containers stored under the canopy. Fishing was more difficult in the rough weather so, in an attempt to conserve energy, they ate half the morning catch and reserved the other half till the evening. They were both ill that night – Maralyn particularly so. Ill, she felt more depressed than before and, when their thoughts turned inwards upon themselves, they said hurtful things to each other. In her log she wrote: 'Here every day becomes more of a nightmare. If only a ship would see us; it would be unbearable to have another pass us by.' Later on she was able to be thankful for the endless opportunity for discussion about themselves and their relationship. They had time to analyse their feelings and opinions, and afterwards could reflect that, in a sense, it was as though they had died and been reborn. They rediscovered each other in a totally different light and, happily, liked what they found.

At last the rain came, clearing away depression and raising hopes. The stagnant water was replaced by fresh and that evening the biggest turtle yet was tipped, with the greatest difficulty, into the dinghy. In the evening another ship was sighted at quite a distance. It rained incessantly. Maurice developed a dry hacking cough which did not at first concern them. So enveloped did they become in the misery of the cold, wet, and seemingly eternal present that when the seventh ship passed quite close they shrugged it off and thought little of the civilization it represented. They had reverted to a simple primeval way of life and for the moment were relatively content.

No more ships were to appear for six weeks, but they clung tenaciously to life and each other.

Towards the end of May Maurice's cough became more troublesome. He began complaining of pains in his chest which Maralyn pretended to attribute to the strain of pulling in the last big turtle. Neither was prepared to face the possibility of his being seriously ill. The time came when he was unable to lift his arm without great pain. Ulcerated sores ate into his flesh and would not heal, while salt water continually wet them. Coughing up blood and suffering continual pain so depressed him that he took virtually no more interest in their survival. Maralyn took over the task of fishing and pumping up the raft and baling out, chattering encouragingly as she did so to hide her fear. She butchered the latest turtle and forced him to try some. He had no appetite at all but, because her willpower was so strong, or because it would have been more difficult to resist, he chewed on whatever she handed him. But even her most exciting find, turtle's eggs, glued themselves to his teeth and throat.

As if they had not enough to contend with already, sharks now put in an appearance and behaved in an alarming manner. Either out of curiosity or in idle sportiveness they would charge at the large protrusions the Baileys' bodies made in the soft floor of the raft and hit them with a sickening whack. Maurice particularly suffered greatly from the attacks as the sharks' aim was very good and often scored a hit on one of his sores, which then bled. After a

week their very bones felt bruised but they could not think of a safe way of driving the sharks off.

June 5 was recorded by Maralyn as their worst day. What started out as a normal squall in the afternoon developed in the evening into a storm. All night they baled and pumped, Maurice's chest problems forgotten in the face of this new menace. Daybreak revealed angry seas which wrenched the raft and dinghy apart one second and flung them violently back together the next. Sheets of driven spray nearly obscured the glowering grey sky above. After hours of watching the waves and keeping the dinghy dry Maurice decided they must fish and eat or they would become too weak to keep the raft afloat. He made a perilous transfer to the dinghy and baled it out, though the salt water and rubbing against the rubber seat had so aggravated his sores that any movement was agonizing. It was a fruitless exercise as the fish had all disappeared – presumably to ride out the storm well beneath the surface of the sea. Maurice shouted to Maralyn that he would tidy up and come back to the raft: he was just too late. As he shouted he saw with horror a huge wall of water rearing up behind Maralyn. The raft was lifted up on to the wave crest, where it seemed to hesitate for a moment, then Maralyn found herself charging down the breaking face towards the dinghy. She braced herself for a collision but instead the dinghy and Maurice were enveloped in an avalanche of breaking water and disappeared beneath it. Maurice felt the chilling blackness envelop him, pushing him down and down, while he fought to swim upwards. He broke surface first underneath the upturned dinghy and in renewed panic dived back down to escape it. Next he found himself surfacing beside the dinghy, caught a glance of Maralyn's terrified face staring from the raft, and felt an overwhelming relief that they were both still all right. Getting him back inside the raft took all their combined strength. While he lay gasping on the floor Maralyn pulled in the dinghy and began to detach the oars, water containers and compass which were tied on with lines. Together they began the exhausting task of turning the dinghy over. Time after time the wind defeated them, but eventually it was upright and everything was tied back inside.

The night passed agonizingly slowly. Most of the time the raft was half awash. At best the water was never lower than their hips and several times huge waves completely immersed them. When Maralyn realized how easily they could be overwhelmed she asked Maurice what would happen if they capsized. Although he was angry at the question – because he thought she could work it out for herself – he attempted to reassure her that it was unlikely. Nevertheless he suggested getting together the last of their tinned food, putting it in a haversack and tying it to the side of the raft. 'I don't feel like dying, not tonight anyway,' said Maralyn as she groped in the darkness for his hand. It was then, thought Maurice, that he really appreciated the extent of Maralyn's tenacity for life. It would not be any failing on her part if they did not survive.

The storm lasted for four days and after it subsided they celebrated by killing two turtles. A booby bird took up roost on the dinghy and proceeded to make a mess there, to the annoyance of Maurice who made a swipe at it with a paddle. Instead of flying away it squatted on the water close to the raft and by way of thanks regurgitated four whole flying fish at the surprised Baileys. A fine supplement to their supper, they thought, as they scooped them out of the water. The next time a booby landed on the dinghy Maralyn thoughtfully fed it some leftovers from their last meal. The booby looked agreeably surprised. The next minute it found itself dangling by one leg from Maralyn's towel-clad hand. It retaliated by sinking its beak deep into her thumb, and smartly got its neck wrung. The raw red meat made a pleasant change from fish.

June 16 brought another four-day storm and all its associated fatigue and pain. Maurice was soon reduced, because of his open raw sores, to a state of abject misery, from which Maralyn laboured constantly to distract him. One wound on his spine, which he fortunately could not see, was three-quarters of an inch across and very deep. Their dreams of life after rescue com-pletely disappeared. When they dreamed now it was of dry warm weather and a particular cut of turtle steak. The world beyond their immediate environment meant nothing. During the storm the dinghy overturned twice, once with Maurice in it. He was flung out but discovered, in answer to Maralyn's anxious enquiry, that he still had their last precious hook clutched tightly in his hand.

On the last day of the storm they managed to capture a medium-sized turtle which Maurice anchored to the floor of the dinghy by one flipper. Once more the dinghy was overturned and although Maralyn tried desperately to haul in the frantically swimming turtle her hands slipped from its shell as the rope came loose. Morale slumped to a new low.

The next day, as Maurice dozed, Maralyn idly ran her finger down the back of a two-foot shark swimming by. A few seconds later, almost without thinking, she had it by the tail. Maurice was aroused by her frantic shouts and came to the rescue. While Maralyn kept a fierce grip on its tail, Maurice wrapped a towel around its business end and proceeded to whack it on the head with the knife. After 15 minutes it expired. Maurice began gutting it but Maralyn went back to her fishing. A few minutes later he responded to her excited cries of another catch. Hardly was that one dispatched when Maralyn had yet another by the tail. Maurice implored her to stop as he was running out of hands to deal with them. Their depression turned rapidly to gaiety at the absurd sight of Maurice trying to cope with three sharks, one dead, one half alive and one frantic in his arms. The picnic was not yet quite complete. As they dealt in high good humour with the sharks, a booby perched itself on the side of the dinghy next to Maurice. A glance at each other spelt its doom and seconds later Maralyn had it by the neck. Shortly afterwards a second booby landed in the spot recently vacated by its friend and began its toilet. The Baileys looked at each other in amazement. That bird also joined its friend and the sharks in the dinghy. They dined royally that day.

The marine life seemed, if anything, to increase as they drifted into the Doldrums. The

After an ordeal lasting 117 days deliverance comes from a Korean fishing vessel

ition he fished, ate or just gazed at the multi-coloured layers of fish swimming around and below them. When they had sufficiently recovered from the effects of the storm they started tentatively to discuss their next voyage on *Auralyn II,* as their new yacht was to be called. Maurice professed a life-long interest in Patagonia and began to instruct Maralyn on every aspect of the country that he had ever read or heard about. Soon, everything was forgotten in the euphoria of being somewhere else; a lonely, windy, wild place, to be sure, but perhaps because that was more in keeping with their present lifestyle it lent reality to the dream.

When most of their improvised hooks had broken or been lost Maralyn turned her ingenuity towards designing a fish-catcher – without a hook. The trigger fish were so anxious to be caught that it was sometimes possible to lift them out of the water with a bucket. This gave her an idea. From the old kerosene container she fashioned a trap by cutting a big hole in one end. Then through the opposite end – with the spout – she threaded a baited line, so that the fish had to swim into the container to get at the bait. It worked wonderfully well – after she had fooled the fish into complacence by hand feeding for an hour or so. The other trigger fish did not appear to notice their friends' absence but queued up obligingly to be next in the pot. Sometimes they caught as many as 40 fish a day.

The next two weeks passed in the now familiar routine of quick squally showers, hot sunshine, endless fishing and contented discussion. They had acquired pets of two baby turtles who splashed about in the water in the bottom of the dinghy. Many of the creatures swimming past, from sea snakes to the very rare spotted whale shark, lingered long enough to be closely inspected. The sea provided an endless spectacle which they never tired of examining.

June 30, their 118th day at sea, began inauspiciously. The dawn promised a hot day and as the sun climbed the Baileys sweated in the heat under their bleached canopy. They slept in the late morning, ate lunch, and carried on sleeping, Maurice was dreaming that there were three people in the raft, the third an American they

weather improved considerably although, despite being so close to the Equator, the nights were cold. Maurice found some relief from his sores by kneeling in the dinghy. From this pos-

had met briefly in another world: a voice kept insistently trying to interrupt his thoughts and he angrily told it to go away. Someone shook him. As he struggled to wake, Maralyn's voice dragged him slowly back to the present. 'Get out to the dinghy. A ship is coming.' She was waving her yellow oilskin jacket but for a while Maurice could not see what she was waving at. 'Wave your jacket, it's there, behind you!' she insisted. He turned around and saw a small white rusty ship coming from the east. He began to wave his jacket and together they watched, without speaking, as the ship drew level with them about half a mile away. It slowly went past. Maurice stopped waving. He called to Maralyn to give up and save her strength, but she ignored him and began imploring the ship to stop. Maurice knelt in the bottom of the dinghy and ignored the ship, allowing his thoughts instead to refocus on the scene around them. Maralyn was now quiet but still slowly waving her jacket. Maurice glanced again in the direction of the ship's stern and his gaze was arrested. He stared long and hard in disbelief and then heard Maralyn say quietly: 'It's coming back.'

Within a very short time the ship was alongside and a rope was being lowered to them. Maurice caught it and tied it to a rowlock. Strong hands pulled the two craft to the rope ladder up forward and the Baileys were assisted up on to the deck of the ship. They discovered that their legs would not support them. The crew of the Korean fishing vessel laid them on a blanket and hovered about uncertainly until the cook appeared with two glasses of hot milk. As they sipped Maurice and Maralyn looked at the smiling faces surrounding them, then at each other. For a moment they were oblivious to the crew's questioning eyes. Maurice said quietly: 'We've made it.' Maralyn, blinking back tears, nodded and replied: 'Now for *Auralyn II* – and Patagonia!' They got there, too, eventually, and in *Auralyn II*.

Maurice and Maralyn each lost about 40 pounds in weight although physically Maralyn survived in better shape than her husband

Against all Odds

At about the same time as the Baileys were embarking on their long ordeal in a liferaft the Robertson family were just concluding the written account of theirs. The Robertsons' yacht sank in June, 1972, on the western side of the Galapagos Islands: the Baileys lost theirs on the eastern side in March 1973. One might have thought that the Baileys would have heard of the other family's experience; apparently not, as they never mentioned it. Cruising about on a yacht one does not necessarily keep up with world news. Anyway, they would have seen no comparison between themselves, merrily going about their business in a wellfound and well-equipped yacht, and perfect strangers whose boat was sunk by whales. It was certainly not likely to happen to them . . .

The Robertson family's yacht Lucette *sunk by whales near the Galapagos Islands in the Pacific*

Like the Baileys, the Robertsons' ordeal is a study of physical deprivation. But, more interestingly, because of Dougal Robertson's honest and fearless account, it reveals the human mind at work and at variance with its neighbours. In this most testing of circumstances, lost in an alien environment and entirely dependent upon themselves, we can see how these few ordinary people coped. It is a test we might all wish to experience without having actually to do it: to discover if, cooped up in a nine-foot, six-inch space with another five human beings, our courage, humanity and strength would measure up to our expectations.

The Robertson family comprised husband and wife, daughter of 16 – who was not aboard for the fateful voyage – son of 15 and twin sons of nine. Dougal had spent the past 15 years struggling vainly to keep up a decent standard of living from an upland dairy farm in North Staffordshire but somehow, on one Sunday morning in the autumn of 1968, he knew he was losing the fight. The discussion that morning as the children bounced on their parent's bed turned to the first Whitbread Round-the-World Yacht Race which had recently been announced. One of the twins jokingly suggested that they should buy a boat too and sail round the world; his mother laughingly joined him in the game. The remark struck a strangely receptive note in Dougal's mind. He was afraid for the children's future, shut away in their limited environment. His disenchantment with his once hopeful dreams of farming had grown beyond the mutterings of a discontented man into despair of the whole business. It struck him forcibly that they had everything to gain and nothing to lose by doing something totally different. It was out of the ordinary but as far as the children were concerned it would be both educational and fun. And, for him and his wife, perhaps a new start.

Two years later they had sold the farm and bought a 43-foot wooden schooner, *Lucette*. After sailing her back from Malta to Britain she was refitted and they were off to the West Indies, the first stage of their planned cruise around the world.

In February, 1972, following a year of cruising and exploring the West Indies, Bahamas, and ports along the American coast, their daughter left to pursue a life of her own. The kick-off point for the crossing of the Pacific Ocean was Panama, where they halted long enough to sign on another crew member. Robin, a 22-year-old Welsh graduate in economics and statistics, was a cheerful, spirited character who fitted in with their – by now – well-ordered, experienced, shipboard lifestyle.

For the majority of sailors doing much the same as the Robertsons the Galapagos Islands are the first stop en route for New Zealand. Here the Robertsons briefly took in the wonders of wildlife and the geography of the various islands in the group, the last one of which, however, did not meet their expectations. Scruffy birds, dead animals, and a seal covered with boils, combined with the harsh volcanic lava, helped to give the place a sinister atmosphere: they all felt it and were anxious not to linger. The sky had also assumed a sombre grey mantle denoting a wind change which could make them vulnerable to a lee shore. Dougal's wife Lyn reminded him that the date was the 13th. But it was not, Dougal pointed out, a Friday. She was adamant about not sailing on such an inauspicious day but had to acquiesce when both Robin and their eldest son Douglas joined in Dougal's desire to be gone. Soon they were sailing steadily away from the islands and by morning had left them far astern.

It was the morning of June 15, 1972. The sun reappeared long enough to enable Dougal to obtain an accurate sun sight with which he retired to the quiet of the aft cabin to plot. He had stowed the sextant in its box and turned to the plotting tables when the hull beneath his feet heaved upwards in violent motion. The loud crash of splintering wood was immediately followed by the sound of gushing water. A shout of 'Whales!' from the cockpit penetrated Dougal's stunned senses. He picked himself up from where he had been thrown and yanked up the floorboards. The blue pacific depths were clearly visible through a wide gap between two oak frames. He shouted at Lyn to bring him clothes – anything – that would fill the hole. She

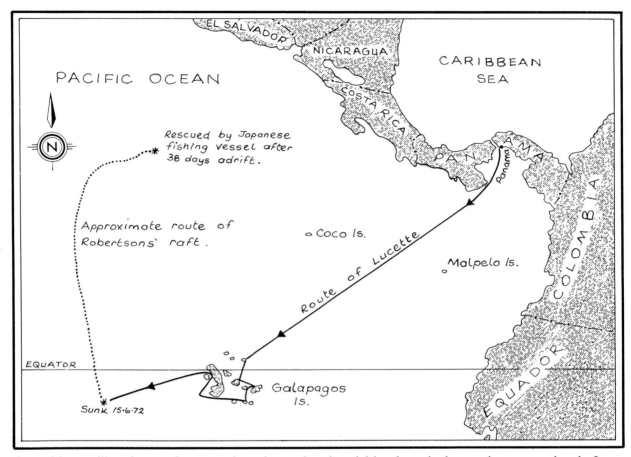

PACIFIC OCEAN

Rescued by Japanese
fishing vessel after
38 days adrift.

Approximate route of
Robertsons' raft.

CARIBBEAN
SEA

Route of Lucette

o Coco Is.

o Malpelo Is.

EQUATOR

Sunk 15·6·72

Galapagos
Is.

threw him a pillow but at the same time shouted that there was another hole under the WC flooring. He stuffed the pillow into the gap, replaced the floorboard and stood on it: the water continued to well up. One of the boys asked from the deck if they were sinking. Dougal heard himself, as if from a distance, say: 'Yes, abandon ship.'

The water was already up to Dougal's thighs and lapping over the batteries in the engine room as he waded through the galley towards the hatchway. He saw a vegetable knife and grabbed it in passing. As he climbed up on deck he saw that Lyn was fastening the twins' lifejackets and Douglas was struggling to untie the inflatable liferaft. Dougal leapt forward to slash at the lashings tying down the fibreglass dinghy to the deck so that Douglas could free the raft from underneath it. Already the yacht was wallowing

sluggishly, her deck nearly at sea level. Lyn had managed to cut loose the emergency water containers and flares and was throwing them into the dinghy while Douglas grabbed the oars. Dougal yelled at everyone to get off as he threw a bag of onions to one of the twins, Sandy, with instructions to go into the raft. Neil, the other twin, was sitting in the dinghy which had somehow become half-filled with water. Douglas, Robin and Sandy were now in the water near the liferaft whose CO_2 cylinders had exploded, noisily expelling gas. Dougal shouted again to Neil to leave the dinghy which was nearly swamped and get into the raft. Neil, holding on to his teddy bear, first jumped back on to the yacht, hesitated a moment, then dived into the sea and swam for the raft. Lyn was still on deck without a lifejacket on: as the deck slipped away she and Dougal stepped off into the sea. After he had helped Lyn into the raft Dougal swam to the immersed dinghy – which Robin still held by a line – and retrieved some oranges and lemons which were floating away. The water containers and flares had disappeared. As he swam back to the raft he caught a glimpse of *Lucette*'s masthead, with sails spread below, sinking slowly out of sight.

They sat in the raft and looked at each other in numb disbelief. It was hard to take in the fact that, in the space of about two minutes, their lives had been wrenched from a steady, harmonious routine into precarious disorder. The two youngest sobbed, not because they were frightened they told Dougal when he tried to comfort them, but because they had lost their most precious possessions. Dougal, like Maurice Bailey, was overwhelmed by feelings of guilt and remorse. A critic's arguments that he was jeopardizing the children's lives by exposing them to the hazards of the elements now seemed crushingly justified. 'How could I have been so foolish as to trust our lives to such an old schooner?' he asked himself. But later, when reason came to his aid, he exonerated himself from that charge. The planking had taken a blow that nothing but iron could have withstood and a modern fibreglass boat would have sunk even sooner. (They were not insured – in fact most people who do this sort of cruising find that the insurance premiums are so prohibitively expensive that they prefer to take the risk. In any case, being insured might have made him feel a little better but it was otherwise of no help in their present predicament.)

Lyn said the Lord's Prayer out loud and then sang 'Eternal Father Strong to Save' to comfort the twins. 'We had better find out how we stand,' was her next remark, prompting Dougal to collect his thoughts and check through the survival kit. He laid the provisions out on the floor of the raft; some fortified bread, glucose, a bag of onions, a one pound tin of biscuits, half a pound of glucose sweets, 10 oranges and six lemons – plus 18 pints of water. Dougal's despair showed stark on his face as he looked at these and calculated how long they would last. Lyn put her hand on his and said: 'We must get these boys to land.' Dougal tried to say something reassuring but his mind was occupied with the hopelessness of their position. 'Tell us how we stand,' Lyn asked Dougal again and glanced at the others. They all appeared to want to know his thoughts. Rather than saying what he really thought – that they were all going to die as soon as their food and water ran out – he spelt out the options. It would be impossible to row back against the wind and currents to the Galapagos Islands; the coast of Central America lay 1,000 miles away on the other side of the windless Doldrums; the Marquesas Islands lay 2,800 miles to the west, but the islands were small and all their navigational instruments were at the bottom of the sea; and, staying where they were would be pointless as no one would be likely to miss them for weeks. Five pairs of eyes watched him silently as he discarded one option after another and finally came to a conclusion. There was really only one possibility: to sail with the Trade Winds to the Doldrums 400 miles away. The only shipping route lay in that direction, also the best chance of rain in any quantity. A small chance of reaching land also lay that way. An unexpected feeling of confidence came to him as he spoke, then grew a little when he saw that the others were reacting positively to his tentative suggestions. Douglas' and Robin's faces mirrored their desire not just to sit around and die but to fight for their lives, even while they talked about the privations they were likely to face. The twins had stopped crying and were thinking about food.

First, the contents of the raft needed sorting, and a minute examination of every corner had to be carried out to see what treasures it might yield. The most obvious one was a genoa sail that Douglas had hauled up on the end of some fishing line on a spool which he had seen unwinding in the water. Lyn had retrieved her sewing box as it floated past the raft, a treasure beyond measure as it contained – apart from the usual threads and needles – scalpel blades, knitting needles, pins, dried yeast, copper wire, a bottle of soluble aspirin, and a dozen other priceless items. The few flares, part of every liferaft's safety equipment, seemed to be in good order. Among the usual contents of the first-aid box they found forceps, scissors and seasick pills. Within a very short time these pills had to be administered to Robin and Neil who were succumbing to the unfamiliar motion of the raft. This was a serious worry as it meant they would rapidly lose body fluid.

Lyn and Dougal spent most of the first day detaching the 40–foot long luff wire from the genoa to use as a painter for the dinghy. From the genoa material they cut out a sail for the dinghy and a sheet each to keep out the night cold. Lyn had on a house coat but the others wore only shorts and shirts. As the sun set Lyn prayed again for their safety and sang 'The Lord's My Shepherd'. Dougal sorted out a watch-keeping system and everyone settled down for the night.

Before long their uneasy rest was interrupted by bumps on the bottom of the raft. The watch-keepers could see dorados sporting below and frequently coming into contact with the raft, whether carelessly or as a result of trying to catch smaller fish keeping close to the raft they could not tell. These were soon joined by sharks. The long uncomfortable night wore on. Breakfast next morning consisted of one quarter-ounce biscuit, a piece of onion and a sip of water. Neither Robin nor Neil could eat but took an extra sip of water with a seasick tablet. Dougal and Douglas next refloated the dinghy and found to their delight the vegetable knife that Dougal had thrown in. The rest of the day was spent rigging the sail to the dinghy and trying to find leaks in the raft which refused to remain properly inflated. None could be detected so the loss of air had to be attributed to seepage through the raft's fabric.

As dusk approached Dougal trimmed the sail for maximum speed which he estimated to be about one knot. He reckoned they would also be helped along by about a knot of current. Robin and Neil had recovered sufficiently to share their dinner of one and a half square-inch of biscuit each and a small piece of glucose. Before settling down to rest they each wrote farewell letters to absent family members, sealed them in waterproof wrapping and stowed

Left to right: Douglas, Neil, Lyn, Sandy, Dougal and Anne, who left before the fateful voyage

parcel away in a raft pocket. Neil, particularly, seemed depressed at the task and as he lay there afterwards, eyes staring into the distance, Lyn whispered to Dougal that she would not permit Neil to die alone. Her shock and distress as a mother, as the implications of their situation sank in, was deepening. Dougal did his best to reassure her.

At dawn the weather deteriorated and Robin and Neil were seasick again. Dougal nearly pitched himself into the sea as he tried to reef the sail, causing the dinghy to half capsize and only frantic baling prevented it from being completely swamped. He had toyed with the idea of abandoning the raft and making a much quicker passage in the dinghy but this incident changed his mind. By the afternoon the swells were 20-foot high with breaking combers on top. Lyn prayed desperately for better weather and fresh water. She tried to enlist their joint participation in supplication, but Dougal, when he saw that her insistence was embarrassing Robin, reminded her that it was up to each individual to choose their own way of dealing with the crisis. Robin cut off a facetious remark as Lyn, surprised at Dougal's words, continued to pray and sing to the twins.

The weather eased during the night and by morning the seas were calm enough to allow the two vessels to move more easily through the water again. It was time to start fishing. The only fish they had tasted so far were some flying fish found stranded in the bottom of the dinghy. Dougal crossed from the raft to the dinghy and tried to tempt the dorado with a shiny spinner. The fish chased it with apparent interest but would not strike. Three smaller female dorado swam a little nearer and Dougal hastily threw them the spinner. Unfortunately he had omitted to attach the end of the line to anything. He watched in dismay as it sank out of sight. His first impulse was to jump in after it but a quick look around made him pause, as on the other side of the dinghy cruised a white-tipped shark. Instead, he cursed his stupidity and delivered himself a lecture on the probable results of such crass carelessness. All the morning he toiled in the hot sun, first to make another spinner and then to fish, but to no avail. Lunch was a piece of orange, including the peel, and half a biscuit, washed down with a small mouthful of water.

In the heat of this afternoon, as in most others, they rested under the canopy to avoid the sun's rays while Lyn kept the twins occupied drawing pictures or playing games. She began a regime of leg and arm exercises for the twins which she made them adhere to, despite their grumbles. The day wore on into night, an uncomfortable repeat of the previous one.

When the weather was fine a routine developed of fishing in the morning – usually without success – followed by 'lunch'. The afternoon was drowsed away. Odd jobs like hunting for and mending leaks caused by friction on the lines attaching the two craft kept the older members of the group occupied and apprehensive, unwilling yet to voice their fears of what more leaks would mean. The twins seemed to be adapting to their environment remarkably well. Lyn administered to them and worried over them constantly, especially at night when Dougal could sense that she was lying awake. He hardly slept either, there was too much to occupy his mind. He taxed his brain continually for ways of catching fish and collecting a drinkable supply of water, instead of the brackish unpalatable liquid which was their only reward from two

short showers.

On the fifth night they heard a loud heavy breathing noise close to the raft. Douglas, on lookout, announced that their visitor was a huge whale. The twins and Lyn were instantly frightened at the thought of another attack, although Dougal tried to reassure them that this was a different sort of whale altogether, the sort preyed on by other big fish and not likely to be interested in them. Lyn would not be comforted and prayed loudly and desperately to be spared another attack. The whale stayed with them for half an hour, but long before it departed the twins had lost interest in it and had gone back to sleep.

Early next morning everyone was abruptly awoken by the sound of flapping and crashing about in the dinghy next door. Dougal leapt through the hatch and pounced on a large dorado. It had obviously found the dinghy an obstacle in its flight path after flying fish. It got an even ruder shock when Dougal attacked it with the knife and cut its head off. When the general jubilation subsided everyone settled down again, but with the happy anticipation of a feast in the morning. At 4am the raft was once more in an uproar when Lyn received a wet flying fish in the face, a shock great enough to send her into hysterics. Sleeping was abandoned for the rest of the night and as soon as dawn threw enough light on the dinghy Dougal climbed in with his victim to prepare their breakfast.

Several hours later they were replete for the first time – even Neil who seemed to find his hunger more trying than the others. Lyn had marinated the pieces of fish in the last of their lemon juice and they still had an onion to flavour it. When everyone had finished eating and the bulk of the meat was hanging in strips in the rigging Dougal took away the flying fish head and some offal to have another session of fishing. Whatever he tried failed: either the bait would be taken by small scavenger fish or, weighted and sent deep, sharks took it, line and all.

Lying gasping in the torrid mid-afternoon heat Dougal studied Douglas' sunken cheeks as he sat in the watch-keeper's position, teeth

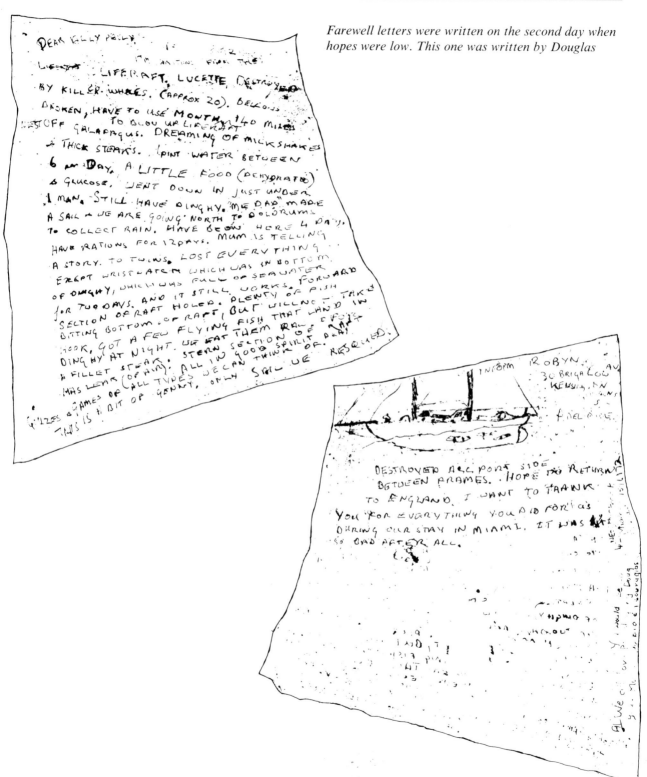

Farewell letters were written on the second day when hopes were low. This one was written by Douglas

clenched against the dryness of his palate, and tried again to think how to catch fish. A spear seemed to be the only answer and how to fabricate one exercised his mind the whole of that night. For the first time the wind had dropped away completely, leaving the dinghy sail limp and the two vessels gently undulating on the glassy swells. Large dorado exploded out of the water in showers of startling phosphorescence and crashed back into a glowing sea of green fire. All six occupants of the raft twisted and turned on the rubber floor in an effort to ease aching limbs or to take the pressure off their developing salt-water sores. Thirst had become a torture as their water supply had dwindled almost to nothing. Dougal wondered if this was the end of the struggle. They were still 150 miles from the Doldrums and rain.

At the approach of dawn the watch-keepers gazed intently at the gathering clouds obscuring the stars and then the horizon. A rain squall was heading their way. All the empty containers were made ready and the collecting tube was fixed into position on the canopy. Soon after daylight the squall hit them. It rained steadily, washing the rubber off the canopy till the water ran clear and pure from the tube. They drank until they were awash.

Morale was high again and the night's torments forgotten. They lay around talking of food and watching the water bags swinging from the canopy roof when they were disturbed by an excited shout from Douglas, as ever in his favourite position by the hatch. 'A ship!' They all stared in wonder at the vessel, still low down on the horizon. Dougal estimated that her course would bring her within three miles of them, sufficiently close, they thought. (If they could have known of the Baileys' experiences their hopes would not have been so unjustifiably high.)

In scarcely containable excitement they set off the raft's rocket flares and hand flares, their expectation of deliverance absolute. When the ship sent no answering signal, Dougal fired off several more hand flares and their last rocket which singed his hand. For a short time the vessel was obscured by cloud but when she next reappeared her stern was disappearing fast over the horizon. 'Set fire to the sail!' cried Lyn. It would not light. From his place in the dinghy Dougal's shoulders drooped in mute dejection. He felt their loneliness like a searing pain. When he glanced at Lyn she smiled brightly and explained that she had previously told the twins that the first ship would not see them, so they had not really expected it to stop. The haunted expression on Douglas' face showed that he had been deeply affected by the incident.

Dougal glared at the empty flare cartridges and reflected bitterly on the ship's officers and crew who had, because of their failure to keep a proper watch, condemned the six of them to death in the Doldrums. Abruptly, his feelings underwent a transformation. If other people would not help them they would just forget about rescue and learn to survive on their own. Hate against the ship turned to a savage aggression against the sharks and killer whales that prowled on the doorstep, waiting. Those predators would not have them: the Robertsons had brains and a few tools and they would learn to adapt to this foreign and unfriendly environment. They would fight for their lives and make it to land, even if it took six months. From that moment on, he felt like a savage.

That afternoon a turtle – a large male – thumped on the bottom of the raft and then surfaced to give the assembled crew a close inspection. It became the first of many creatures to die under the new regime. As Dougal slit its throat he was careful not to allow any blood to fall into the sea, on the assumption that if the sharks knew of the source of the blood they would attack the inflatable. (It is interesting to note that the Baileys were able to discard all the unwanted gory bits and pieces of turtles and fish without fear of attack from their shark entourage, which never showed the slightest interest in the leftovers.) When he did eventually tip the contents of the dinghy into the sea it was instantly pounced upon by the scavenger fish, whose activities seemed to excite the sharks, who in their turn attacked a dorado swimming innocently by. Some time later, Dougal actually managed, to his great satisfaction, to catch a shark. 'Sharks would not eat Robertsons, Robertsons would eat sharks!'

They had been adrift for eight days. It was becoming increasingly difficult to keep the raft inflated due to leaks, some of which they plugged with rubber bungs and other suitable water-proof material, but some could not be reached. It was only a matter of time, Dougal knew, before they would have to abandon it and transfer to the nine-foot six-inch dinghy.

One aspect of their well-being was causing increasing concern to Lyn. Only Robin had had a bowel motion since joining the raft. She had practised as a nurse right up until the time they had left Britain so her word in these matters carried weight, although one of her suggestions to right this particular shortcoming was viewed by most of the crew with misgivings. She wanted to administer enemas so that the undrinkable water could be utilized. Dougal professed himself to be rather perturbed at the difficulties involved, but a few days later Lyn expertly administered enemas to them all except Robin, whose refusal was adamant and unshakeable. They did not, however, have the desired effect.

On the 11th day they were within striking distance of the Doldrums, having travelled some 250 miles. With the sail set at an angle of 45 degrees to the wind they had been able to obtain a good course. Dougal instructed Douglas in navigation by way of sun and star observations and the set of the underlying swell so that, in the event of anything happening to him, Douglas could take over.

As the floor of the raft was now constantly wet their sores rapidly worsened. Lyn kept up the twins' exercises and tended to all their ailments, scolding them into a routine of hygiene and ignoring their groans and grumblings. As the water was again getting low she prayed hard for rain and Dougal had to chastise Robin for an intolerant remark directed at her faith. His angry tone of voice startled Robin who apologized to Lyn.

That night Dougal and Sandy decided to test out the dinghy as an alternative to sleeping on the wet raft floor. They got very little sleep. The hard surface was unforgiving on their salt-water boils and the cold was more severe. On his return to the raft Dougal pulled in on the towrope and watched it drop from the raft into the sea. It was easy enough to paddle to the dinghy but Dougal reflected soberly on their good fortune: if it had happened in bad weather and the raft had become separated from the dinghy the occupants would not have lasted long in the rapidly disintegrating raft. Their precious dried food and water would also have been lost.

Personality differences now began to be more acutely felt, particularly between Robin, the only outsider, and Lyn and Dougal. Lyn's overt display of religion irritated Robin, although he professed – somewhat surprisingly to me – to being a non-practising Christian and not an atheist or an agnostic. Dougal felt the need to protect Lyn from any scathing remarks, but all the same even he was a little exasperated that she could not keep her fervour more to herself. On the other hand, Dougal had to force Lyn to take her share of the water. She preferred to give it to the twins and only when Dougal prevented anyone else from drinking did she acquiesce. No doubt she resented being unable to sacrifice her share, which she felt she could well do without, while the twins would benefit more from it. She also resented the fact that Dougal allotted Robin a greater share of food and water. Robin was over six feet tall and needed more to retain the equivalent body condition. Dougal was painstaking in his attempts to be fair, well aware as he was of Robin's feelings as an outsider, but it created disharmony between husband and wife. Robin chafed at being made to do things at Lyn's request, like drying bedding, which she insisted must be done properly if at all. Dougal had to intervene on such occasions to make sure that Robin pulled his weight, willingly or not. In Dougal's opinion, Robin was – through no fault of his own – the pampered, self-opinionated, impractical product of an eight-year educational system, but now he was learning reality the hard way. To use Dougal's own words to Robin: 'We all have to do things we don't like, Robin, especially now. Left to your own devices you would be dead already. If any one of us dies because you don't feel like doing what you're told, I'll kill you! I mean that as a promise, not a threat.' Robin, apparently, took him seriously.

By the 14th day the water containers were practically empty again. In Douglas' gaunt face, which remained haunted by the failure of the ship to rescue them, Dougal felt he could see the shadow of death lurking. Goaded by his son's futile questions as to whether or not there would be rain that night Dougal made an irritable reply. What comfort could he give when Douglas must know, like everyone else, that if it did not rain for a week they would all be dead. Later on though, he was able to say that he thought there *would* be a possibility of rain that night.

Rain poured down at dawn. Once more they felt reprieved. Again, optimism and hope rose as their thirst was sated and they looked at the full water containers. But their contentment was rudely disturbed by a desperate yell from Douglas: 'Dad, the dinghy's gone!' Dougal leapt for the entrance to see the dinghy sailing off, already 60 yards away. Without hesitation he dived into the sea, ignoring the horrified cries of Lyn and the twins and swam, head down, after it. From the raft they watched him move swiftly through the water in a racing crawl. He was gaining on the dinghy which had slowed a little as its sail momentarily collapsed. They could also see two sharks, one close behind Dougal and one to his right. He glanced up at the dinghy now 30 yards away and increased his speed. The water churned from his feet while his stomach shrank at the thought of the sharks. Then he was in the dinghy, grabbing at the sail to haul it down, before falling to his knees in exhaustion. After a minute's rest to catch his breath he picked up the oar. It took almost half an hour to paddle back to the raft where the others greeted him with tearful delight and relief.

The 16th night was later rated by everyone as the most miserable of all. Pumping was now continuous and mouths were raw and cheeks aching from all the blowing. Stamina and fortitude disintegrated rapidly. Despite their efforts three inches of water remained in the aft section; even the forward one where they rested could not be baled out fast enough to remain dry. They could not remain in the raft much longer.

Everyone knew this, but for various reasons most were loth to accept the necessity to move. They argued this way and that: it was colder at night in the dinghy and in the day there was no shelter from the sun; the fibreglass and wood construction would be so painful to their boil-infested limbs that everyone shrank from the thought of contact with the hard surface; worst of all there was the unknown quantity of survival in a dinghy as opposed to a liferaft. Fully loaded the freeboard would be reduced to six inches. Dougal had already demonstrated how easy it was to capsize. How would they manage to keep it trimmed – or stow food and water?

Dougal had long been puzzling these problems; nevertheless, for him it was a question not of if, but when. After another tortuous night he suggested a move the following day. To his surprise most demurred and thought they ought to remain where they were a few days longer. He looked at the exhausted shrunken faces of the group and made the decision for them.

The transfer took place that afternoon. The twins, Lyn, and Robin climbed in first and stowed what little gear was left after everything dispensable had been thrown over the side. Dougal and Douglas cut off all the ropes and useful appendages from the liferaft, particularly the flotation chambers, which Dougal later fitted to the dinghy's bows to add buoyancy. The butchered raft had nearly sunk by the time Dougal abandoned it. When everyone had settled in they were encouraged to see that the dinghy was reasonably stable – provided anyone who contemplated a move told the others so that someone else could be used for trimming purposes. That night they suffered acute discomfort from the unforgiving hull but there were definite compensations in not having to pump or bale. Gone also was the unwelcome prodding in the posteria from inquisitive turtles and fish. The next morning they set sail for the coast, 600 miles away.

Once they had got used to life in the dinghy they made comparisons in living standards. Some preferred it, others not. Sores dried up in the sunshine, which compensated for the lack of comfort at night, but no one except the twins could lie down and even they had to lie over or under someone else's limbs. Robin was six-foot one and had been thin even before getting into the raft. His extra height meant that he was more cramped than the others but they suffered from his bony elbows, knees and feet. Many a time, turning in the night, he dragged a sheet off someone, or unwittingly banged someone else on a painful spot, until the night was filled with curses and thumps. During the day, if there were no turtle to butcher, the boys played word games or talked about food while Lyn worked with great perseverance to forestall the disintegration of their garments. Robin talked of his many travels or helped to make up menus for 'Dougal's Kitchen', which they planned to open on their return to the Leek district, which the family knew well. They did not talk of further adventures at sea. The twins in particular were most comfortable with the notion of solid land under their feet, in a place they recognized, with a cat to cuddle and ordinary things to eat.

On day 21 the weather began to deteriorate again. Towards evening Dougal instructed the older members of the group to steer, using the sail as a rudder to keep the dinghy's bows heading into the waves. At 4am he took over the steering himself for everyone feared a capsize. The waves were large and menacing, and coming from different angles, due to several big wind shifts. Lyn and Robin baled continuously. Dougal sat in the stern, water slowly saturating him under his inadequate sheet until he felt as if the wet was penetrating through to his bones. All that day he sat, while the waves increased in size and those baling worked incessantly. It rained all night without pause.

At some time in the early morning the wind eased but to their astonishment it rained even harder. The cloud-burst was accompanied by deafening peels of thunder and lightning that hurt their eyes and hissed as it struck the sea around them. (Electric storms in the Doldrums are one of the most awe-inspiring and frightening phenomenon one can come across at sea. In my mind's eye I can see advancing faces of rolling hills of water, and crests flattened by the brutal force of rain that blinds you with the ferocity of hailstones. In the absolute darkness, in between flashes, not even a hand in front of your face can be seen, until the scene of psychedelic brilliance leaps into focus again. I was in a large boat – 53 feet long – and the hissing combers that rolled up and over the deck, pushing the boat around like so much flotsam, were not particularly dangerous, I felt. It was the distinct possibility of a lightning strike that frightened me. How it must have felt to be there in a nine-foot dinghy – devoid of protection – defies imagination.)

Above the noise of the maelstrom Dougal could hear Lyn praying and a child sobbing, whilst those baling worked with increasing desperation. After half an hour of intense cold Dougal seized up and Lyn shouted to Robin to stop baling and do something to help him. Robin crawled over to him, pummelled his inert form for a little while to force back the circulation, then resumed his baling. Suddenly Douglas shouted 'Sing!' and they sang as hard as they could, every song they had ever known, to keep themselves alert and their circulation going. When they were too tired to sing any more Lyn thumped and massaged life back into their bodies. The rain eased as the wind increased, a sign that they were getting nearer the edge of the disturbance. When the wind threatened to tear the sail Dougal was forced to move his frozen torso so that he could gather the sail into the reefed position. Now that the rain had lessened, those baling were at last gaining on the water, and the spray that washed over them felt comfortingly warm compared to the cold downpour. Slowly, the wind and rain eased.

At dawn they were still baling, but occasionally falling asleep in their crouching positions against the thwarts. At 9am Dougal was able to leave his position in the stern and, helped by Lyn and Robin, worked feeling back into his frozen limbs. As they breakfasted Lyn told the others that she had seen a seventh person in the dinghy during the storm, a presence, rather than a person, helping them to fight the elements. Robin and Douglas voiced scepticism but Dougal was of the opinion that if it had helped her, it had helped them all. Everyone had been needed to do his part and the failure of any one may have prevented the others from keeping the craft afloat.

For another two days the rain kept on, freezing them to the marrow and polluting their dried food. All thoughts, hopes and fears were suspended in a haze of exhaustion as baling went on around the clock. At last, on day 24, the sun reappeared. The baling ceased, and everyone – except a watch-keeper – slept.

Sunshine and calm seas over the next few days soothed their battered spirits. A steady diet of turtle meat, blood, eggs, and whatever else the commodious reptile had to offer, had already begun to have a beneficial effect on their health and spirits. As the exhaustion of the previous few days disappeared their improved bodily condition contributed to a better state of mind. Fears of capsizing had lessened now that their skill in trimming the raft had grown, but the cramped conditions of the dinghy remained a grievous aggravation. Bitter reproach and arguments broke out whenever someone stepped on someone else. But to temper those outbursts were moments of lightheartedness when someone felt moved to reminisce or sing. Dougal felt that they had now gone beyond merely thinking in terms of survival: they now believed that they would reach land without anyone else's help. They felt self-reliant and very much part of their environment. Dougal amused himself with thoughts of living permanently at sea, but decided, on balance, that it would be impractical. They were learning to get along with it, but it remained, in Dougal's words, 'the savage sea'.

The spell of calm weather did not last long, alas. On the 26th day they were again grimly coping with another line squall which lasted a full two days, but at least the wind was in the right direction which meant steady progress towards the coast. Each day Dougal estimated their run. Sometimes it was an excellent 20 miles; sometimes 15; and occasionally, when they had to stream the sea anchor fully open, he put down the same position as the day before. Better, he thought, to see land before they expected it.

As soon as the weather calmed down again Dougal made his second spear (the first had

broken off at the barb on contact with a fish). This second attempt did not fare much better. It was not the right line of thinking, he decided, and began instead to make a gaff. Several turtles turned up in quick succession and were skilfully dispatched and their meat hung to dry in the hot sun. There was a mishap with the water for which Robin, who had become petulant and quarrelsome under the pressure of Lyn's exacting instructions, was blamed. Dougal was doubly annoyed for it was up to him to check

that Robin followed instructions properly and the failure to do so on this instant amounted to a grave error. Only the day before most of their water was found to be contaminated and now, with the loss of water from their biggest container, their supply was reduced to six good pints and two brackish ones which could only be used for enemas.

The returning menace of thirst cast a pall over the afternoon and added fuel to a bitter row between Lyn and Dougal. In the quiet early hours of the morning while the others slept they talked again of their life on the farm which hardship and poverty had slowly reduced to a despairing existence. Dougal passionately hated the new methods of treating animals as business machines, turning them into neurotics ridden with stress, existing only as long as a profit could be made from them, after which they were heartlessly slaughtered. Talking about it brought all the despair back; how deprivation and toil had eroded the happiness from their lives. Now, even their attempt at a new life had gone terribly wrong, and although the closeness of death had forced them to overlook the divide between them it was now reinstated in all its former bitterness. Dougal berated Lyn for the years of nagging and misery until she wept and he lapsed into contrite silence.

For the next three days their total liquid sustenance came from tiny sips from the water bottle several times a day, supplemented by marrow fluid and the eyes of dorado. Thirst drove all emotion but misery from Douglas' face. Robin was in better shape, and perhaps because of his guilt concerning the spilt water, made more effort to co-operate with Lyn's tireless badgering about cleanliness. She made them attend to the small things that contributed so much, if only momentarily, to their comfort. She massaged the twins with turtle oil, wiped the pus from their eyes (they all suffered this condition), gave them enemas, and if that did not cause a bowel motion, gave them oil enemas instead. She bathed everyone with sea water when they were hot and rubbed them when they were cold. It was her weakness and her strength to worry over small things as though their lives depended on them: to her mind they did. But the fussiness and ministrations which her family tolerated for their own good – particularly for the good of the youngest members – Robin obviously regarded as officious pettiness. His 22-year-old spirit rebelled against having to take orders and be forced into taking a passive role in his survival.

Increasingly, bad feeling erupted between

After 37 days their ordeal is over. Dougal has poured turtle oil into the sea to calm the water

members of the group when someone hogged an extra inch of space, or more importantly, when Douglas – and then Robin – lost turtles after they had been told by Dougal not to attempt to bring them in without his help. At such examples of stupidity and disobedience Dougal lost his temper, slapping the offender with his hand while haranguing him on his shortcomings. His acrimony moved Lyn to deliver him a lecture on his former inability to provide a decent living on the farm, reminding him how they had all suffered at the lack of money and the conditions they had been forced to put up with. Dougal was equally savage in his response until they were silenced by the twins' distress, Lyn's tears and Robin's attempts of conciliation.

A passing squall on the 34th day deposited a miserable pint or two of water on them before shifting off elsewhere, leaving them feeling more hopeless than before. The sun shone blisteringly upon their meagrely covered bodies and at night they huddled together, unable to sleep for thirst.

Dawn on the 35th day brought rain. This time, Dougal calculated, they could collect enough to last them to the coast, less than 400 miles away. Later in the day they killed and butchered two turtles. As much meat as they could find space for was laid out to dry. Soon, they would be close enough to make a dash for the shore, which would include rowing at night. Extra food and water would be needed to compensate for the exertion. That night Dougal received a nasty whack on the side of the head – through the side of the dinghy – by a shark bigger than the tiny boat. He jabbed at it fiercely with a paddle and the fish took itself off.

The morning's attempt at fishing broke the gaff but the dried fish and turtle meat already hanging in the rigging would ensure their survival, even if they were unlucky enough not to catch another turtle. The following day, Dougal decided, they would start rowing. That evening they ate their supper and talked about 'Dougal's Kitchen' and whether or not it should have a wine licence. Dougal gazed out past the sail, pondering the delights of Gaelic coffee, when he suddenly became aware that he was staring at a ship. The dinghy rocked with the excitement of the others tried to catch a glimpse of it. Dougal warned everyone to keep still and remember that the last ship had not seen them. All eyes were glued upon him as he lit their last but one flare and held it aloft. It singed his fingers badly as he waved it to and fro, then threw it up as far as he could into the air. It illuminated two sharks gliding past at a respectful distance. The second flare would not light. He cursed it wildly and shouted for the torch. But as he looked again for the vessel he could see its bows turning towards them. He relayed the information to the others crouching low in the dinghy watching him with breathless anticipation. They had been seen.

Dougal sat down abruptly on the thwart as the others cried or cheered. Robin cried and cheered at the same time, and thumped Dougal on the back. 'Our ordeal is over,' Dougal said quietly to Lyn and felt, as the ship came alongside and hands reached down to lift them to safety, that he could cheerfully have died in the moment of exquisite contentment.

When Dougal reached the deck of the Japanese fishing vessel he discovered, like the others, that he had lost the use of his legs. Lyn, the children, and Robin were lying in a row on deck, looking around. The seamen who had rescued them were holding their noses and shaking their heads in disgust as they cast the dinghy away. Dougal started up in dismay, gesticulating in a wild attempt at sign language. At a word of command from the bridge the men grabbed boat hooks and hauled it back again. They yanked it up against the ship's railings and shook it till everything, including mast and rigging, fell out. A hose pipe and brushes were produced and they started scrubbing. Dougal expressed his unintelligible thanks to the bemused crew and joined the captain in the chart room to check on their position. His latitude reckoning was only five miles out, but his longitude was 100 miles adrift. However, as this put them 100 miles closer to the coast than he had reckoned he was satisfied. They had travelled 750 miles. In less than three weeks, all going well, they would have reached their goal on their own.

The Robertson family and Robin posing with the crew of Toka Maru II, *their rescuers*

Storm Force Ten

Margaret Winks watched her husband cast off the shore lines, push the yacht away from the quay, and jump aboard. He waved to her and joined the rest of the crew in a burst of song as *Grimalkin* motored smoothly out into the channel and headed off towards Cowes. The weather was lovely – it was August – and they were about to embark on one of the most famous races in the northern hemisphere. It never entered Margaret's head to feel apprehension or worry on their behalf. Neither she, nor they, nor any of the almost 3,000 competitors, had any premonition that they were heading out into a force 10 storm – the worst summer storm for 30 years.

The yacht Ariadne *drifting after most of the crew had taken to the liferaft. Four of them lost their lives*

Her owner and skipper, David Sheahan, steered *Grimalkin* across the starting line off the Royal Yacht Squadron, Cowes, Isle of Wight, a few seconds after the gun fired. He was first across the line. Fifty-eight yachts jostled for position, tacking and cross-tacking, and attempting at the same time to avoid collision with the 245 boats in the other classes, milling about waiting for their starting guns. Class V worked their way towards the Needles, the chalk cliffs at the western end of the Solent. It was the smallest of five groups, and, at 30 feet, *Grimalkin* was one of the smallest in her class. Nevertheless, she was as quick on the wind as many larger boats and held her position near the front of the fleet as they squeezed through the narrow gap off Hurst Castle before passing the Needles and heading towards the Lizard. The wind was in the south-west, a steady, moderate breeze. The forecast was for much the same the following day, Sunday, August 12, 1979.

Sheahan was an experienced dinghy and day-boat sailor but had taken up big boat sailing quite recently. Because of his lack of off-shore experience and because he was, in any case, a meticulous planner, he had gone into every detail of the equipment for the boat and crew with greater thoroughness than many of the other competitors who were more used to the routine. He wrote out and posted a six-page memorandum to the crew with details of the course and the length of time he envisaged spending at sea (six days). Also included were notes on safety gear – liferaft, flares, and safety equipment for a man-overboard emergency – reminders of fuel capacity, insurance, and first aid. But, he added, each man would be responsible for his own medication. (His particular concern on the subject of safety possibly sprang from the knowledge that one of his crew, Gerry Winks, was arthritic and another, Nick Ward, was an epileptic. With their own medication these two men led perfectly normal lives and were valued for their specialized skills on sailing boats – one acted as Mate and the other was the sail trimmer.)

David Sheahan recommended that everyone have a pre-race dental checkup and to notify him if there were any special dietary problems; and to bring the minimum amount of clothes for racing 'as we will break with our normal tradition and not dress for cocktails or dinner.' Sheahan's caution even extended as far as equipping the yacht with three high-frequency marine transmitters and receivers (although none was mandatory in the race rules), and he fitted life lines along the decks and in the cockpit to which the watch could clip their safety harnesses.

It is unusual for a skipper to go to such lengths – not to equip his crew for safety, everyone does that, but to be so thorough in his attempts to acquaint every man with all the equipment on the boat. Paradoxically, when the storm came upon them they were one of the worst affected boats in the fleet.

Like most of the other racing boats, *Grimalkin* hugged the south-west coastline to minimize the effects of contrary tides and currents. The wind, also south-west, kept the boats tacking on to every favourable wind shift to maintain the best course to Land's End. Although the sea was fairly flat, David Sheahan suffered a bout of seasickness so common to many sailors, but he soon recovered and put through a call to his wife with a progress report. They were doing well. Many boats 15 feet longer were still tacking alongside them. The weather forecasts, which were broadcast four times a day on BBC Radio 4, had remained almost unchanged since Friday: sou'westerlies, 4 to 5, possibly 7 or 8 near the Fastnet Rock on Monday.

Force 8 is a gale: not pleasant at the time but it always adds spice to the stories in the yacht club bar afterwards. After force 8 comes a severe gale, most unpleasant and potentially dangerous, especially for small yachts. Force 10 is a storm, described in the Beaufort scale as 'Very high waves with long overhanging crests. The resulting foam in great patches is blown in dense white streaks along the direction of the wind. On the whole the surface of the sea takes a white appearance. The tumbling of the sea becomes heavy and shock-like. Visibility affected.' This dispassionate description gives the uninitiated no clue to the brutal savagery of a storm-driven sea.

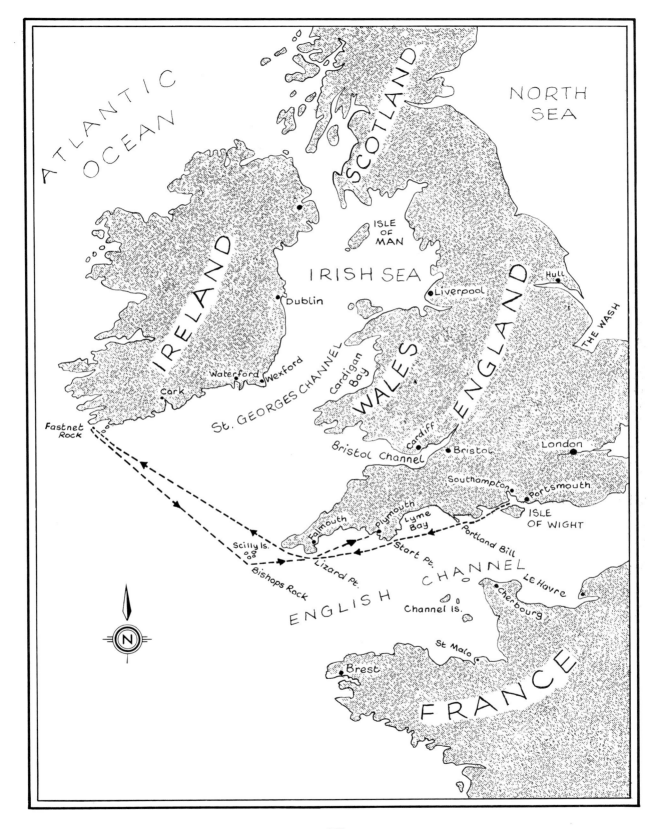

With 70 mile-an-hour winds behind them freak waves can form out to sea, often on top of a underlying swell. They are the result of a combination of factors, such as several converging wave patterns caused by a sudden change in the wind direction and an underlying current pulling strongly against the direction of the wind. Shallow water will sometimes act as a break to the sweep of waves coming from a long distance. The Irish Sea is relatively shallow. There, in a storm, all these factors gang up together to whip the water into a cauldron of steep, dangerous waves. Out of several hundred small boats heading into such a storm, it was inconceivable that all would escape unscathed.

On Sunday the fleet ran into fog. This was rather unusual considering the high but steady barometric pressure (1020 millibars) which pointed to stable and fair weather. But on Sunday night the fog cleared away, and at dawn on Monday the boats wallowed about in a flat calm. Those nearest the shore put down kedges while the rest fretted and played with limp spinnakers in an effort to keep enough momentum going to beat the tide. This normally hair-pulling state of affairs was somewhat alleviated for the keenest competitors by seeing all the boats around them in the same predicament. A few hours later, wind appeared suddenly from the north-east – behind them – and spinnakers flew aloft along the length of the coast. *Grimalkin* cleared Land's End at 10am and, on entering the Western Approaches, Sheahan set a new course for the Fastnet Rock.

As they sailed clear of the English coast the boats climbed up and over the heavy ground-swell at the end of its long fetch across the Atlantic. Some noticed that it seemed to be getting higher as the afternoon wore on. There were other signs, too, that pointed to an unfavourable change in the weather. The barometer had dropped 10 points and the western sky had taken on a blackish-blue hue. The wind was veering also, from north-east, to east, to south-east, and strengthening. The 5:50pm weather forecast had changed its tune somewhat but as yet there was nothing to alarm the competitors. The Irish Sea and Fastnet areas were

The fast moving centre of cyclonic disturbance crossing the Irish Sea. It decimated the fleet of 303 yachts taking part in the Fastnet Race

to have southerly winds, force 4 to 6, increasing to gale 8 locally. The Meteorological Office now had its eye on a depression centred, at that time, 250 miles west of the Fastnet area, but assumed it would pass to the north.

Several hours later David Sheahan heard another forecast in French which cast quite a different light on the situation. This forecast winds of 8 to storm 10, with higher gusts likely. Whether this was because someone in their Met. Office had jumped to a hasty conclusion, or because they really knew something the British Met. Office did not, the men on board *Grimalkin* had no way of telling. Another boat had also heard the French report and had become alarmed enough to call the Land's End Coastguard Station to confirm the BBC forecast. They were informed by the Coastguard that the BBC was, indeed, correct. *Grimalkin*'s crew monitored both calls and felt a little easier.

The sun set at 8pm that evening on a rough sea and a still rougher-looking sky. The gloomy cloud cover was much lower and bits of ragged grey cloud skidded low overhead. The men on *Grimalkin* watched anxiously as the weather deteriorated. The wind was up to 30 knots.

What no one on the English side of the Atlantic knew as yet was that a small intense depression had taken shape over the hot Great Plains in the north of America. Instead of just heaping destruction on the heads of the long suffering people of Minnesota and thereafter dying away, this little depression had worked up enough venom to continue south-east across New York and New England, wreaking havoc along the way. Yachts dragged their anchors and went ashore, roofs were blown off, and trees were blown down (a woman was killed by a falling branch) as it moved very quickly towards the coast. When the Fastnet Race started on Saturday the depression had left the shores of the United States and was racing at a speed of 50 miles an hour out into the Atlantic.

For some reason this depression was ill-defined in meteorological terms. It had no distinct shape or centre and even the American tracking systems had had difficulty seeing precisely where it was and where it was likely to go. After leaving the US coast it became sandwiched between the Azores High to the south (where it always loitered at that time of the year), and a very large depression moving slowly from Canada to Iceland. The top of the Azores High was generating south-west winds; so, too, was the bottom of the 1,000-mile-long depression in the north. Along the valley in between rushed the little spinning cell of furious air – so fast that it crossed the Atlantic in a mere five days. Unfortunately, before the big Icelandic Low reached the coast it paused for a couple of days, just long enough for the mini-depression to overtake it and be deflected north-east towards southern Ireland and the Western Approaches.

The yacht Camargue *whose eight-man crew were lifted to safety by Royal Navy helicopters*

The Met. Office had received only scanty information from a few ships in mid-Atlantic about the storm and came rather late to the realization that it was heading for the Irish Sea, where the fleet of 303 yachts was also heading – too late to put out the sort of gale warning that might have persuaded some of the smaller boats to stay within reach of the English ports. When they did realize the seriousness of the situation, the warnings came too late for the standard forecast times that all yachtsmen listen to. They went out instead with other news flashes but a racing yachtsman listens only to the standard forecast times. By the time the next bulletin came out and the impassive voice announced the imminent arrival of a force 10 in the Fastnet area, the boats were well out to sea and grappling with a rising wind and sea.

By 11pm that Monday evening David Sheahan knew that they were in for some nasty weather. *Grimalkin* pounded into the wind and heavy sea at six knots under a minute storm jib. Her movement was violent; too rough, Sheahan decided, to stay below in the cabin where much of the food and general equipment had become unstuck and careered around like missiles. The six men sat, well wrapped up in their foul-weather gear, in the cockpit with their harnesses hooked on to the safety lines. Although disturbed by the sea conditions they were still racing towards the Fastnet Rock; and, with no way of knowing it, they were also heading straight for the eye of the storm.

Gerry Winks was steering at this stage and having difficulty seeing through the spray and driving rain which stung their exposed skin and found its way down the necklines and up the sleeves of their waterproof suits. After a time he asked to be relieved and went below to change. It was 3am. He was shivering with cold and very tired. A little food and dry clothes warmed him up a bit but he was dimly aware that he was already suffering from exposure. Although it was sheltered from the wind and weather the cabin was not an inviting place in which to remain. The jumble of gear rattled about noisily as the hull pitched and rolled. He climbed the companionway steps again, and joined the others in the cockpit.

Nick Ward was steering and looked awe-struck at the sight of the massive waves rising towards them – 'like blocks of flats but three times as wide' was how he described them. At 4 am Sheahan decided that it was too dangerous to continue sailing into the seas. The race would have to be abandoned. Coping with these enormous waves was the priority now.

The storm jib was handed and a rope, several hundred feet long, was paid out astern to check the speed of the yacht as she tried to surf down the waves. The rope made virtually no difference. As each wave built up astern the boat was carried higher and higher until the forward momentum of the water began to propel her,

bows down, along with it. Straight down the face of the wave she would fly until one of several things occurred. If she was lucky, the wave would flatten out and she would slow down in a welter of foam and bubbles at the bottom. But on other occasions the crew, looking in horror over the bows, would find themselves suspended over the crest of a wave which was pouring into the deep trough behind the wave in front. The boat would hurl itself into the abyss and, eventually, thrust her bow into the black wall of water of the next wave in front.

But the most deadly ones, the worst situation of all, caught her when she was hardly moving. The boat would falter at the bottom of a wave and, before she could right herself, another sea would rear up and smash down on top of her, throwing her on to her beam ends, into a half capsize. Five times in the next two hours this occurred. No amount of holding on could withstand the huge weight of water that hurled each man to leeward into the guard-rails, or catapulted him into the sea. Their safety harnesses brought them up short with a vicious wrench that strained shoulders and muscles, and inflicted severe bruising. Those who could scrambled back on board and helped untangle others from guard-rails or stays. On the fifth knockdown Nick Ward felt himself flying through the air, hitting the water and simultaneously feeling a seering pain in his leg. Sheahan and his son Matthew helped him back on board with great difficulty as his leg had become tangled in the harness line and his shoulder was on fire with pain. Sheahan left Ward lying in the cockpit and went below to put out an SOS.

By the time the Land's End Coastguard Station received *Grimalkin*'s call for help they had a major disaster on their hands. Mayday calls jammed the airwaves from every part of the 180-mile stretch of water between Land's End and the Fastnet Rock. All the available lifeboats from the south coast of Ireland had already been called out, and the air bases at Kinloss and Culdrose had been alerted and their helicopters and Nimrods were standing by for a dawn take-off.

At 6am six helicopters and a Nimrod took off. Three helicopters headed for the Western Approaches, where the Nimrod, high above, was trying to unscramble the distress calls, which were jumbling one on top of the other into her powerful radio receivers. The helicopter crews began their hazardous rescue operations. Visibility was very poor and it was more good luck than good management that brought a helicopter within view of a stricken yacht – more often than not, a different craft from the one she was looking for. Most of the crews had had such a battering that they were desperate to get off their foundering vessels – many of which were rudderless, dismasted or holed – and onto dry land. Many of the yachts were abandoned to their fate. Some sank, others were later rounded up and towed into port.

In those first few hours more than 70 yachtsmen were air-lifted to safety. *Grimalkin*'s first distress call had been picked up before dawn. The helicopters had orders to search for her but could not locate her in the position she had given. A short while later the St Ives lifeboat was dispatched to find her but got waylaid by another vessel, which required a tow into port. At 7:15pm another helicopter, having delivered its passengers to the sick bay at Culdrose, set off immediately in search of *Grimalkin*. It returned an hour or so later, unsuccessful. At 10:30pm a Sea King helicopter took off to search the area in which the yacht had last been sighted by another competitor. They gave her position as 65 miles north-west of Land's End, more than 30 miles away from her previously reported position.

Meanwhile, David Sheahan had called to the men on deck that he had managed to get their Mayday call through, and that spotter planes and helicopters were on the look out for them. He had just reached the cockpit again when the yacht suffered her sixth knock-down. As the boat came upright Sheahan found himself sitting on the cockpit floor, blood pouring from a cut in his head. His son Matthew and several others got him below and put an antiseptic on the wound and sprayed it with plastic skin. Putting a balaclava and oilskin hood up pro-

A stricken yachtsman is plucked from the sea

tected the cut from the wind and spray, but it continued to bleed. Seeing that the cabin looked totally wrecked they went up top again and huddled close together for warmth. Both Gerry Winks, who by now was suffering severely from hypothermia, and David Sheahan kept passing out. Nick Ward was in a bad state, too, from the pain in his leg which he thought was broken.

A discussion was started as to the advisability of getting into the liferaft. The men, especially those who were hurt, had had more than they could take of the conditions on board and felt that the liferaft offered a safer refuge than the uncontrollable yacht. But before they could put the idea into effect a massive wave curled up over the beam and rolled the yacht over before it. Down she went until the keel was uppermost

in the water. There she hesitated for a considerable time before another wave thumped into her keel and pushed her the right way up.

Just what happened to the crew during the capsize is not clear. Some were thrown into the water, others were trapped under the cockpit. David Sheahan's harness prevented him from being helped back over the life lines so it had to be cut. Very weak and no longer able to help himself he drifted away from the boat and disappeared.

The yacht was now half-full of water and the five men left were suffering either from injury, hypothermia, or shock. Nick Ward and Gerry Winks lay unconscious in the cockpit. The other three examined them and decided they were

Grimalkin sent out several distress signals but at first could not be located. At last she is found and a winchman is lowered to the deck

beyond help. Even if they were still alive, they would not last long. They quickly launched the liferaft, climbed in and were swept away on the next wave. They were picked up half an hour later by a helicopter.

Sometime later Ward regained consciousness as water closed over his head. The boat had rolled again and he was in the sea. As she righted herself sluggishly he fought free of the mess of tangled stays from the broken mast and managed to heave himself back over the rail. He then saw Gerry Winks suspended half overboard by his tangled harness. Forgetting the pain in his leg, shoulder and head, Ward attached a rope to Winks' harness, wound it around a winch and slowly winched him back onboard. Winks looked nearly done for. Ward laid him on the floor of the rolling cockpit and breathed air into his mouth until he regained consciousness. For a while Winks seemed all right but his injuries were too great and a short time later Ward saw that he was dead.

Ward looked about him and tried to assess his situation. It was daylight. As far as he could see he was the only one left alive on the boat although he had not been aware of the others abandoning ship. They had been talking about it before the capsize, though for all he knew they may have been swept overboard, along with the raft. With no liferaft and no flares, his only chance of survival, he realized, was with the boat. He heaved himself to his feet and felt the pain coursing through his body. Down below, one of the four original buckets remained, the smallest, and with it he started to bale. Every hour he took some time off to rest and eat the few odd bits of food he could find that were not spoilt by salt water. His medicine, which was supposed to be taken every four hours, was nowhere to be found. For a few hours the baling made no impression on the level of water and he wondered if water was coming in through the hole where the speedometer had been. It was a small hole, and as long as the hull was sound, he thought he could keep pace with the intake. (Most likely, the extra water was running down from the lockers and drawers which had filled when the hull was inverted.)

During the afternoon the weather began to moderate. The waves remained very high but were less steep – the venom had gone out of them. When Ward allowed himself to think at all he was angry with the others for having given up on the boat. He began to reflect, as he baled, on the possibilities of hoisting a jury rig and sailing back to port, but he knew he could never manage it on his own. He shouted in frustration at the heavens and continued baling.

It was not until 6pm that he heard the first spotter plane. He leapt up from his rest on a soggy bunk and scrambled into the cockpit, but the plane was already well past and heading away. Hoping that it would make another pass in his direction Ward settled himself in the cockpit beside the inert form of Winks. Instead, another yacht appeared. Ward blasted his fog horn in her direction and watched her alter course and come within shouting range. She had no transmitter but her crew fired off several flares which attracted the attention of yet another yacht close by. She did have a radio and sent off the last of the many distress calls on *Grimalkin*'s behalf.

By this time it was nearly 9pm. Ward was wondering if he was going to have to spend another night on board when he heard a helicopter approaching directly towards him from the east. It was just on dusk. The helicopter flew straight up to him and hovered 40 feet overhead, manoeuvring carefully to keep pace with the rise and fall of the boat, and an airman dropped onto the deck at the end of his winch wire. First, he attached Winks' body to the harness and signalled to the winchman to take it up into the helicopter. When his turn came, Ward was weeping uncontrollably and talking about retrieving some clothes from below. The airman clipped

A helicopter crewman helps hoist the body of one of the crew of the Hestrul: *one of the 15 victims of the Fastnet disaster*

him into the harness and gently handled him into the correct position to be taken off. As he looked down from the helicopter at the abandoned boat growing smaller and smaller, Ward regretted her loss and thought sadly of how, with someone else's help, he could have saved her. She had done a good job keeping him alive.

In all, 15 people lost their lives, in this, the worst maritime tragedy of its kind in Britain. Nineteen of the yachts abandoned were recovered; five sank.

A yacht called *Ariadne* suffered an even more appalling loss of life than *Grimalkin*. Before dawn on the Tuesday she had suffered a knockdown during which one of her crew received a severe head wound. The mast had broken and a lot of water had entered the boat, but the rest of the crew baled her out. At dawn, just as things were looking a little better, she was rolled again and another crewman lost contact with the boat – either his harness broke or whatever it was attached to did – and he was swept away. The skipper, a man in his sixties whose powers of endurance were limited by his age and the effects of an accident suffered some years earlier, made the decision to abandon ship. No one disagreed with him. The liferaft was inflated and the men climbed in. Two hours later they saw a small freighter whose attention they attracted with a flare. As the ship approached, the raft was either caught by a wave or upset by the men shifting position, and it capsized. The men stayed in the water, hanging onto the outside ropes, and waited. The freighter's captain brought his vessel expertly alongside the raft and someone jumped for the ladder. He caught the rungs and pulled himself up to the waiting hands of the crew. The skipper tried next but missed. He fell back into the water, was carried away by a wave, and disappeared. Two of the crew who were injured were now helped by a third member onto the upturned bottom of the raft and were instructed to hook on to it, but not to forget to release themselves before jumping for the ladder. As the ship swung slowly round for another pass, the fit crewman and one of the injured jumped. The fit crewman reached the deck but on looking down saw with dismay

that the injured man had not disconnected himself from the raft. As the ship surged the man was plucked off, and he and the remaining man on the raft, who was too weak to jump for the ladder, disappeared, along with the raft, under the stern of the ship.

Most of the other fatalities occurred in separate incidents, either when harnesses failed or, in one case, when a decision was made to abandon ship after a capsize. The only crewman who got into the inflated raft from this yacht, *Gunslinger*, was thrown out when it capsized. He failed to reach it again. The remaining crew were forced to stay with their yacht but, after some hours of frantic baling, they discovered that she was not sinking after all. They were picked up by helicopter a few hours later.

The crew of another yacht, *Trophy*, were answering a distress call from another boat when their yacht was struck on the beam by a breaking wave and the rudder jammed at an angle. This probably contributed to a capsize soon afterwards. The yacht was completely inverted but quickly righted herself. The skipper was thrown over the side, and hung there, tethered by his harness until the other crew members could get him back on deck. This they accomplished only by hacking away his harness and life jacket. Two other crewmen, seeing their skipper overboard and, in their view, done for, took it upon themselves to inflate the liferaft. Once inflated it either had to be used or cut free, so the crew had little choice but to abandon ship. Another yacht drifting by offered to take them aboard but, as that vessel looked in a bad way herself, the eight men elected to stay in the raft. It was a tragic decision.

The raft capsized once, and then repeatedly, each time throwing the men into the sea. On the fifth occasion it split in half. Two men were swept away by a wave and, although the others tried to paddle towards them, they disappeared. The remaining six men now clipped themselves on to the rope handholds on the outside of the raft, except for the skipper whose harness had had to be cut. Again and again the two raft sections were turned over, each time tipping the men into the water.

Some hours after sunrise, when they had been in the water over seven hours, a wave separated the two sections. One half, with just one man in it, floated away and disappeared despite the others' efforts to reach it. A short time later a 44-year-old sailing instructor in the other half of the raft succumbed to the cold and died, and the others believed they would soon follow him. Then a helicopter sighted them, first the single man and then the others, and they were quickly hauled into the safety of its cabin and taken ashore.

Of course a major enquiry had to be carried out after a disaster of such proportions. As a result some changes were recommended in yacht design and equipment, particularly in the area of the rudder. In general it was accepted that many of the boats were too small for the severe conditions, but short of forbidding boats under a certain size to enter these short offshore races

Thanks to the magnificent air–sea rescue operation the potentially enormous loss of life was minimized

(and who can decide what that size should be?) no useful answers to the problem were form-umulated.

Much has been said in defence or condemnation of those who lost their lives, or got into serious trouble in the storm. Human error counted for many of the deaths. I imagine if any of the participants in this race were to run into the same conditions again the same number of lives would not be lost. But blaming people for making mistakes in such impossible conditions is a fruitless exercise. The blame for these disasters lies fairly and squarely on the weather. It is a salutary reminder that nature at her worst is not a force to be trifled with.

Rowing across the Atlantic: Tom McClean

I can hardly imagine anything worse than rowing across
an ocean. I have done a bit of rowing in my time from the
shore to the boat against the tide and I found it a bore. All
that physical effort for so little gain. One can achieve great
speeds rowing a light skiff in flat water but try loading it
up with a hundred days of food and water, plus all the
extras, and the weight would sink it. To cross the Atlantic,
you must have a vessel big enough for all these things, and
that boat will be very much harder to propel through the
water. Actually, I do believe that a woman would have to
be an Amazon to succeed in such a venture and a much
braver woman than I even to attempt it.

*Tom McClean's first try at the oars on the day he set off to cross the
Atlantic*

SUPER SILVER

Tom McClean was sitting in a clearing in the Borneo jungle with his fellow paratroops, brewing up a pot while they waited for new supplies, when he was shocked to see a couple of old mates of his, Chay Blyth and John Ridgway, grinning up at him from the page of a three-week-old newpaper. They were just about to row across the Atlantic together. 'What a great caper,' thought McClean and continued to think about it as he patrolled the jungle.

A few months later, after Ridgway and Blyth had returned triumphant, McClean found himself hauled up in front of his Squadron Commander to explain why he – McClean – had been asking for detailed information on the Atlantic. Was he planning to desert or did he have some other sinister plan in mind? 'I want to row across the Atlantic alone, Sir'. As he uttered the words, McClean was a little surprised. It had only been a vague idea up until that moment; a yearning to be involved in something that would make his mark in the world. But as he said it, he knew in his bones that this was the opportunity he had been waiting for all his life.

The officer looked at him closely, all five-foot six-inches of him, and recommended that he talk to his Commanding Officer. His CO merely asked, with some curiosity, 'Are you absolutely sure you want to tackle this?' 'Yes, sir.' was McClean's reply. The officer suggested he try rowing non-stop for a few hours when he returned to England, then to have a chat with Ridgway and Blyth, and then to see if he still wanted to do it.

Months later (Christmas 1968), with permission from the War Office to do the row, he had purchased a slightly smaller (20-foot) version of the Yorkshire dory that Ridgway and Blyth had used, costing £200, for which he had enough savings of his own. Then his money ran out. But he soon made an extraordinary discovery: although almost everyone said he was mad, an odd impulse that grips certain people when they see someone else setting out to achieve what they themselves wish they could do, moved them to give McClean the help he required. The fact that he had no rowing experience – apart from the few hours his CO had

ordered – and no idea of seamanship or navigation, did not deter his helpers in the least. Three sets of special oars were donated by a Herefordshire businessman. Everything else, food, drink and navigational equipment, was given or loaned by other companies in exchange for advertisements or publicity in the unlikely event that he was successful.

By the following April the dory was ready. McClean had had buoyancy compartments fitted fore and aft, stuffed with polystyrene, and a shelter of sorts built out from the aft compartment. When all the food, water and stores were loaded there would be just enough space left for him to wriggle down under the canopy next to the radio, rubber dinghy, and perishable foods. One hundred SAS field-ration packs constituted his staple diet. These he intended to flavour lavishly with curry paste – apparently an indispensable survival aid for a paratrooper.

McClean flew to St John's, Newfoundland, in the first week of May, 1969. The sea beneath the aeroplane was ice-bound as far as the eye could see. As he stared morosely down at the white wilderness a passenger nudged him and said, 'If it's like that all the way across you'll just have to get your skates out.' McClean laughed and could not help wondering if his fellow passengers thought his laughter bravado, nerves, or just stupidity. He had opted to start from St John's because it was closer to England. It was certainly colder that far north but he wanted to take the shortest route. The reason for this was that he was desperately keen to be the first man to row the Atlantic alone, but delays had already put him a week behind schedule, and during this time John Fairfax, another Englishman, had set off in his rowing boat from the warm Canary Islands. As far as McClean knew, he was already steadily clocking up the miles towards Florida.

Super Silver was waiting in a customs shed where she had to remain for a few days while the necessary formalities were seen to. McClean contained his impatience as best he could and got to know a few of the local fishermen. They had plenty of advice on seamanship and procured for him some oiled wool mittens from a

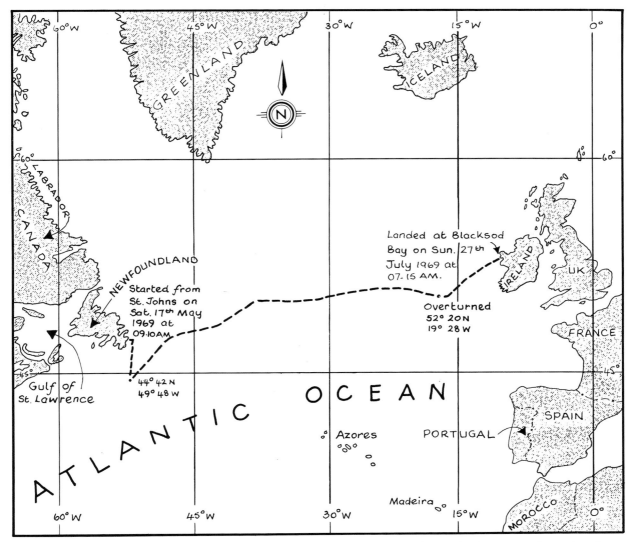

Portuguese fishing vessel. They proved to be invaluable. As he watched the boat being lowered into the water, McClean felt a surge of relief and confidence. She was quickly loaded up with her stores, then reloaded several times to make sure her trim was to everybody's satisfaction. Then McClean announced that he was ready to go.

The faces of the fishermen at the quayside turned gloomy as McClean rowed his first few strokes into the harbour. He had the distinct impression that they considered him a doomed man. Not that he could blame them, he thought,

as he fought to keep the boat steady and pointing in the right direction. As he had never rowed her before he was not at all sure how to go about it. He shook off the creepy feeling of disaster the faces had instilled in him and bent to the task in hand. He had been told emphatically to keep on rowing until land was out of sight, otherwise the tides and currents would suck him back in again.

When he was 10 miles out to sea the last of the accompanying boats turned away. He was alone. A few minutes later he shook himself and started rowing again; without realizing it he had stopped to watch them leave. It was mid-morning. At 4pm he stopped rowing and took stock. The coast had all but disappeared, but the wind had got up and was driving him south while he wanted to go east. To cut down the drift he put out the sea anchor and decided that seven hours rowing was enough for one day. He settled down to sleep. When he surfaced at 5am there was no sign of land.

That day the blisters began. By midday they were so large he could hardly get his hands around the handles of the oars. The treatment? He popped them, of course. He bit a little hole in the centre of each with his eye teeth and drained out the water. Several immersions into cold sea water and they felt dead enough for him to be able to resume rowing.

At dawn the next morning *Super Silver* was covered in frost. It was a lonely, empty day. A child's potty floating by steered his idle thoughts into speculation on its owner and from there to his own childhood in an orphanage. He had not liked it much at the time but realized now that there had not been a lot wrong with it as an education. He had learnt to be tough and to look after himself. He was with foster parents for about a year before he was off to see what the wide world offered, only to find himself in with a group of louts, stealing bikes and getting caught. A chance meeting with an old friend from the home recommended him to the Parachute Regiment. It suited him perfectly. The stupidities stopped and all his energies were directed into the life of a paratrooper. He was a loner, though. There was no one to miss him particularly, he mused as he rowed.

The next night he was thankful there was no one but himself to worry about his violent initiation into the might and fury of the Atlantic. Soon after dark the wind began to whip up spray from the cresting waves and send it horizontally into his doorless shelter. Within a short time everything was soaked and freezing. The seas rose higher and higher and the boat began to jerk violently, rising steeply up the face of a wave one minute and falling hard into the trough the next. Ridgway and Blyth's boat had taken this punishment, he knew. These were deep-sea

boats, small though they were, used by fishermen off Nova Scotia. He had to believe the boat could survive if he could only prevent her from being swamped. Every 10 or 15 minutes a wave swept right over the boat, depositing floods of cold phosphorescent water which swirled around his knees. He pumped furiously until it was around his ankles, then caught his breath and waited for the next one. It seemed the night would never end.

But daylight, when it came, brought no relief. The cold light of dawn illuminated wave-tops rushing at him from a great height, roaring with the fury of an avalanche. The dory rose gallantly up the face of them; it was only the awkward ones that caught her dithering at the top and then their foaming crests poured on to her decks. Wondering if a change of tactics was required, McClean retrieved the sea anchor, got out the oars and attempted to row. In half an hour he rarely managed to get both oars in the water and on those occasions when he did they were nearly wrenched out of his grasp. He shipped the oars again and left the boat to run before the wind. This meant less water over the decks but every mile drifted south added to his total distance.

The following night was again spent at the pumps. McClean had cause to be thankful for his rigorous Army training. Imbued with the belief that he could cope with anything he averted his eyes as much as possible from the heaving frothing sea, and pumped. When morning came and the seas and wind were as high as ever a tide of frustration swept over him. The situation was utterly beyond his control and he knew it could go on in this way for days. Sleep was impossible. Hot drinks were achieved only by spending 15 minutes and half a packet of matches just getting the stove lit. Hot food was out of the question. An odd, dull ache in his feet warned him that there was something amiss there, but he ignored it.

Halfway through the day the wind suddenly dropped and he grabbed the oars and rowed as if for his life. If opportunities had to be grabbed in between storms then he would row when the lulls came, never mind his feet, hunger, or anything else. He rowed until 9pm and for the first time went to sleep happy.

At dawn he was up again, had a quick bite to eat and settled down at the oars. But the wind, although only 15 knots, was coming from the east. It was pointless trying to row against it. McClean spent the whole day fretting, but that was only the beginning. The easterly wind went on and on. The days passed. Four days and then six, and he had not moved an inch to the east. He was being sensible, he told himself, just waiting for the wind to change and not trying to struggle against it with the oars, but frustration and helplessness ate into his soul. In an effort to busy himself he made up for lost food consumption by heating his meals properly and eating them slowly and deliberately. The flickering gas jets were a comfort as well as a small source of heat, but their warmth could not reach his feet, which were swollen to twice their normal size. A little experimenal stamping had sent excruciating pains shooting from the toes to above the ankles. When the pain had dulled to a throbbing ache, McClean debated the problem of getting his boots off, or leaving them on to protect his feet from further cold. In the end he left them on, vaguely aware that he was avoiding the issue.

On Sunday, a week out of St John's, the wind finally went around to the north-west. McClean began rowing at 4pm. His mood switched from gloom to elation as the hours flew by. His course was still a little to the south but it was basically in the right direction and a good following wind added speed. When he next looked at his watch it was 1:30am. He snuggled down into his sleeping bag and immediately fell asleep.

The sound of a ship's engines woke him somewhere around dawn. He ignored it until it was no longer possible and then realized in a panic that he had left it too late. The ship was bearing down on him just a few hundred yards away. McClean grabbed a flare and was about to light it when the fact got through to his befuddled brain that the ship was going to clear him easily. He sat down as *Super Silver* rocked in its wake, and the engines receded into the darkness. He was annoyed with himself then for not having

Camera set up to click automatically, McClean has a swig of Dutch courage

attracted its attention so that he could get a position fix. As he had done no navigation since leaving he had only the vaguest idea where he was.

The next day dawned mild (it was nearly 50 degrees Fahrenheit) and almost clear. The wind was in the right direction but something told him to attend to his feet before going any further. it took 20 minutes to ease off his boots. His feet were a revolting shade of grey, grotesquely swollen, peeling, and totally numb. According to his medical book, which he consulted with considerable alarm, they had to be kept dry and warm at all costs. Going indoors, as the book suggested, was obviously out of the question. So was warming them on the stomach of a true friend. (He sincerely doubted this test of friendship, even if one had been present.) Wrapping them in oiled seaman's socks solved the problem of warmth, but keeping them dry taxed his ingenuity somewhat. He finally wrapped them in plastic bags from food parcels, tied securely at the top.

Conditions were perfect for rowing, although very cold and grey, and he kept at it all day. Towards evening, when he stopped for the night, the wind was getting up but it was pushing *Super Silver* along nicely. McClean had his supper and settled down happily.

In the morning the wind was blowing once more from the east. Like a barometer his spirits dropped. Out went the sea anchor and the oars remained lashed. In an effort to shake himself out of a feeling of lethargy, McClean decided to get out a new ration pack and cook himself a big feast. But he did not quite get himself into a steady position as he leant over for it. A small tilt from the boat at a critical moment had him fighting for his balance. The ration pack splashed into the sea as the deck tilted further, and he fell. A lightning reflex grab of the hand made contact with the handle of the bilge pump. The boat was now heeled right over, his feet were higher than his head and the top half of his body was over the side. A wave flicked up and doused his head. Gasping and spluttering he hung on desperately until the boat slowly began to right herself.

He was shaking, for he knew that total immersion in those freezing temperatures would probably have meant exposure and hypothermia. But the Atlantic was determined to get him that day. The call of nature could not be ignored for ever, even if the conditions were anything but perfect for this outdoor acrobatic act with the bucket. In mid-performance a silent wave curled up from behind and wacked him on the backside. The force of the water sent him sprawling in the bottom of the boat. A recipe for constipation, if ever there was one.

A report over the radio said, 'Lone Atlantic rower Tom McClean has not been sighted since setting out from St John's two weeks ago . . .' Squashed up in his little shelter with his ear to the radio, Tom did not need this reminder that no one – himself included – knew where he was. It was obvious that 'shipping experts' had been consulted, and ships in the area had been asked to keep a look-out for him. It sounded as if they considered him a goner. He shrugged it off, and

the insinuation that he was a nuisance. Navigation *was* something of a problem though. The best he could come up with in his rough calculations was a huge zig-zag but he could be over a hundred miles out. Without the sun – it had not appeared at all yet – he could not get a better idea of where he was.

The next two days provided great rowing weather. He started at dawn and did not stop till 9pm. But getting down to rowing on the second morning was agony. The previous 16 hours at the oars had done dreadful things to his hands – not just the blisters, or the muscles, but the bones themselves seemed to be on fire. For half an hour, eyes shut and teeth grinding, perspiration running in rivulets down the contorted muscles of his face, he concentrated his mind on anything other than the pain in his hands. It worked. After an hour the pain had either worn off or he had got used to it.

The third day started well but by midday deteriorated into a brooding overcast sky. He lashed down the oars, rechecked that everything was secure and positioned himself resignedly by the pump. It was a night he would never forget. He relates: 'My God! It was a nightmare of a night. *Silver* pitched and rolled as if deliberately trying to throw me overboard. She seemed to have developed a sudden frenzied hate for me personally. There was no sleep at all. *Silver* shipped water all through the night. I pumped, I bailed and I clung to her like a limpet. There were moments I am sure, when she was completely out of the water. I could feel those waves carry her high into the air as if trying to throw us up into the black void overhead . . . when she hit the water again I literally bounced on the floorboards.'

The water was about a foot above the floorboards all night despite his efforts to pump or bale it out. Towards dawn he vented his fury and anger above the din of the storm. Later, he stopped yelling and prayed instead.

The storm spent itself shortly after daybreak. Aching, exhausted and hardy able to move, McClean searched the empty grey seas and sky for some sign of life. He felt the need just then for reassurance that he was not the only living

creature in this vast expanse of barren sea. Even the birds seemed to have deserted him. He gazed long and hard at the horizon till eventually he spotted several birds flying east, towards England. The reflection that they would be there long before him only increased his loneliness. He thought longingly of a companion, anyone, to share the hardships and problems, but reminded himself that the whole purpose of this exercise was to be alone. Otherwise, there would have been no point whatsoever in doing it.

After a while he pulled himself together and brewed up a cup of tea. The scalding liquid hurt as it went down and turned his thoughts to the question of food. Part of his problem now was the lack of proper nourishment. Up until that day he had believed that rowing mattered above all else, even to the exclusion of food. That had been a mistake, he told himself, as he stuffed boiled porridge cakes, biscuits and strawberry jam into his mouth.

These sort of glassy sea conditions were perfect but rare

As he ate he looked around, at his sodden sleeping bag and various items of clothes which he had left lying on the floor of his shelter, at the bits of seaweed that the storm had thrown up, and at the six inches or so of dirty water that swilled around the floor. It looked a bit squalid. A quick tidy up, though, was all that was needed to put things back in order, he thought. The wind might dry the sleeping bag a bit if was tied on to the roof and the water would not take long to pump out.

He fell to contemplating the horizon again. There was a ship. He sat bolt upright and stared at it. Pictures of laughing people filled his mind. Merry people, drinking around a bar, or eating hot, fresh food, or wallowing in a steaming bath. They would have a doctor on board who would treat his salt-water sores and blisters, and his frostbitten feet. The ship was miles away and not even sailing in his direction. Would he have been able to withstand an invitation to go aboard, he wondered. He was shortly to find out.

Tired of looking at the empty sea he lay back and stared at the sky instead, drifting off into pleasant memories of harvest time and fresh-cut hay. His reverie was rudely interrupted some time later when the sound of a bell right behind him made him leap in the air as though he had been shot. A few yards away was a fishing boat. Fishermen were shouting and waving from the rails – Portuguese, he recognized instantly, from seeing them in St John's. The skipper leant out from the bridge as it passed and shouted, 'Hey! you all right, eh? You want anytink, eh? Help maybe? You in trouble, Eh?' McClean grabbed a chart and waved it at him to indicate that he wanted a position. The skipper understood and a few seconds later shouted it across to him, but his offers of food, water, or anything else, were politely declined. The boat began to drift away. The grinning Portuguese raised their hands again, some in the Churchill salute, as the boat gathered way. It steamed off to resume fishing.

McClean was full of elation. The position he had been given confirmed his hopes that he was about to leave the cold Labrador current at last. And best of all, he had resisted the temptation to accept help. The simple contact with people had left him full of energy and high spirits. His luck had changed, he felt sure. Could it be that the worst was over and the Atlantic would treat him more kindly now?

As if to confirm his hopes the next four days were perfect. The wind blew steadily from the west and the temperature rose to 48 degrees Fahrenheit until McClean could imagine he was on the Côte d'Azur on a summer's day – even though the sun was struggling to peer through a high cloud layer. Super Silver sliced swiftly through the water, forming a high bow wave and throwing off sparkling drops into the clear deep-blue sea. On the fourth day the sun broke through. McClean hurriedly stripped off his clothes and roasted back, front, and sideways for a few minutes, washed off the accumulated salt crystals that had caused boils and chafe marks in all the creases, and then changed into clean clothing. He felt marvellous.

The oars dipped in and out. Steadily, not too hard or fast for that would just use up too much energy. Just a steady rhythm than even allowed for dozing off. Tom found his Army training once again coming to the fore. His mind clicked into a sort of overdrive, where only a small per cent of the active mind or body was needed to keep the oars going.

The trouble was that the overdrive was hard to shake off when he was not rowing. He noticed after a while how slow his reactions were becoming. Because of the warmth and repetitive pace of successive days the hours began to slide by without being noticed. He was losing his sense of time. (He did not appear to think this had anything to do with solitude, but as every other single hander suffers in this way it must have been a major cause in his case too.) By the time he realized what was happening he had lost track of the days. He could not even be sure that he had been rowing all the time. He suspected that although he had gone through the motions the oars had not made much impression on the water. He scratched at his face and discovered he had a week-old beard. The oars hung over the side as his thoughts went round and round, attempting to work out how he was going to impose more self-discipline.

He dithered through another day of indifference, not rowing much – Super Silver was being pushed along towards the east by a moderate following wind – but trying to work out what should be done to improve the boat's trim. He realized suddenly that he had been using the drinking water from containers stored in the stern. These containers acted as ballast so that now the boat was down at the bow. The empty containers had to be refilled with seawater and restowed in their original places. As soon as this had been done the wind veered to the north, and for a few hours he rowed hard to counteract the drift south but gave up when he got tired.

When he made the effort to work out which day it was he had a pleasant surprise. It was a Sunday, the day that he was to open one of the letters given to him for that purpose. By chance, he chose the very letter he needed. It was written by the unit's Education Officer and it was about why so many started but so few succeeded. He wrote of willpower and belief in one's self. Tom could feel the message penetrating his dulled brain and reaching down to where his own self-motivation had sunk underneath the force of the Atlantic. It started him thinking. He folded the letter away and looked around. A fog was rolling along the sea towards him. Fog meant only one thing in this area; he had entered the Gulf Stream. It meant that, theoretically at least, the worst part of the trip was over.

Rowing through the wet, impenetrable mist was not a pleasant experience, McClean soon decided. At first the absolute silence and density of the air, which clung to him like a blanket, felt comforting after the weeks of wind and noisy seas. His shouts bouncing back off the solid-looking white walls of fog sounded so much like someone else that he kept it up for a bit, but then the idea of a ship bearing down on him unheard and unseen made him keep silent. Every few minutes he had to stop rowing, hold his breath and listen. The fog stayed throughout the day and was still as thick as ever when he gave up rowing at 10pm.

The heavy sleep into which he fell as soon as he climbed into his sleeping bag was violently shattered some hours later. *Super Silver* quivered and rocked, and the sound of a loud crash echoed in his ears as he fought to free himself from the sleeping bag. A series of bumps and scrapes sounded down the boat's side as he got to his feet and looked all round into the close black air, expecting to see he did not know what. There was nothing at all, no lights or sounds of a ship's engines. A quick search in the water astern showed no signs of logs or other large objects either. But the fright from being woken so roughly from a sound sleep refused to be quietened. Certain that there must have been damage from the impact he examined the boat from end to end. Amazingly she appeared to be sound as ever, but his relief was quickly tempered by the thought that the hull might have sustained some damage that could not be seen

Finesse in eating or cooking arrangements was not something McClean aspired to

from the inside. He baulked for a little while at the idea of going over the side to look, but eventually decided that it had to be done. Stripping off all but the plastic bags around his feet he plunged into the still black surface and felt his way carefully around every inch of hull. There was not a scratch on it.

It was not easy to get to sleep after that. McClean lay there thinking, considering how lucky he had been so far. He even offered up a prayer of thanks and grinned at himself in the darkness as he thought of the changes that had taken place within him since his wild brash days at the boys' home. How he had scoffed then at the idea of church.

The next day, just to remind him to keep on his toes, the fog cleared and gale-force winds came rushing in to take its place. However, they did not last very long. For the next five days steady winds blew from the west and the sun even came out once or twice. Still, McClean realized that he was not feeling as jaunty as he ought to have been, considering the favourable conditions and lucky escape he had had. As he rowed slowly along the seemingly endless ocean to the east he tried to think what exactly was bothering him. It took quite some time for the truth to sink in. There was a bone-deep soreness that had spread to every part of his body; it was as though he was bruised all over. Instead of a steady hour's stint at the oars getting rid of the usual stiffness and aching muscles, he slowly became aware that he hurt more, not less. Rest might remedy the problem but then again, how long should he rest? A few hours or a few days? He struggled against the temptation to put the oars aside. This is the meaning of endurance, he told himself. Stopping to rest now when the conditions were so good for rowing was the thin edge of the wedge. It will wear off, he argued; it was a simple matter of pacing himself more sensibly and not getting unreasonably tired. Instead of rowing for as long as he could stand it when the weather was right he decided to row for three hours and have three hours off – off rowing that is. But there were other things to be attended to which he had put off till now, like inspecting the rudder and rechecking the trim.

That evening he felt a little more cheerful again. It was June 12, he noted, three and a half weeks since setting out. Unfortunately, he still had not got around to navigating except by dead reckoning. Basically he was lost, but as his general direction was always east it was only a question of whether the drift and currents had carried him too far north, in which case he might miss Ireland, or even Scotland, altogether and end up in Greenland, not a cheering thought. But there was a way he could get a rough fix if only the sun would shine at the right time. If, as he imagined, he was still on more or less the same latitude as Greenwich, all he had to do was to time the sun rise where he was, look up the Almanac to see what time the sun rose at Greenwich, and then divide the difference by four to find the degrees west of Greenwich. This, he reasoned, must give him a fix within 15 miles.

The sun stayed obstinately behind the clouds. Three difficult, tiring days went by. McClean kept up his schedule by an enormous effort that left him both drained and fed up. The only incident he could remember later with clarity was the cooker blowing up. He had not been able to light it because the matches were damp, but forgot to turn off the jet while he searched for another box. When he lit the new match there was an explosion which scorched his hands and eyebrows. He consoled himself with the reflection that he was so saturated in salt water that nothing short of a forest fire would have set him alight. The next day he recorded a perfect sunrise which put him close to the halfway mark.

The weather was kind and progress was good but McClean still felt out-of-sorts and a little dispirited at the thought of the distance to go. He was apprehensive, too. Deep in his mind he knew that the ocean had not yet exhausted her reservoirs of ill temper. The longer the weather remained mild the more likely it seemed that something horrible would happen to balance it out. He did not have to wait very much longer for his fears to be confirmed.

On Tuesday, June 17, 70-mph winds came screeching out of the night to harass and batter the little rowing boat with bone-shaking violence. McClean fought to keep himself in the boat, and the water out. There was a point when he thought that the brutality of such a storm could drive a man to the brink of insanity. But if the will to survive is strong the mind will keep terror at bay, particularly if survival is dependent on one's own actions. While there was breath left in him, he snarled, he would fight. He shouted at the boiling sea as he baled, and when he tired of that he shouted at himself to keep pumping while the sea swept over him, pouring into his eyes, nose and mouth till he could hardly breath. The nightmare went on and on. As yellow streaks of dawn touched the ravaged cloud cover scudding low overhead the wind plucked and tore at his oilskins, intent

on ripping them off his back. Throughout the morning it raged. At noon it stormed off to wreak vengeance elsewhere.

McClean sat by the pump utterly spent, watching the rapidly calming seas warily. The wind had departed so swiftly that he fully expected to find that he was in a vortex and the tempest would begin all over again as soon as he moved away from the pump. The gnawing void in his stomach could not be ignored, though. Vortex or no, he had to eat. He stood slowly and flexed taut, complaining muscles, then set to work to brew up the biggest meal he had yet eaten. A huge curry, followed by beer, sardines, biscuits and cheese, a tin of fruit and two spoonfuls of honey, all finished off with a long swig of rum. Feeling replete he retired to his sleeping bag for a snooze. Two hours later

It was not physical hardships that made sustained effort so difficult but mental fatigue

the wind was still light and from the west. Wearily, he got out the oars and started rowing.

The calm did not last for long, alas. In the evening the wind returned with renewed malevolence. For 48 hours it scourged, mauled, chastised and punished him, as though it wished to obliterate him from the face of the sea. McClean prayed and imagined he could hear others back home praying too. His blisters peeled in the constant wet, formed again and broke. The old salt-water sores itched and the new ones burned. Salt piled up in every crease and chafed the skin raw. Two days and nights at the pumps reduced him to the state of catnapping where he crouched, waking to the feel of cold water swishing around his knees, making him automatically work the pump again with hands as stiff as claws.

When the wind eventually eased McClean slumped down beside the pump and sank into oblivion for some hours. The weather was unchanged when he awoke except that a thick cloud had descended to sea level and coated the boat in glistening rain drops. It was a depressing sight. McClean searched his mind for something more cheerful to while away the time until he could start rowing and hit on the happy notion that, now that he was half way, the RAF Shackletons might be within range on their Atlantic patrols. He had a radio, which he had occasionally used, but so far no one had responded to his calls. He put out a call now but there was apparently no one within 200 miles of him, or no one listening at any rate. His forlorn appeal for a response came back at him dully from the foggy cloud bank pressing in on all sides. His surroundings seemed even lonelier now than before.

His brooding was disturbed some time later by the sound of a ship's fog horn. At first he was convinced that it was not getting any closer, but then, abruptly, it was echoing all around him. He sprang to his feet in excitement at the thought of people so close. Peering frantically this way and that, unable to ascertain the precise direction of the sound, he finally saw the ship break through the fog. It was heading straight for him. His excitement turned to alarm and then to panic. The sea anchor was out and bringing it in so as to row out of the way was impossible. He snatched up the radar reflector and waved it in the air above his head, realized his stupidity, and threw it down. Abandon ship, get into the liferaft and paddle away – get the hell out of it, were the thoughts clammering in his head. With one hand on the ring about to inflate the raft he suddenly stopped. The flares! Why had he not thought of the flares? He snatched one up but before he could set it off the ship altered course and slid by him.

McClean found himself shaking uncontrollably from fright and anger at his stupid behaviour. Before the shaking had stopped the fog horn blared out again, very close to him. He leapt up, flare in hand, and saw the ship approaching him very slowly, its engines just ticking over, until it stopped, just 20 yards away. As she glided past he could see people hanging over the rails and waving at him, way down beneath the massive steel walls of the ship's hull. It was a West German freighter. In response to a shout he waved a chart above his head. His position came floating down from the bridge via megaphone, along with the inquiry: 'Are you all right?'. He shouted up that all was well. The captain, leaning over the bridge, shrugged, waved a salute and gave the order to move off. As the ship turned away and gathered speed the crew continued to wave. She disappeared quickly into the fog.

The next part of the journey was hard; harder, in a way, than the first month. As the incident with the ship had shown, his mental processes had slowed to the extent that he no longer trusted himself to take proper precautions or notice when things were going wrong. The weather was good so he should have been able to chalk up good mileages every day, but the fervour of the first few weeks had deserted him. He had not considered – it had never occurred to him as a possibility even – that his own mental attitude could defeat him, not the physical hardship. But faced with the prospect of another month or more at sea alone, he felt daunted.

One morning he spent the whole time huddled under his shelter, wallowing in self-pity. The airbed had a hole in it and he had forgotten to bring a repair kit. It was an insignificant mishap and he did not care about the loss of the airbed; but the mere fact that he no longer cared about what he had previously thought the greatest luxury disturbed him strangely. A warning note sounded somewhere in his tired brain. There was something very wrong in this attitude, he tried to convince himself. This was not the sort of exercise where one could just accept defeat and give up, go home and accept that the undertaking had simply been too much. Defeat here meant death. Apathy, lack of concentration, and diminishing willpower, all added up to the lack of resources to fight. The sea would accept no second-rate efforts. It would bide its time and strike in his weakest moment. The appalling meaning of his predicament, how close he had come to accepting that dreadful situation, hit him like a ton of bricks. He staggered out of the shelter and gasped for breath as though he had been punched in the stomach. Then his legs started to shake and he sat down. It was not a tremble, but a violent contortion of the knees, thigh muscles, and feet. It was as though they were having convulsions. He grabbed his knees, leant his arms, head and shoulders over them and hung on till the shaking stopped.

He decided on a drastic cure, and worked out a proper regime of rowing, sleeping, maintenance and exercises – anything to keep busy – and clung to it. Up at 5:30am, then a cold wash in sea water to get the reflexes working. Making and eating breakfast, watching the clock all the while, tuned his mind into the daily schedule. One hour's rowing, 10 minutes of exercises throughout the morning with exactly half an hour for lunch. Then a repeat of the morning. Oars away at 6pm, supper, writing up the log, drinking cups of tea, etc., with bed at 11pm. It was more a case of keeping the mind occupied and away from the prospect of being in mid-ocean, like being at the top of a mountain which looks as though it will never slope again into the valley. It was a struggle to keep the mind along sane lines.

Half of him stubbornly carried out the schedule while the other half did its best to disrupt the timetable. By the time a week had gone by he told himself he was winning. He was doing the routine things more or less without having to force himself by the clock. He felt more alert and the time had passed productively. He could also pick up the BBC now and the American stations had faded out, an encouraging indication, but on Wednesday, July 5 the radio went dead. No amount of juggling, shaking or cajoling succeeded in producing the faintest crackle. He felt more lonely and depressed than at any other time.

The days crept on. With the continuing mild weather the apathy crept back. Another shock was needed, and it was not long coming. A thunderstorm struck with the force and noise of a thunderbolt. It wakened him and brought him alive again to the real dangers of wind and waves, spiced this time with lightning and a deluge of rain that was frightening in its intensity. When it eased, McClean got out the oars and rowed as he had never rowed before. He rowed with an urgency born of desperation. Pain coursed through his hands and arms like fire but he took a perverse pleasure from the feel of it. It made him feel wide awake and alive for the first time in weeks.

The following day, July 9, was the start of 10 days of westerly winds and the beginning of the last lap. The previous rigid schedule was even more useful now. His increased vitality and elation made the oars fly and the days marched steadily by in a haze of rowing, eating and unconscious, dreamless sleep. Another ship appeared on a sparkling, clear day and steamed severely by, in spite of all his efforts to attract its attention. He badly wanted a position fix and this was the first ship he had seen for weeks. When it was obvious ordinary means were of no avail, he fired his biggest flare which rose to 2,000 feet and exploded into a shower of sparks. The ship did an abrupt about-turn and motored up to him. It was an English ship. After getting his position he handed over some films for his sponsoring newspaper and declined an invitation to go aboard for a bath and a meal. As she disappeared he looked up the position. There were just 600 miles left to go. His mood as he bent to the oars again was euphoric. The only thing missing, which he absolutely craved, was someone to tell the good news to. He was winning. He would make it.

For the next two days he sang as he rowed. The run of good weather had to end sometime and McClean was therefore not surprised when towards evening the waves began to build, but not even the prospect of another night at the pumps could destroy his good mood. In the early hours of the morning, he was huddling beneath the shelter, trying to sneak a short snooze, when his world was erupted by a new cataclysm. The moment the wave struck he was wide awake, tensed and waiting, in those few seconds after impact when it seems the world stops. Then he was spinning out of control, crushed against the sides, roof, and floor of the boat while his arms and legs flayed in useless attempts to save himself. Water rushed over him as the boat turned over and over; it filled his ears and mouth, and floated his clothes free of his body. He held his breath until his head felt it would burst. Then the spinning stopped and he fought to get away from the water. Above his head he could feel the canvas roof of the shelter, as heavy as lead and unyielding to his shoving. 'Christ, oh my Christ!' ... the words ran through his brain over and over again in desperate, frantic repetition. He managed to wriggle past the life-raft that had got itself wedged against parts of the canvas, and then broke the surface of the water. Gulping in great lungfulls of air McClean looked around. The boat's gunwales were nearly under the water. The only thing keeping her from sinking out of sight was the polystyrene in the buoyancy compartments.

McClean hurled a stream of filthy abuse at the sea, the sky, the boat and himself, and felt a little more normal for it. Then he started rocking the boat, running from one side to the other and pressing down on the gunwales until he got the momentum going. The water started to slop out over the sides. The bucket was still lashed down in its place, and he cut the string holding it and baled out at the same time. When dawn came the boat was empty. As soon as he stopped baling the reaction set in. The shakes came again, this time all over. When they finally stopped McClean propped himself up against the wet floorboards and slept.

As soon as he came to he checked everything carefully and was relieved to find almost no damage. A water container had gone, some food, a kettle and a cup. The sea anchor had caused the problem, he discovered. One of the two lines attaching it to the boat had worn through and the result, when caught by an awkward wave, had been a tripping effect.

The next time McClean worked out a rough position he estimated there were only 250 miles to the Irish coast. A good wind blew him along due east, exactly where he wanted to go. The days flew by. On the 26th he spotted a long dark cloud on the horizon and tried to kid himself it was Ireland. A few hours later it turned into land. His delight was hard to contain and impossible to express adequately. Yelling at the top of his voice had to suffice for the time being. Some hours of hard rowing later he estimated by the chart that he was 10 miles off the Mullet peninsular in County Mayo. Almost bursting with excitement he rowed on. Curious fishermen hailed him and asked if he was all right. McClean replied that he had never felt better and asked them if the land was Mullet. They confirmed it.

Hours later McClean realized he was not going to make a landfall before dark. He settled down to an all-night session at the oars to prevent the wind and tide from driving him onto the rocks, glowing eerily in the moonlight. At dawn he rowed in.

The wind was strong, and rowing was hard and tiring. This, and the fact that he was pretty exhausted, gave him the excuse to beach the boat at the first feasible-looking landing spot. There was none that looked even remotely possible. In desperation he closed to within 20 yards of the rocky coast. *Super Silver* could be battered to pieces, he knew, but judgement deserted him at that critical moment. He thought he had to land just there, regardless. In he went. The vessel struck the rocks and he threw himself into the surf and staggered up the rocks. She went broadside on and started to pound. The realization of what he was doing to the boat that had been his sole means of survival these last weeks brought him to his senses. Staggering back against the pounding waves he reached the boat and heaved against her bows, pushing them back towards the sea. Holding her in that position he waited for an outgoing wave to lift her up, and jumped in. He grabbed the oars and rowed madly. It took an hour to escape from the clutches of the surf but eventually he managed to row a safe distance from the shore. Abruptly, the wind fell away to nothing and he rocked in a calm sea. He looked towards the shore and could not believe his eyes. There was a perfect landing place, a sandy beach with no surf. He cursed himself for a fool and rowed *Super Silver* in.

A little way above the beach was a cottage. An elderly woman was watching him. As he approached he called out: 'Good morning, ma'am. I've just rowed the Atlantic. Can I take your photograph?' She looked at him as if he was mad, and made to shut the door. 'Then can you please tell me where I am?' he asked, and heard, just before she closed the door, 'Blacksod bay'. A little further along he could see a pub. He sauntered over to it.

The other Briton, John Fairfax, rowing from east to west on a more southerly route, landed in Florida after a 180-day crossing, one week ahead of Tom McClean.

McClean, the right character to row the Atlantic

Twice is More than Enough

At some point during the final frantic few weeks of preparation for my circumnavigation I was handed a large hard-cover book by a friend. 'Put this away on your shelf – don't look at it now.' There was an air of nonchalance about him which did not go along with the title, 'Heavy Weather Sailing'. He said: 'When you're getting near the Roaring Forties you might have time to browse through it and get some ideas.' I put it aside and got on with my preparations. It was not until I had been on my own at sea for several months and was approaching the area where I could expect bad weather that I remembered the book and dug it out. 'Heavy Weather Sailing' by Adlard Coles; just what I need, I said to myself, how thoughtful of him.

I had not allowed my imagination to run riot on the subject of storms. It was not that I was hiding my head in the sand exactly, but there just had not seemed to be much point in worrying about hypothetical situations unless they materialized. I had not got far into the book before I was riveted to my seat. The photographs in the book of gigantic seas and freak waves were impressive and very relevant indeed. I began to look around the boat to see what had to be done.

I find it curious, reading back through my logs, that I was not more apprehensive. My defence mechanism was obviously working well, or perhaps the isolation led me into believing that it could not happen to me. Whichever, it seems now that I was not taking in what I was reading in that book about Cape Horn seas. Instead of heading for the nearest port I spent the following two weeks doing whatever I could to the boat to make her more secure, and pressed cautiously on.

Now, 10 years on, I have re-read 'Heavy Weather Sailing' and am aghast at the photographs and accounts of other people's Cape Horn sailing. Like me, they ventured into the Southern Ocean believing that their boats were up to the conditions. Their experiences seem to prove that no vessel can boast total protection against such severe weather. My experience only goes to prove that some are luckier than others.

Among the unlucky ones was the yacht *Tzu Hang*, owned and sailed by Miles and Beryl Smeeton. They had the idea of returning to England via Cape Horn, leaving Melbourne, Australia in the early summer and spending several months in the high latitudes before rounding the Horn. Few – if any – small yachts had taken this route at that time (1956). Most started off from New Zealand and therefore stayed north until dipping down around Tierra del Fuega. The Smeetons, however, were not keen to attempt this route on their own. Their 15-year-old daughter, who had sailed almost everywhere with them, had just returned to school in England, but even had she stayed they would still have taken on someone with more experience in deep-sea sailing. So they enlisted the help of John Guzwell, a single hander who had already sailed around the world, although not round Cape Horn. Guzwell was happy to lay up his own small boat and join *Tzu Hang* for the experience.

The yacht was a 46-foot ketch, built of teak with a flush deck, canoe stern and a bowsprit. She was a good-sized boat, not too big, not too small. There was no self-steering but three people could steer her 24 hours a day without undue effort. She also sailed well on her own if the conditions were right.

Christmas eve that year (1956) was a cheerless, unwelcome occasion, reminding the Smeetons of their absent daughter. On Christmas Day they were prevented from departure by the weather but on the following day the anchor was broken out and stowed away for the last time. The feel of the wind in their faces, and the rising and falling of the yacht as she lifted over the waves, filled them with pleasure and anticipation. Beryl's face was aglow: she had ceased to worry about her daughter. John, at the wheel, sang at the top of his voice. Miles stood astride the cockpit seats, leaning against the doghouse – or on the bridge as I used to call it – out of the wind, staring forward towards the open sea and thinking. He was reminded of the turret of a Sherman tank. (To me it was always like swaying in the branches of a tall tree with the whole countryside as far as the eye could see spread out around me.)

The days settled down into the routine familiar to them all. John was a carpenter, always on the look-out for things to improve, or searching for a little more speed by fiddling with the trim of the sails. He loved *Tzu Hang* even though she was not his. (Some sailors imbue their vessels with feelings and personalities, even talking to them as though they were alive in a human sense. A ship has been called a 'she' as far back as we know, but then the ancient seafarers were a very superstitious breed of men. I do not think of myself as superstitious at all, yet I think it is impossible, when you trust your life to a vessel, not to feel that she is more than just an inanimate object.) Among other things, John utilized pieces of wood and oddments that Beryl, an inveterate hoarder, had collected, and changed the door on the aft end of the doghouse to washboards which would make it safer in the event of a heavy wave coming aboard.

Beryl did all the cooking and stood two watches to the men's three to compensate. She did not trust anyone but herself with the primus stoves as they tended to give trouble if not handled in just the right way. Every morning the smells of porridge and bacon came wafting up through the hatch to Miles on the helm, eager to end his three-hour dawn watch.

Their route took them below the off-lying islands to the south of New Zealand and from there the course was more or less a straight line for the Horn. The days turned into weeks. Halfway to South America the wind steadied to the normal pattern of fast-moving depressions approaching from the west, which blew the yacht before them. Then, after a day or two, she would be overtaken by the low pressure system and left to wait in the unceasing swells for the next one.

John filmed the sometimes boisterous seas and cold, blue skies but commented to Miles that he preferred the weather further south where the waves were likely to be really impressive. This preference prompted a discussion on the nature of the sea, whether it was cruel, or impersonal, whether it deliberately set out to get one, or whether vessels like *Tzu Hang* were so insignificant that the sea just did not notice they were there. Although neither Miles, Beryl or John were of the Moitessier persuasion, Beryl let slip her feelings about the sea's benevolence. The men's feelings appeared to be much the same as mine. The sea is only the salty water in a rock pool on the beach multiplied millions of times. Power is added along with volume but not intent, benign or otherwise, although John liked having something else to blame sometimes besides himself.

On February 5 the twin headsails developed an idiosyncracy when the wind reached force 8 – flapping at their peaks. This was the start of a run of classic heavy depressions from the north-west swinging to south-west, mostly force 7 or 8 and sometimes gusting higher. This pattern continued for nearly two weeks.

Early on the morning of the 14th, Miles was aroused by the persistent drumming of the head-sails and the increased whining of wind funnelling through the rigging. The yacht's movement had abruptly changed to a new tempo as she lurched over the tops and swooped down the sides of the gale-driven seas. Once up and on his feet, Miles felt the urgency of the boat's movement. Hurriedly throwing on oilskins, boots and safety harness he shook John on his way up the hatch and poked his bare head out for a look. Breaking wave-tops were being driven into long white streaks of spume along the back of the swells which loomed up in regimented rows behind the yacht. She was going too fast; the sails had to come off. He jumped below again to hurry the others into their oilskins. Beryl snapped her harness onto a mizen shroud and took the tiller while the two men carefully moved up the deck holding on against the sharp movements of the deck and the buffeting wind at their backs. (I was reminded of a warning from a fellow single hander when I read that they had made their harnesses fast onto the rigging. If a boat should turn over the mast would be pointing downwards. Working on the deck in rough seas I frequently had this vision of myself during a capsize, sliding to the top of the mast when it was under the water, then swinging up on the end of it as the boat righted, before beginning an undignified descent down the back stay. Consequently, I always fixed my harness to lines or strong points on the deck.)

The halyards were let go and the madly flapping canvas was shoved through the forehatch. Before John and Beryl went below they paid out a thick rope from the stern to slow the boat and assist the steering. Under bare poles *Tzu Hang* still achieved a reasonable speed with the wind and waves behind her. Miles felt exhilarated by the sight of the storm, the same exhilaration, he realized later, that he had felt in battle or mountaineering, which ought to have warned him that trouble was at hand. He wondered as he stared at the advancing waves if there was something more he ought to do to make their situation safer. There was a can of engine oil on board but it was not enough to have any calming effect on the waves for any length of time. Anyway, the weather did not seem extreme enough yet for oil. The yacht was handling well, even though several waves had come over the stern. The weight of one washed him out of the cockpit, at the same time ripping the canvas dodger protecting the helmsman from the wind. As the hours passed and she rose over each huge wave he felt increasingly confident that this was, despite his belief in lying a-hull, the correct approach to this storm. The sea was dangerous, he knew, but lying a-hull (lying beam on to the waves without sails) he felt would make the risk of capsize far greater.

Beryl came up to relieve him at 9am, colourful in her yellow oilskins and with a big grin on her face. She looked more serious as she glanced aft at the approaching seas, sometimes with a distance as great as a quarter of a mile between them. *Tzu Hang* would begin the long ascent up to the crest of a wave, shoot forward a little way at the top, before dipping her stern as the wave passed underneath and then sliding down the other side. When Beryl had got the feel of the tiller Miles left her, not really wanting to go below and shut her out, but it was pointless to stay on deck.

He divested himself of wet oilskins and retired to the comfort of his bunk and their Siamese cat who parked herself on his stomach. John did some filming of Beryl fighting the big seas and then he also came below and sat in his oilskins on the edge of his bunk. He put his feet on the heavy tool box securely tied to ringbolts on the lockers while he loaded another roll of film. The cabin was warm and cosy despite the high-pitched whine of the storm and the occasional roar of a collapsing wave as it cascaded against the hull.

Beryl, far from comfortable or warm, sat with one hand gripping the tiller and the other bracing herself against the boat's fairly wild movements. She turned from watching her compass course to check the next wave and to make sure the yacht was square on to it. A slight veer off the face of one wave was easily corrected with a little push on the tiller and at the bottom

of the trough she glanced back to the next one. To her horror immediately behind her the sky was blocked by a mountainous wave, and *Tzu Hang* was almost stationary in the trough at the bottom of the wall of water. Down it a torrent of breaking white crest was pouring towards *Tzu Hang*. Beryl's only thought was: 'I can't do anything, I'm absolutely straight.' Her next sensation was of being hurled forward through the air.

Miles, in the Smeetons' book, 'Once is Enough', remembered the occasion thus: 'As I read, there was a sudden, sickening sense of disaster. I felt a great lurch and heel, and a thunder of sound filled my ears. I was conscious, in a terrified moment, of being driven into the front and side of my bunk with tremendous force. At the same time there was a tearing, cracking sound, as if *Tzu Hang* was being ripped apart, and water burst solidly, raging into the cabin. There was darkness, black darkness and pressure, and a feeling of being buried in a debris of boards, and I fought wildly to get out, thinking *Tzu Hang* had already gone. Then suddenly I was standing again, waist-deep in water, and floorboards and cushions, mattresses and books, were sloshing in wild confusion around me.'

Shock was replaced by panic and fear as the knowledge that Beryl was at the helm burst into his mind. That she could have survived the force that had hurled the boat head over heels he felt instantly to be impossible. John was just emerging from the water in the galley as Miles fought his way to the companionway crying out: 'Oh God, where's Bea, where's Bea?'

John, on his back, stared up at a large square of light above him, wondering what it was. He watched Miles climb up the companionway and out onto the deck before it dawned on him that he was looking up at the sky where the doghouse had once been. He climbed up after Miles and straight away saw Beryl in the water, about 30 yards away. Her face was covered with blood but she was smiling and waving her arm to them as she swam towards the mizen mast, which was floating in several pieces to leeward of the yacht. She reached it and pulled herself up to the boat which was lying so low in the water that there was virtually no freeboard. Miles grabbed her hand and called to John to help him. John was standing stupefied on the deck thinking: 'I might as well jump in alongside her.' But he moved to Miles and knelt on the deck, and said: 'This is it, you know, Miles.' Miles nodded. Before they could pull Beryl aboard another wave roared up alongside them. *Tzu Hang* lifted sluggishly over it, the weight of water inside her reducing most of her buoyancy. Together Miles and John hauled Beryl back on board, at the same time thinking that there was little point in it as they would all be in the water soon. But Beryl thought differently: 'I know where the buckets are,' she said. 'I'll get them!'

John recovered first from thinking that this was the end and dived below after Beryl to search under the water for floorboards, nails, sailcloth and plywood to make a covering for the hole in the deck. Water was lapping in with every lethargic roll of the boat. Miles roused himself to grab the pieces as John threw them up, until John emerged with his tool box, retrieved from the galley sink. While he worked feverishly to block the hole, Beryl and Miles baled out the waist-high water. One of Beryl's arms was nearly useless and prevented her from baling herself. But she could help Miles by filling the bucket while he pulled it up on a rope and tipped the water out through the hole where one of the skylights had been; as both had been swept away. Water continued to splash in through the gaps but Miles was able to block one with his body. As soon as a hasty covering was over the doghouse hole John moved to the other missing skylight and tacked a sail over it. Soon, the yacht began to rise a little in the water.

John next went around and let go all the rigging screws so that the masts would lie clear of the hull. He hoped they might act as an anchor for the bows to swing to, but as soon as the weight of the vessel came on to them, now attached only by the forestay fitting, they broke loose and floated free.

Beryl's steady cheerful voice saying 'Right' as each bucket was ready to be hauled up went on and on. Towards mid-morning Miles had to call a short break to warm up as he was working on the exposed deck without his oilskins. They rested a few minutes below looking at the jumble of gear that seemed to half-fill the boat, and chewed on some Horlicks tablets. Beryl gave Miles her oilskin jacket and they continued baling. At dusk the water was down to the floorboards and they rested again. With the emergency over for the time being, Beryl found that her shoulder and one foot were causing her great pain, so much so that she just wanted to crawl away and find oblivion for a while. The cat was bedraggled and shivering, too, and not looking at all well. They had not had time to do anything about her before, but now they all climbed into John's wide bunk – along with the cat – to try to warm each other up, but Beryl's painful shoulder would not let her sleep or lie still. Each went back to his own sodden bunk to pass the night away in fitful dozing, thinking, and listening to the waves as they hit the side of the yacht, and to water dripping in through the temporary coverings.

Dawn after a storm, no matter what dreadful confusion it illuminates, bestows relief and calm. No situation seems quite so bad when exposed to the reassuring light of day. Beryl was the first up to make breakfast – egg on lifeboat biscuits – and together they planned their campaign of action for the day. John's first priority was to construct a water-tight hatch over the six by six-foot hole where the doghouse had been as the temporary cover leaked and would not have taken any weight if anyone had fallen on it. Although the wind had dropped a lumpy sea made it difficult to keep a footing on the deck. Miles and Beryl began the daunting task of tidying up below. Several heavy, bronze portholes, once part of the doghouse, were unearthed from the debris and heaved over the side, along with Beryl's sewing machine and their decapitated teddy-bear mascot. Tins without labels, broken glass, coal, the insides of 70 eggs, soggy charts and books were all bound together in skeins of wool from a part-made jumper. String and twine, integral components of an orderly life on board ship, added to the mêlée. Beryl's injuries forced her to lie down for the afternoon with a dose of pain-killers, having first lit the coke-burning stove to dry out the cat. The poor creature was in a sorry state still and did not seem to have much interest in living any more in a world that had dealt her such a blow.

The work continued all that day and the next. On the third day Miles made another discovery: they were without a rudder. Noticing that the top of the post was not moving he leaned over and watched as the stern came out of the water and saw that the rudder had broken clean off at the stock. Considering the catastrophe they had already lived through this added problem did not cause the concern that it would otherwise have done. John announced that he would make a steering oar as soon as he had finished constructing a mast which was the work in hand at the moment. That same evening he stepped the mast but the wind was too strong for the flimsy contraption, so he took it down again and strengthened it.

Beryl could only manage a little sleep at night with the help of sleeping pills and cushions to stop her from moving too much as the boat rolled. The following night it blew hard again and she got no rest at all. The mast could not be tried again until the next afternoon but this time it was stepped successfully. By the evening they were sailing slowly in the general direction of Chile.

Optimism rose and bets were laid as to the number of days it would take them to reach a port. The likeliest place was Talcahuana in Chile, about 900 miles away. Several days later it blew very hard again. The mast had to be handed and a long rough night endured until it could be restepped in the daylight.

The days crept by, filled with tidying, mending, and drying out, and, for Beryl, with nursing herself and the cat back to health. She also tried to nurse the stove into working. Smoke issued from it at each rise and fall of the bows and, as the chimney had gone, swirled about the cabin looking for a place to get out while Beryl, kneeling in front of it with the trembling cat, poked at the damp sticks and coke. Miles and John were forced to make frequent visits on

deck to escape the fumes but Beryl sat it out, getting blacker and more dishevelled-looking by the day.

Without a rudder steering was a precarious business. It could only be achieved with sufficient forward speed and nifty positioning of the sail. *Tzu Hang* occasionally refused to come about. Once, the two men struggling to force her around got on each other's nerves so much that Beryl finally suggested they stop trying and go below for toast and tea. It was the first time for over a week that she had even put her head out into the daylight, and the incongruous sight of her, covered in soot and with dried blood stains still on her head, restored the men's good humour.

On Thursday, February 21, phase two of the journey to the coast began. John made a steering oar. They tried it the next morning and were overjoyed to find that they could steer. With the boat sailing in the right direction for the first time it looked as though they had a good chance of survival.

Sailing along in more or less the right direction at one to two knots was all very well to start with, but ambition soon prompted John to start designing and building a new mast. Miles and Beryl unpicked the spare mainsail to use as a lugsail while John ferreted about amongst the piles of wood that Beryl had hoarded in the forecabin until he had enough to do the job. The time was passing pleasantly now. A greater sense of comradeship had grown among the three, which John felt particularly. They had all leant on each other in their various times of need and no one had failed in the crisis. Each thought the others' contribution had ensured their survival. By the time the new mast was up and the two sails pulling, there remained no longer any doubts about their ability to make land. They even felt rather sad that the adventure was coming to an end, and could never be repeated. On March 22, they made a landfall in Arauco Bay, crossed it with *Tzu Hang* sailing well under her jury rig and makeshift rudder, and anchored off the town.

Most sailors would hope to survive a lifetime of sailing without pitchpoling or capsize, and, if unfortunate enough to experience such a calamity once, I would imagine that the likelihood of a repeat experience to be as improbable as being twice struck by lightning. Confident that they had had their full share of ill-luck the Smeetons began to discuss the refitting of the yacht for a leisurely trip back to England the easier way, through the Panama Canal. With the help of the Chilean Navy the yacht was lifted out of the water at the Navy yard at Talcahuano, and the huge task began. They had hoped to stay only a month or two at the most, but it did not take long to find out the impossibility of that assumption.

As the trip round the Horn was off John was anxious to get back to his own boat, but, to the great relief and pleasure of Miles and Beryl, he offered to help with the repairs to *Tzu Hang* first. He built a new doghouse (stronger and better shaped than the other one), new hatches, masts and the wooden part of the rudder. An enormous amount of help and kindness was also extended to them by a large number of people, but there were still interminable delays. The right wood for the masts was impossible to find and John had to make do with scaffolding planks which he grudgingly planed down to the correct size. Nothing was available in brass or any other suitable material for a rudder stock. In fact, there were virtually no brass or bronze fittings to be had in the whole country. Chile simply did not cater for yachts. Four months raced by and still the boat was nowhere near ready to go to sea. Eventually, a rolled, bronze propeller shaft, once part of an old, unused launch, was turned down on a lathe and fitted as a rudder stock. Other shortfalls were made up by ordering items from England. But this process turned out to be fraught with difficulties, too. Packing cases from England failed to turn up at the right time or right place, and when they eventually did arrive they had been plundered. Still, they contained enough rope, sails and important equipment like the compass for the yacht to receive the final touches and be put back into the water.

All the while, in the back of his mind, Miles was conscious of a niggling apprehension. He and Beryl had decided to continue their journey home via the Panama Canal. They had tried the southern route and it had not worked, but only, they believed, because of bad luck. There were practical and attractive reasons for returning via Panama but whatever reasons he had given for returning that way Miles now knew the real one: he was afraid of going back into the Southern Ocean. Although he and Beryl did not discuss their feelings on the subject he was certain that Beryl had been as deeply affected by the catastrophic event as he, and very likely felt equally apprehensive.

They consulted the captain of a large square-rigger moored in the harbour on the subject of storm tactics. He advocated lying a-hull. Another friend, an admiral, also thought this the best strategem in the case of a small yacht. These opinions comforted them as lying a-hull was the approach Miles had favoured before the big storm. However, at the commencement of that onslaught he had been forced to conclude that lying a-hull would be too dangerous. The final remedy to their personal fears, they had to agree, seemed to be to go south and face the ordeal of another storm.

At last the yacht was ready for sea. On Monday, December 9, they collected the cat which had been boarding in a villa and conveyed her on board. Despite screaming indignantly at being uprooted from her recent life of indulgence, she settled into her usual position on the engine casing and purred her happiness. The Smeetons felt immensely grateful to her for showing no signs that her old home had become abhorrent. Now fully crewed, and with nothing but a few cans of petrol still to be collected, they slipped away from the pier.

The weather could not have been better for the first three days but Miles was depressed, weighed down by having to face the uncertainties of the Southern Ocean weather, Beryl's health, and doubts about their abilities without John to assist them – he had gone back to Australia to continue his solo wanderings. Beryl, however, revelled in being back at sea with *Tzu Hang* and was able to talk Miles out of his unease. They moved unhurriedly south and did not have their first taste of bad weather until they reached the Roaring Forties proper. It was a small gale, but enough to warrant lying a-hull. The barometer had dropped during the gale, and dropped a little more for another gale a few days later, but instead of rising again it continued a steady decline. This was viewed with considerable apprehension by Miles. The following day was Christmas Eve. It was not a cheerful one. As they opened their Chilean friends' special parcels of wine, cigarettes and biscuits the force 7 wind whined over their heads and spray lashed the cabin ports. Before their feast was over they were donning oilskins and dousing the running headsails.

Tzu Hang ran on through the night under storm jib but by daybreak the unmistakable sounds of a storm drove them on deck once more. The familiar, disturbing sight of a foam-streaked, angry sea met their gaze. As yet it was not as violent as the previous storm but rough enough to warrant storm tactics. Together they lowered the jib and brought the yacht beam on to the seas, and she rolled and side-slipped under the onslaught of the heavy waves. Beryl lashed the helm and followed Miles below.

There was nothing left to do but batten down all the hatches and wait. (How vividly I recall waiting for a capsize in the South Atlantic. When it happened it was not a 360-degree roll, more a 130-degree knockdown, which does less damage.) The hours passed with agonising slowness. At about midday, having spent the morning lying in their bunks trying to read, or staring at the green water pouring over the windows, they discussed using the sea-anchor, but eventually decided against it. They had never used it before, and even the thought of getting it out of the forehatch with the wild motion of the boat was off-putting. They decided to trust in luck and to the tactics they had adopted. After all, the crisis might not happen.

Miles was about to get up and make some tea when *Tzu Hang* heeled sharply, and kept going over and over into darkness and swirling water. Miles later wrote: 'Again the water burst violently into the ship, and again I found myself struggling under water in total darkness, and hit

on the head, battered and torn in a kind of mob violence, and wondering when *Tzu Hang* would struggle up. I could not tell what was happening to me but I knew all the time what was happening to the ship. I felt her heavy and deep as the keel came over, and felt her wrench herself from the spars deep below her.'

As he got to his feet he could see Beryl struggling to stand up in the forecabin. 'It's all the same again,' he said to her as they waded aft through knee-deep water to view the carnage on deck. Both masts had gone; the doghouse was partially stove-in on one side; one of the skylights had gone; and the guard rails were bent and twisted out of shape.

Beryl jumped below again to fetch the jib to nail over the broken doghouse as Miles viewed the damage. He said loudly: 'By God, we've done it once, and we'll do it again,' and then felt the foolishness of his heroics – especially as Beryl was already doing something about it without wasting time in amateur dramatics. He jumped below to help her and together they hammered the sail into place. The easiest way to bale out was again through the missing skylight, with Beryl passing the full buckets up from below. There was a lot less water in the boat this time and before long they were down to the floorboards. They then returned to the deck to nail another jib across the cockpit which was also partly stove-in. Darkness was falling by the time it was tacked on sufficiently tightly to prevent another deluge of water. After this they went below to heat up something hot to eat. The cat was rescued from her hiding place and found to be wet but not so devastated in appearance as the last time. They all lay down together for warmth and to talk about the next step.

As the enormity of their situation hit him Miles let slip a groan of agitation, which made Beryl start in surprise and some alarm. 'It's the thought of going back,' he said. It was almost exactly a year since the pitchpole – they were not far from the very spot now. All that work in Chile had come to nothing and they were going to have to start all over again. But then a lucky thought struck him. This time, *Tzu Hang* was insured. The repairs would not have to be

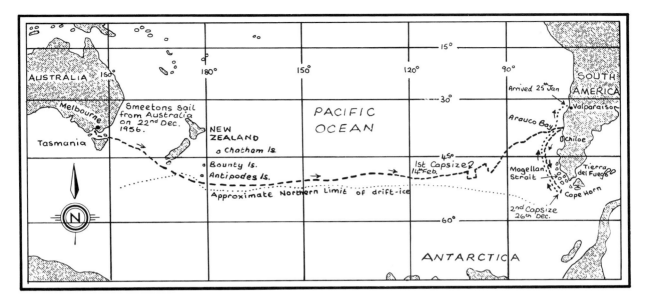

the same cost-saving exercise as last time. The sleepless night wore on.

Three days later they were moving slowly towards the Chilean coast under a jury rig made from a staysail rigged on what was left of the mizen mast. Another day passed and they had a better rig made with the mizen boom as a mast and a piece of John's old jury rig which Beryl had carefully put away. This rig gave them greater speed and manoeuvrability but Miles knew they could not go to windward with it. The wind at present was in the wrong quarter for a landfall but they hoped it would change to the south as they got closer to the coast. Some terrific runs of 70 miles brought them to within 80 miles of the land. The continuing north-westerly wind caused Miles one of the most harrowing nights he had ever spent as he pictured *Tzu Hang* going ashore on Isle de Chiloè. But early the next morning he was woken from a fitful sleep by the feel of a cool southerly breeze on his face. He woke Beryl to give her the good news.

Confident now that they would make Valparaiso (the nearest port from which arrangements to have *Tzu Hang* shipped home could be made) they chalked up more excellent runs. On the morning of January 25, they crept past the breakwater on the edge of Valparaiso Bay and were becalmed. A harbour launch offered to tow them into the dock, where they could see the tall masts of the square-rigger whose captain had given them so much assistance in Arauco Bay a few months earlier. Minutes later they were tied alongside and received a surprised but very kindly welcome.

Many months later, in England again and reunited with their daughter, Miles was asked if he would have another go at the Horn. His answer was emphatically, no. Twice they had tried and twice been unlucky. He hesitated, though, to attribute all their problems to bad luck. He wondered if *Tzu Hang* was too small for those sort of seas. Would a much bigger boat have escaped their predicament? The pitchpoling may have been avoided but larger vessels than *Tzu Hang* have come to grief through capsizing. There are usually a combination of factors involved: size, faulty equipment, unseaworthiness, poor sailing techniques, but the most important factor by far is the unpredictability of a storm-driven sea.

A Round Britain Victory

'It's flat calm down there. Couldn't be better.' Rob was obviously thinking of the problems of manoeuvring a large trimaran in confined spaces. 'Thank goodness for that!' I muttered in thankful agreement as we looked down at the glassy water of Plymouth Sound from our hotel room on the top of the Hoe. Today was the start of the 1982 Double-Handed Round Britain Race, and I dreaded it, not just the start but the whole thing. Getting across the line was the least of our problems in my view. Other, more personal ones, had my stomach churning over in earnest now as I remembered the ghastly trip over from Ireland a few weeks before. And my elbows, damaged by too much wall building, had been injected with four star cortezone (the two star had not worked), and I wondered if they would stand up to winding in those miles of genoa sheets. We would look stupid if they did not. At least I was not going to disgrace myself within sight of our sponsors . . . The unworthy thought cheered me up as we threw our few things into sea bags and dashed down the hill to the docks. It was very early but every boat had orders to be out of Millbay Dock by 8:30am.

On one of our sea trials in the Solent we overtook a tanker

Family and friends crowded on board for the last few minutes before we let go the lines from the quay and moved out through the dock gates, aided by a dinghy tied alongside our main hull. Our trimaran, *Colt Cars GB*, was very light but very wide – 40 feet. Considering that she was 60 feet long and that each of the three bows was extremely pointed and delicate, she represented quite a trial of tempers and skill (Rob's mainly) to move her around without touching anything and possibly breaking off a vital bit. Once outside the dock gates, we dropped our tow and sailed towards the start area in a light sou' easterly. There were several hours to kill.

I made a pot of tea in the galley. Actually, it was not only the galley, but navigation area, sail stowage, and where we dozed between watches. Whatever function was required of the space below, it fulfilled. There were two bunks right forward but at sea they presented a dubious resting place unless the conditions were pretty flat. I searched for sugar in several boxes stowed on the two-foot-wide floor space. The thought of producing food in that airless place, with a leprechaun grinning malevolently out from behind a pile of food cartons (an artistic friend had painted it on in an attempt to liven up the cavern-like interior) made my stomach turn over. It had to happen, I could not get away from it. No matter what I tried – acupuncture bands, patches behind the ears, all the latest pills – even used all together, I had a force 4 barrier, beyond which I just had to be sick. On my own in a slow, proper sort of boat I had always had time to cope with it, but this boat was different. Alien, unpredictable, and unruly as it was, I had felt at something of a loss ever since I had first stepped aboard. I felt she had some potential nastiness: it made me nervous.

'God, why do I go sailing?' The forecast, coming over that moment on VHF radio, mentioned possibilities of force 9 in Fastnet. I climbed up the hatch and handed Rob his tea. 'Don't worry about that forecast,' he said gayly. 'They're just being cautious after the cock-up they made of the Fastnet race.'

We sat on the stern watching the other boats moving about in the start area. Rob was not concerned about my lack of experience of multi-hulls and even less about my lack of racing skills. 'Never mind about that,' was his answer to the doubts I had felt it necessary to express. 'Just do as I tell you and you'll be fine. Let's just do this race and then you can forget all about the sea and bury your head in your wood shavings or whatever else you want to do.' Thinly disguised under my protests was certainly the desire to try living a normal life for a change – if you can call carving, stone wall building and the like normal. I did. The thought of sitting at a work bench in a warm room without a squall or a wind shift to worry about seemed immeasurably dear just then.

Perhaps my nervousness was getting to Rob for just before the start he put a reef in the mainsail. The wind was up to 15 knots and in view of the forecast he thought he would err on the cautious side. With a few minutes to go to the gun we approached the line on starboard tack, a little ahead of the other large multihulls. Just in front of our main rival, Chay Blyth's trimaran *Brittany Ferries*, Rob tacked and shouted to me to take the tiller while he wound madly on the genoa sheet winch. Sitting on the line ahead were two small multihulls but Rob grabbed the tiller, dodged in behind them as the gun went, and we shot over the line.

After some minutes of careful steering while Rob trimmed the sails I looked astern and saw that we were easing ahead of the fleet. Rob also glanced back and satisfaction temporarily erased the look of tense concentration on his face. But it was shortly replaced by concern when we realized that the wind was dropping instead of increasing. All the other boats which had had reefs in had shaken them out. We hurriedly followed suit, losing some ground, but by the time the Eddystone Lighthouse slipped by we still had a couple of minutes lead.

At present, the water was flat but I knew from the wind direction that as soon as we reached open water the sea would rise and I could expect the worst. However, the next forecast had toned down its dire warning of a Force 9 Gale at the Fastnet to the possibility of Force 6 to 7 winds. I felt a little more optimistic.

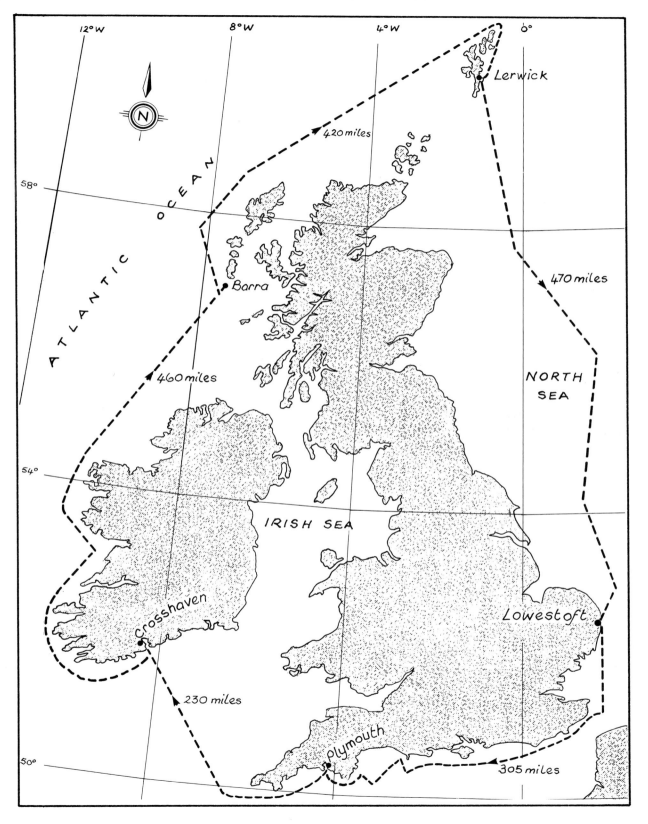

I steered a good deal of the long afternoon while Rob checked and rechecked the opposition astern to make sure they were not going to sneak up on us without our noticing them. He spent most of his time navigating and trimming the sails for another half-knot of speed while I alternated my gaze from the horizon to the compass and, occasionally, to watching him. He was a slightly different man during a race, I realized warily. Gone was his usual light-heartedness and good humour. Instead, he was a competitor: calculating, tense, obsessed almost, it seemed to me. I thought of the rocking-horse in my workshop that I was restoring to its former Victorian glory, and sighed.

Towards evening we altered course to pass the Scilly Isles and hoisted a spinnaker. The shortest course was close by Bishop Rock – the closer the better from a racing point of view. As very careful helming and sail trimming was required to keep the spinnaker set I perched out on the windward cross-beam for an hour and called the luff of the spinnaker to Rob, who steered and worked the control lines at the same time. Spiky fingers of black rock jutted out of the sea quite a distance from the actual Bishop Rock. We were getting uncomfortably near to them, I thought. Rob was engrossed with the spinnaker; a shiver went up my back. This situation was horribly like a dream I frequently had where my boat and I get stranded in the middle of a mass of jagged rocks. (Only in the dream the boat climbs gently up the rocks and sits in a field of yellow flowers.) The sail suddenly collapsed. Out on the float I gasped as Rob steered straight for the rocks and I scrambled back towards the cockpit. Behind me the spinnaker filled noisily and Rob rounded up again. He laughed at my discomfort. It was the first of several corners we shaved comfortably close in the pursuit of the lead. Me, I would have given them another mile of so – and finished the race near the back.

As soon as it was dark Rob considered it safe to gybe (if we had gybed within sight of the opposition they might have tried another course, hoping to find better winds). There was little to do from now on but steer. The wind was a steady south-easterly and looked like remaining that way – the forecasters had forgotten strong winds. 'It will be a dead run all the way to Cork,' said Rob as he settled himself in the cockpit for his stint at the tiller. 'Go below, I'll call you when I've had enough.'

I dozed a little on the bench underneath the leprechaun, bracing myself easily against the boat's gently-swaying motion. I was thankful for the reprieve, but with several thousand miles to go it was very unlikely that I would escape seasickness. Several hours later I relieved Rob, who tried unsuccessfully to pick up the Irish Radio Direction Finding beacons, before lying down on the bench. He was asleep immediately.

It was a dark, quiet night, broken only by the swish of water past the hulls. A thousand images of past nights spent at sea washed gently over my thoughts as I sat steering and peering ahead into the impenetrable gloom. Fears and disquiet were for the time being submerged under the soothing peace of the ocean. I felt a sense of belonging, and regret that it could not always be this way.

By dawn the wind had backed a little and now blew on to our starboard beam, but far enough off the bow to carry the spinnaker. One of the Kinsale gas rigs hardened up ahead in the murky haze. Rob had hoped it might have been further to leeward but admitted that this wishful thinking had been based on optimism, not navigation. Navigation became even more of a problem when land appeared. As we were exactly between two RDF beacons it was not possible to tell whether we were to the left or right of the harbour entrance. I did not recognize the configuration of the land (though I had had ample time to study it when a girl friend and I had brought a boat over the summer before) but argued that we must be on the east side. Rob was not convinced. We really ought to have known as we had lived off and on in Cork for three years. By the time he was quite sure we were too far upwind and had to bear away for the harbour entrance, five miles away. So much for local knowledge.

Rob became very twitchy again as we sped towards Roaches Point Lighthouse, one end of the finishing line. 'Oh no!' he groaned. 'There's someone just about in.' I looked hard at the sail he was pointing at and told him not to be stupid. It was a day sailer, all of 20 feet long. Closer in I, too, was nervous of finding another trimaran moored up ahead of us. Rob's disappointment would have been awful. He knew that if we could not win in this sort of weather, we had no chance at all. There was no one there. We picked up a mooring and stepped ashore just as *Brittany Ferries* turned the corner into the river, 20 minutes behind us.

The stop-over in Crosshaven was a very enjoyable one for us as we could stay with friends at Currabinny – which had been our base when we had lived in Ireland – keep *Colt Cars GB* in view at her moorings, and watch the rest of the fleet rapidly fill up the estuary. One morning's work on the boat was enough to get her back into shape for the next leg; the rest of the time we spent in the yacht club discussing tactics with our rivals – that is to say, Rob talked tactics. I listened and enjoyed the friendship between even the closest competitors. I liked being part of the scene, without thinking of myself as anything much more than a supporter. I wanted to win for Rob's sake and our sponsors, but I could not think of myself as even being in the same league as the other crews, many of whom were as experienced as their skippers. They were competitive: I was not. The men were friendly, but there was no doubt in their minds that Rob was the expert and I was along for the ride.

Early on the morning of the 13th we were out early and hoisting the mainsail with the help of friends. This huge sail was almost impossible for just the two of us to handle until it was up; then winches and other modern devices brought it under control. We arrived at the starting line in a rapidly dwindling breeze, which died away to nothing a few minutes after we crossed the line. Chay Blyth must have had a grin from ear to ear at the sight of us struggling to get the big spinnaker to set. (Starts were staggered; the stop-overs were exactly 48 hours for each boat.) After half an hour of frustration (Rob nearly blew a gasket) a tiny zephyr came up from the

south-east and we moved away from the harbour entrance. Our lead was down to just two miles.

The wind remained fluky all the way down the coast towards the south-west corner of Ireland and at times maddeningly died away to nothing. The Fastnet Rock Lighthouse moaning out its dreary signal into the fog added further aggravation to the worst of all conditions for the competitively minded – lack of wind. In your mind is the absolute certainty that the boat just out of sight behind has picked up a little whisper of wind and is furtively passing you.

At last, in answer to Rob's desperate entreaties, the wind sprang up from the north. I watched the windspeed meter with growing alarm. Within an hour it was force 5 on the nose and I was feeling dreadful. I emptied my mind of all thoughts of resistance and my stomach dutifully followed suit. All night we beat into the rising sea and absolute darkness, filled only with wind and spray. When I needed to be sick I moved to the leeward side of the cockpit, which was quite close to the side of the boat, and got on with it. *Colt Cars* was slamming heavily into the seas and not sailing very well. Ideally, we should have changed to another headsail and not rolled up the furling jib, but Rob did not have the heart to ask me to help him accomplish this awkward and rather dangerous manoeuvre, and could not attempt it on his own.

By the morning we had force 6 dead ahead and a very uncomfortable sea. The trimaran pitched badly and slowed down on every wave. About mid-morning another trimaran approached us on port tack and passed about a mile under our stern. It was *Brittany Ferries*. Another trimaran was in view four or five miles to windward. Rob was silent and looking pretty grim.

At dawn on the third day we had cleared the north-west corner of Ireland and had eased sheets slightly for the 180-mile reach to the Isle of Barra. Rob, after seeing the two other boats, decided to continue on inshore, towards the Arran Islands and flatter water, and, although we did not know it at the time, this tactic helped our position enormously.

I was at the helm at 8am and feeling much better now that the pitching had stopped and my stomach was as empty as it could possibly be. Two miles away was a boat which I was daring *Colt Cars* to catch. She charged at the waves at 18 to 20 knots, sending spray and sheets of green water over the deck every time a wave caught her on a cross-beam. It was exhilarating sailing. Now that I had a quarry in sight I found myself enjoying the excitement of a chase. When Rob appeared on deck shortly after 8am he glared intently at the boat ahead, decided that it was *Brittany Ferries*, and prowled around the deck for a while to make sure that nothing was about to break. He was a bit worried at the way the waves were hitting the cross-beams with such force, but as the alternative was to reduce sail and let Chay get away from us we had to try to ignore it. The fairings, the thin aerofoil mouldings put on the cross-beams to reduce drag, had already failed us once in Ireland and had been strengthened.

'She's taking a hell of a hammering but those fairings are pretty strong now.' No sooner had he said it when a crack appeared in the join between one of the beams and its fairing, which rapidly came unstuck along its lower edge. The next time a wave hit it, there was an alarming jerk as the speed was reduced by half, which threw Rob off his feet into the bottom of the cockpit. I tried to ease the boat through the waves while Rob watched to see how the mast was reacting to the treatment. It seemed to be absorbing the shock but I wondered what would happen when we landed a big wave. Rob could not stand the strain of looking at the mast. He went below for a while to navigate. Standing by the chart table he was unable to anticipate the impending jerk when we hit a wave, and was thrown violently against the bulkhead each time. After a few minutes of that punishment he erupted on deck and started to wind in some jib. Our speed dropped and the boat ahead began to pull away. Half an hour later Rob was desperate. 'Put the helm down, I'm going to cut the fairings away'. Hove-to on port tack, we were making five knots back towards Crosshaven.

For 15 minutes he attacked the fairings with every sharp instrument he could lay his hands on, but the top flange refused to budge. He gave up in disgust and we put the boat back on course. Upset and annoyed at his anger and frustration I suggested we put on full sail and carry on regardless. 'There's no use dribbling on here losing the race,' I pointed out. 'Let's go for it or bust.' Rob rolled out the jib again, and we bashed on.

The other yacht had disappeared over the horizon. It could not have got too far away though, I thought, as I braced myself against shock after shock as the waves exploded against the deep, vertical face of the fairing. I had plenty to do at the tiller and left Rob to worry about the spectre of a broken mast, sponsor's reactions, etc. I did not enjoy his despondency but I perversely enjoyed forcing the boat along like a bucking bronco, trying to steer her away from the worst-looking crests that reared up on our beam, but often as not being caught out by rogue waves that sent solid water over me.

The mast stayed up and Rob looked more optimistic as the day wore on though the fact that it did not break astounded him. The wind held all the way to Barra Head and there, in the lee of the island, and in flat water, we heaved sighs of relief and shook out the last reef for the final 10 miles to Castlebay.

After crossing the line a launch came out to meet us and very obligingly held us head to wind while we tackled the mainsail. It came down ominously quickly. The headboard at the top of the sail had disintegrated and had ripped off about two feet of luff tape which connects the mainsail to the mast. The only consoling thought was that it had happened now. Any earlier and all 78 feet of luff tape would have gone.

Once safely under tow we dared to ask what our position was. *Exmouth Challenge*, a 53-foot trimaran, had beaten us by 90 minutes and *Brittany Ferries* by 30 minutes. Rob was amazed and pleased. All was not lost.

The Isle of Barra was a lovely place but did not offer much in the way of suitable repairs. The fairings could simply be dispensed with but the slugs required to put the headboard back

The start of the Round Britain and Ireland Yacht Race. Colt Cars *was good in light to medium winds but we had problems in heavy weather*

together were in Lymington. Rob sent an SOS to our sponsor, who flew them in the following morning by helicopter – to the surprise of the local fishermen and gull population. We spent the afternoon and following morning effecting repairs, then took some time off to stretch our legs cycling around the island. As usual performances were chewed over in the evenings and, thanks to a comment from Chay, Rob decided to move the sails not in use from the sleeping compartment to the all-purpose living space aft. It helped to reduce our pitching moment, though it raised the floor by 18 inches.

We arranged our tow out to the start line in good time to watch the other two boats cross the line. They did not set spinnakers for the half-mile run around the little island before clearing the course down to Barra Head. I ventured to suggest that it was hardly worth the effort. But our spinnaker went up, and came down again a few minutes later.

When we reached Barra Head we could see the others through a gap between the islands. It was getting dark when we tacked but we could see that our new course would take us half a mile clear of the corner and on course for St Kilda. Unfortunately, just as we were to windward of the cliffs, the wind dropped away completely and we were becalmed within shouting distance of the shore. Cursing himself and wind-shadows in general Rob used every trick he knew to get away from the cliffs, but failed miserably. If we tacked, the boat stopped dead and it took 20 minutes to build the speed up to four knots – back the way we had come – only to be stopped dead in our tracks again by the backwash of waves hitting the cliffs. The tide started to turn and pushed us further in towards the rocks. An hour and a half later Rob was beside himself with fury and frustration, and I wanted to retreat below to get out of the flak. I was sure we were going to hit the cliffs. The ignominity of our situation was particularly hard to bear: 'Trimaran wrecked off Barra Head in zero wind . . .'

After two hours we managed to drag ourselves away from the area and picked up a little wind. (We later discovered there was a general lull in the wind, which lasted several hours.) Rob vowed to steer clear of headlands in future.

Thankful, at least, that no one had passed us while we had been stuck we pressed on for the rest of the night and St Kilda appeared dead ahead shortly after daylight. Rob steered us round the desolate-looking rock-pile at a respectful distance and bore away towards Muckle Flugga, the northernmost corner of the Shetland Isles.

The wind was increasing quite rapidly and it was a relief to be sailing before it again. I was no longer troubled by seasickness and was feeling quite sanguine about the business of multihull sailing. My delusions were about to be shattered.

After a hasty breakfast I rather rashly suggested to Rob that we ought to hoist a spinnaker. We were going along at pretty well top speed anyway but Rob agreed that we might as well try it. I steered while he took care of the nasty work on the narrow foredeck, which meant working over the water moving past at more than 20 knots. The spinnaker was in a squeezer, a long thin bag which traps the spinnaker until such time as one wants to let it loose. When all the sheets and guys were arranged I furled up the jib while the auto-pilot steered. As Rob pulled up the squeezer, I sheeted in and the sail set with a bang. Rob leapt aft and grabbed the tiller. The former bucking bronco now turned into a turbo-charged racehorse and accelerated.

At first it was great fun to see the fantastic speeds we were achieving. The wind speed varied between 12 knots down to virtually nothing as we out-surfed it, but what I failed to appreciate initially was that if we had been sailing on the wind, we would have been sailing in a near gale. While we sailed with it, the wind speed was reduced by our boat speed – which was fine so

long as we kept going with it. After a little while I noticed that Rob was having to use quite a lot of strength on the tiller to stop the boat going off course when waves tried to slew us around.

The sight of the boat rushing along under brilliant skies and rough seas suddenly reminded Rob of the severe ticking off he had been given by the BBC at the end of the last leg for not doing enough filming, so he suggested I get the camera out. What a sight, I told him as I filmed over his shoulder. Spray was flying in all directions and *Colt Cars* was positively humming along.

At that precise moment Rob lost control of the boat. He had not been concentrating quite as hard as he might have been and a big wave caught him steering slightly up on his course. The yacht started to surf and Rob could not get her to bear away. I dropped the camera and jumped in to add my weight to the tiller, but it was too late. We had reached the trough of the wave and as the apparent wind drew to our beam the lee float started to dig in. The next wave crest threw the stern round. Our acute degree of heel had put the rig so far to leeward that its drive was outside the lee float and was helping to pivot us around. Within seconds we were beam on to the 30-knot wind, stationary, with the spinnaker and full mainsail driving the lee float completely under. I looked in horror at Rob. He was holding the helm hard over with one foot while he released the spinnaker sheet from its winch. He shouted to me to get on the foredeck and pull the squeezer down. I ran forward and pulled on it with all my strength but the sail was flogging so wildly, it would not budge. 'I can't do it!' I screamed above the commotion of flailing canvas. 'We'll have to bear away again!' Rob held the tiller up and waited for a wave to push the bows away. I reached the cockpit again as a wave knocked us off the wind. The yacht picked up speed and turned swiftly downwind until the spinnaker filled with a crack like a rifle shot. We were back under control, but I was shaking a bit. 'Can't we get rid of the spinnaker while we're all still in one piece?' I asked Rob. He laughed, gave me the tiller, and lowered the sail without difficulty.

While I steered, feeling decidedly apprehensive, Rob disappeared below to work out where we should be heading next. The seas had grown to match the force 7 wind and *Colt Cars* was swooping down the waves with the sort of power that unnerved me. Our speed wavered around 23 to 24 knots at the height of each surf and fell back to under 15 if we went down on our course slightly and out-surfed the wind. Each time that happened the mainsail tried to back (with dire consequences to the full-length battens which were not supposed to be bent backwards), but as we had a preventer line on the main boom the mainsail could not go far. Unfortunately it was not always possible to stop the boat coming up or going down slightly on her course. The waves were powerful enough to exert enormous pressures against the rudder and sometimes the boat refused to answer the helm until the greater force of the water released it. By the time this happened one was usually off course and desperate action was needed to prevent a broach to windward or a gybe.

I was finding at times that it was necessary to use all my strength against the tiller and the boat's refusal to answer immediately made me angry. Rob appeared again and announced that we needed to gybe. We looked at each other and wondered how we were going to tackle the problem of gybing a fully battened main on a fractional rig, short-handed, in near-gale conditions. The biggest problem was that the mainsail had to be right in to the centre-line before the lee backstays could be wound up and the others let off, otherwise there was simply nothing holding the mast up. It was impossible to get the lee stays on sooner because the battens would all break if the stays were winched into them, and, anyway, the boom was in the way.

Rob elected to look after the tiller and backstays, and delegated the mainsail to me. It took me all of 20 minutes to wind the sheet in, inch by inch. I was getting to the critical point, with the lee stays still just slack and the sail threatening to gybe, when we lost control. The effect of having the mainsail amidships, and with no spinnaker to pull the boat along, made the trimaran behave like a weathercock. The mainsail

took over and spun us through 180 degrees. We ended up amid flailing sheets and running rigging – facing upwind!

Rob ignored the battens doing contortions all along the length of the mainsail and wound both running backstays up tight. *Colt Cars* was stationary head to wind with the sails and rig shaking violently. 'I've no idea which way she'll go,' he said prosaically. I was staring, hypnotized by the sight of the mast shaking so hard that we could feel the jerks in the cockpit, and wondered why it did not fall to pieces. Then I jumped as Rob shouted: 'Back the jib to starboard – stand by to let off the port runner!' The yacht had started to move backwards. There was a tremendous crack as the tiller was wrenched out of his grasp and hit the stop – we were now surfing stern-first down a wave. At the bottom of the surf the bows swung away to port. 'Perfect!' Rob yelled; then to me: 'Runner off! MAIN OUT!' and for good measure, 'Get some jib in!' This was the moment I fully realized the limits of my puny strength. I wound furiously. The jib came in with agonizing slowness, and *Colt Cars* started to move forward on the starboard tack, luckily the right one. She picked up speed, but Rob was hesitant about bearing away with the wind steadily increasing. 'Here goes,' he said. 'Either she will or she won't.' I did not need a degree of physics to understand what was likely to happen next. If she did not turn fast enough before the full weight of the wind got into the mainsail, she would turn over like a leaf. Rob swung the tiller hard over and the yacht reacted instantly. She ground around on one float, accelerating as though she was jet-propelled. I hung on to the side of the steeply heeling cockpit as the other float whistled through the air. At the worst angle of heel Rob later estimated the main hull would have also been clear of the water before we lurched back upright in the relative calm of sailing downwind.

'Well done,' said Rob, patting my hand and grinning at the look of delayed shock on my face. 'I'm going to put another preventer on the boom and goosewing the genoa. Then, if we do threaten to gybe or broach, we are less likely to get into trouble.' He handed me the tiller and added, 'Only 250 miles to Muckle Flugga,' and scrambled on to the deck.

We settled down as best we could to 24 hours of nerve-wracking sailing. By now we could each steer for only half an hour at a time. The strain on our arms made it necessary to alter position as much as possible, rather than sit by the tiller and steer with one hand as one normally did. I found it best to stand with the tiller between my knees, so that I could throw my body to either side. I gripped the front of the tiller with both hands and sometimes went into contortions to stay on course. Concentration had to be fierce, for one moment's distraction would have been enough to give the boat her head and then it would have been a desperate struggle to regain control. Every 15 minutes or so a rogue wave would lift some part of the vessel and try to screw us off course and it was impossible not to waver slightly. At those times I did not think I could hold her, but, although the mainsail backed occasionally, the preventers held and I managed to straighten up without mishap. Rob was having the same problems so I comforted myself that it was not that I could not steer properly; it was just the extreme conditions and the fact that we were racing. At one point Rob suggested that if the preventers broke, never mind about the course being steered or the rig – just duck!

What worried me most at this stage was the possibility of pitchpoling. Every now and again *Colt Cars* would decide at the last moment to pick up a wave that was almost past, and we would start to career down its face at an alarming angle. It felt as though we must drive under and be somersaulted stern over bow, but somehow, although we occasionally lost the floats – and a couple of times the whole bow – she always kept going forward. On these wild surfs the cross-beams would sometimes catch a subsidiary wave top, slice it clean off and sent it as a sheet of solid water into the cockpit. We had our safety harnesses clipped on to strong fixing points so that we could not be washed out.

Later in the day we began to have more control problems. The mainsail was tending to turn the boat up wind, which caused the genoa to back. As it was well prevented there was not much harm done but it shook the rig badly. Worse, it was too easy to over-compensate with the rudder. Then we would swing to leeward, which sometimes called for both of us to push on the tiller to prevent a gybe.

It then became necessary to reef, something both of us imagined would be just about impossible to achieve. However, it turned out to be quite easy. Each time we out-surfed the wind, Rob pulled down on the mainsail luff until he had sufficient sail down for the reef. We were better balanced with a slightly smaller mainsail and steering became a little easier.

As time went on, I stopped worrying about disaster. I have a theory that one can only keep up a high pitch of apprehension for a limited time; I had found this out on my circumnavigation, and the same applied during this race. It would have been different with nothing to do but that was not a problem just then. In our half-hour off-watch we tried to rest. Rob managed to snooze a little on the floor just below the hatchway, but I preferred to remain in the cockpit.

One of the worst moments came in the middle of the night, when my imagination and the light played a trick on me. It was shortly after we had altered course slightly towards the land and we were broad-reaching instead of running. The yacht heeled sharply on the face of a wave and as I fought the tiller over I glanced to leeward where the float should have been. I saw only foam and boiling water. 'Rob!' I yelled. 'The float's gone!' Rob leapt on deck as we ground to a halt. 'Shall I luff up or bear away?' I blurted out, believing that we were about to capsize. Before Rob could say anything the float dug itself out from under the water and I found that we were now facing dead down wind, and I had to yank the tiller hard the other way. 'So, what's the problem?' Rob asked facetiously. 'Go away', I growled and he went below to finish his snooze.

At daybreak – fortunately there are only a couple of hours of real darkness at 60 degrees north in summer – we found the visibility down to a few hundred yards. The wind was still force

7, the seas high, but I had become inured to the conditions. I had had no sleep for 24 hours but, except that I ached all over, I did not feel too bad. We were only 30 miles from Muckle Flugga. It was a case of hammering on until we sailed around it and into milder conditions.

Eventually we saw land close on our starboard beam and altered course slightly to port. We were sailing very much by the lee as Rob did not want to gybe – it would have wasted too much time – so Muckle Flugga was going to have to be shaved by a whisker. We closed on the cliffs, which now appeared directly ahead. The chart said the coastline was sheer and the wind looked very unlikely to drop just to spite us, so we rounded it with only yards to spare and hardened up on to a reach in the lee of the cliffs. The water was flat but the wind howled off the grey cliffs glinting in the early morning light. They looked utterly God-forsaken, and devoid of all signs of life but for thousands of wheeling, screeching seabirds.

My previous sailing had all been done on single hulled 'normal' sorts of boats. The unpredictability of a fast trimaran unnerved me

The next stretch did not offer the respite I was hoping for – in fact it could hardly have been worse. The mainsail was looking very sorry for itself with broken battens poking out of the sail like bones from a broken wing. We soon had to come hard on the wind and, with our mainsail setting badly, boat speed was terrible. Halfway down the coast our course took us west of south around the Outer Skerries Rocks, and then we really got into a pickle. The sea was a mass of steep waves, too close together to form any sort of pattern. They knocked into us from all sides and we pitched and hobby-horsed in the most frustrating way possible. Rob became incensed, but with no power in the mainsail, and vicious puffs coming off the land and forcing us to luff continuously, we were helpless.

Fortunately for our morale, we overheard

Brittany Ferries reporting their ETA (Estimated Time of Arrival) to the Lerwick Coastguard. It seemed that we had only lost an hour as a result of our contretemps with the wind shadow at Barra, not two. There was no word from *Exmouth Challenge*. I continued to monitor Chay Blyth's conversation with the Coastguard until he asked if anyone knew where we were. We sent him a message saying: 'We're down, but we're not out yet.' We could hear Chay chuckling over the radio as he received it.

The last 15 miles were terribly frustrating. We even missed a tack and got stuck in irons for a few minutes. Heavy squalls of 35 to 40 knots were hissing off the last headland, but Rob was determined not to reef. Luffing like mad to avoid being overpowered he clawed the boat around the point. The line was two miles away.

Rob started to ask me to call up the Coastguard to amend our ETA, but stopped in mid-sentence. 'Ease the main,' he said urgently, while trying to ease the course a little more off the wind. I hurriedly did so and then glanced towards the shore. Advancing over the water towards us was what looked like a huge shoal of jumping fish. My second glance recognized water churned up by wind. 'Ease the jib!' Rob shouted as the squall hit us, and we accelerated like a rocket. The water level came up to the top of the floats as the wind tried to press us into the sea. 'EASE THE MAIN! Look at that water!' It was rushing past at an incredible speed; suddenly the boat felt as though she was airborne except for little quivers and jumps as small waves collided with the beams. I glanced at the speedo; it was hard against the 30–knot stop. We roared across the line. Immediately, Rob bore right away into the lee of the town, and I furled the jib away. Even he looked somewhat shaken by that experience.

Our time for the leg had been fast. In the 24 hours between St Kilda and Muckle Flugga we had clocked up 330 miles, and were back in second place. *Brittany Ferries* was one hour, 55 minutes ahead. *Exmouth Challenge* came in over an hour behind us.

The 48-hour stop-over in Lerwick was largely devoted to mending battens and patching up the holes in the mainsail. Rob as usual joined in the tactical discussions and socializing with friends in the yacht club while I caught up on sleep as the ability to cat-nap at any time had deserted me – not that I had ever possessed the level of refinement that Rob had acquired. He could fall asleep between the soup and the main course. In this sort of sailing even 10 minutes sleep in every hour was infinitely better than none at all, though given another 12 hours at sea and I would have been crashing out like the best of them.

According to the forecast at 6:30am on the morning of our departure, we could expect northerlies, force 4 to 5, which could not have suited us better. Rob went out in a dinghy to watch *Brittany Ferries* shooting away over the line and returned in a fever of impatience to be off. We were an hour too early at the line and had to while away the time till our start. At last we were away.

This leg turned out to be most enjoyable. The sailing was perfect. We executed a series of long reaches at an average boat speed of 12 to 13 knots, with not a single worrying moment or problem. We had regular meals, a lot more sleep than before and managed to find time to film and do general maintenance. Rob's deadly determination to catch the boat in front did not have to manifest itself in frustrated rages this time: the boat was sailing as well as he could hope for, we were a good team, and he believed we had the speed to win.

During the second night we approached land, our navigation helped by the dozens of brightly lit oil rigs dotted along the way. We gybed several times with the spinnaker up (the wind was well below the force 6 impossibility margin) to keep on the best course through the rigs and sand banks. Twenty miles from the line we turned on the VHF and overheard Chay calling the coastguard with his position. He was also fishing around nervously for news of us. They had had spinnaker problems and had expected to be overtaken. We let them stew for a bit and then came on the air with our position. Chay's voice was an amusing mixture of relief and disbelief when he realised they still had the lead.

Not by much, though. They crossed the line at 4:30am, just before daylight. At that point we had picked up a squall and were racing towards the finish at 15 knots. The shore lights, plus the approaching dawn, made it difficult to identify the flashing red buoy that marked one end of the line and also the limit of navigable water (the water off Lowestoft is littered with sandbanks). I saw a red light in more or less the right place and pointed it out to Rob. He altered course towards it. We were still flying a spinnaker, but reaching made it a tricky operation. Rob was concentrating on keeping it set when he suddenly noticed brown water all around us – we were almost on a sandbank. He threw the tiller over. At the same time I noticed another flashing red buoy half a mile away on our port bow. Rob ran off towards it, sweating at the thought of going aground at 15 knots.

We finished 19 minutes behind Chay, thanks to that last lucky burst of speed. Crossing the line, though, was not the end of our problems on that occasion. We had hardly any room to get the sails down, and the squall had stayed and churned up the sea, which was already choppy with wind over a fast tide. Rob lowered the spinnaker squeezer, then quickly gybed the mainsail so that we could point the bows away from the bank which we were drifting onto again. Then I left the cockpit to help him lower the mainsail – with dire results. It came half down but a puff caught the bow and put us beam on to the wind which pressed the top half of the sail tight against the rigging. Meanwhile the rest of it disappeared over the lee float with me spread-eagled in the centre, trying to stop the middle part ballooning up. If that had happened the whole enormous sail would have ended up in the sea. Rob helped me up, cursing and vowing he would never have another fully battened main or luff grove system, and bit by bit we got the luff back under control. I sat on it (I felt about as effectual as a spider trying to hold down a tiger) while Rob stuffed the spinnaker down its hole, which reduced the windage forward, and then we finally managed to haul the mainsail the rest of the way down. By the time we had lashings around it we were exhausted. A boat was standing by with a tow so we threw them a line and made our way into the harbour.

There was not a lot to do on the boat in Lowestoft and not a lot to do off it, except watch the people on the beaches eating ice-creams and turning red in the sun. I entertained some of the family on board and Rob thought about the last leg of the race. He expected it to be the most tricky and most telling. The wind was likely to be fluky and lucky wind-shifts might mean gaining or losing valuable miles. Actually, it was just those conditions that he liked best.

The alarm rang at 3am of the 25th. Rob leapt on deck to view the weather – flat calm! The tide would be against us for hours so it looked like we had a problem. So did Chay, of course. The only person who could afford to laugh about it was Mark Gatehouse, skipper of *Exmouth Challenge*, who was four hours behind us. We hoisted the mainsail in a flat calm and got our tow out only 20 minutes before the start, by which time Chay should have been away. He had dropped his tow five minutes before their start and was now drifting rapidly down past the harbour entrance. Rob asked our tow to hold us on a transit somewhere near the line and with five minutes to go we dropped anchor. By now *Brittany Ferries* had also anchored but not till she had drifted 200 yards down tide. We had regained the lead!

The time passed. Every now and then Rob would imagine a puff and heave up the anchor. I was watching a transit on the shore and after a few minutes I would tell him to drop it again. At last a tiny breeze set in from the east. We pulled up the anchor for the last time and crept up the shore. By the time *Exmouth Challenge* started we were two miles ahead of her with Chay a quarter of a mile behind us. The race had started all over again.

Chay elected to stay inshore while Mark Gatehouse was heading out to sea. We could not cover them both so Rob headed out in front of Mark who seemed to have more wind. A puff brought him right up on to our stern but it died away before we could catch it. *Brittany Ferries* disappeared into the haze; when we last saw her she was moving well.

All that day and night we crept on, trying to get away from Gatehouse and failing. The problem seemed to be that our light spinnaker was too big and too full and would not set in the calm patches. A smaller, flatter spinnaker would have hung in a better shape when there was virtually no wind, ready to catch the slightest zephyr. Occasionally we came within speaking distance of *Exmouth Challenge* but, friends though we were ashore, there was not a lot we had to say to each other in those circumstances. We could not shake her off.

Outside the Goodwin Sands and into the Dover Straits we fought the variable winds every inch of the way. Off Dover we began beating into a light head wind and still *Exmouth Challenge*'s navigations lights were within yards of us.

Suddenly a squall came off the shore and we blasted away. The other trimaran's lights were soon lost against the maze of shore lights. By morning there was no sign of her or anyone else. Passing the Isle of Wight at dawn we searched ahead and behind for another sail but, stupidly, not to windward. So it was well after daylight before we suddenly saw, with something of a shock, *Brittany Ferries* exactly north of us on our windward beam, about four miles away. We smartly got the reef out we had been carrying (it was puffing up to 30 knots at times but Rob now decided that the wind was dropping) and set off up wind to get in behind her. This meant we were losing ground initially but we had to get into the same wind pattern.

Because of the puffs Rob set the mainsail with more twist than usual, which seemed to suit the conditions well. The leeward float was submerged at times but the speed was excellent. By the time we were in line with *Brittany Ferries*' stern we were a mile behind. Within an hour we were abeam of them and edging past. As we drew level the wind dropped and there was a scramble all round to set bigger sails. We watched anxiously as their big genoa set but, very slowly, we increased the lead. We were 100 miles from the finish but, from here on, Rob covered their every move.

A few hours later I went to pull on the control line to lower the centerboard (the wind had come around and we were beating in light winds) and fell flat on my back. The line, seven foot down inside the centerboard case, had broken. All we could do was to luff up hard and jump on the board, then wedge it, but it remained two feet short of its maximum depth.

Conditions remained the same, and by late afternoon we were tacking in towards Start Point. Whatever we did now would be critical. It was essential to stay on the same tack as *Brittany Ferries* while trying to ignore the thought that *Exmouth Challenge* might be sailing wide around us and coming in with more wind. But it was about to get dark and soon we would not be able to see where Chay Blyth was — and Chay was not likely to put his navigation lights on to give himself away. As soon as we lost sight of them we tacked. So did Chay, we later discovered. They could still see us against the western sky but had no alternative but to come on to our course as the wind had shifted to favour the starboard tack.

Soon, we were reaching up past Start Point. The wind had increased, so we went very close to it, past resolutions forgotten. Our sails were brilliantly lit up every few seconds by the flash of the light. From there we reached all the way past Bolt Head at 17 knots and sheeted in for the last 12 miles to the finish.

Every time we saw a navigation light we panicked, convinced that either Chay or Mark was ahead of us or about to overtake.

As the light on Plymouth breakwater came into view the wind dropped. It was a very dark night, made even darker when one of the motorboats hovering around turned on a brilliant spotlight. This blinded us momentarily and made navigation all the more difficult. The wind headed us as we neared the western entrance to the Sound and it was obvious we were going to have to put in a few tacks. I took the helm and the running backstays while Rob saw to the jib sheets. Fortunately we did not miss a tack. We slowly edged our way past the harbour entrance and tried to identify the buoys. More floodlights blinded us as the TV crews moved in. They went out again when Rob cursed them, then a voice

out of the darkness said: 'Well done'.

'Do you think we should ask them if we are first,' I whispered to Rob as the wind died and we slowed to a crawl. 'They might be congratulating us for coming second.' Rob said nothing. He was not at all sure either. We moved very slowly towards the line and then someone asked the magic question. 'Where are Chay and Mark?' We both looked back into the darkness. 'Probably just back there,' I said, and a minute later we drifted sideways across the line. As

The successful conclusion to the race and for me the end of my sailing career

pandemonium broke out Rob gave me a quick hug and a great whoop that nearly deafened me.

Shortly after we got ashore the questions began. 'Did you enjoy it, Naomi?' someone asked. 'No. It was too hard, both physically and mentally. The way you have to drive these boats now is beyond my strength and skills. I'm going to retire now – while I'm ahead.'